The
Mysterious
Mistress

The
Mysterious
Mistress

The Life and Legend
of JANE SHORE

MARGARET CROSLAND

SUTTON PUBLISHING

First published in the United Kingdom in 2006 by
Sutton Publishing Limited · Phoenix Mill
Thrupp · Stroud · Gloucestershire · GL5 2BU

British Library Cataloguing in Publication Data
A catalogue record for this book is available from the British Library.

ISBN 0-7509-3851-X

Typeset in 11/14.5pt Sabon.
Typesetting and origination by
Sutton Publishing Limited.
Printed and bound in England by
J.H. Haynes & Co. Ltd, Sparkford.

The past exudes legend:
There is no life that can be recaptured wholly, as it was.
Which is to say that all biography is ultimately fiction.

Bernard Malamud, *Dubin's Lives*,
1979, p. 20

Read no history:
nothing but biography, for that is life without theory.

Benjamin Disraeli, *Contarini Fleming*,
1832, Part I, Ch. 23

Contents

Illustrations

Acknowledgements

In writing about Jane Shore, the background to her life and her legend, I have received essential and valuable help from many individuals and organisations. Particularly important has been the groundbreaking research by Nicolas Barker and the late Sir Robert Birley concerning her family, their London life and Jane's possible connection with Eton College, published in 1972 in *Etoniana* Nos. 125 and 126. New information also came from Desmond Seward in his 1995 study *The Wars of the Roses and the Lives of Five Men and Women in the Fifteenth Century*.

In addition Professor J.L. Harner of Texas A&M University gave me his unpublished dissertation 'Jane Shore: A Biography of a Theme in Renaissance Literature' and indicated several hard-to-find sources of reference and information.

Other information has come from the Group Archives Unit at Barclays Bank plc, the British Film Institute, the Monumental Brass Society, the Richard III Society, the National Portrait Gallery and Tate Britain, London; many libraries have been helpful: the Bodleian Library, the British Library, the Guildhall Library, the Huntingdon Library in San Marino, California, the Pepys Library, Cambridge and the Poetry Library, London. The *Dictionary of National Biography* (2004) has also been constantly useful.

I am especially grateful to the Billingshurst branch of West Sussex County Libraries, where the staff have been unfailingly helpful in all ways.

I have also received helpful cooperation from Bill Alexander; Professor Sir John Baker (Cambridge); Nick Baker, Collections Administrator, Eton College; Catherine Ellis carried out wide-ranging Internet research. Madge Madden-Colenso and Mike Heritage took me to Hinxworth in Hertfordshire where Mrs Yvonne Tookey, Secretary to the Parochial Church Council, showed me the Lambert-Lynam family memorial brasses in the church of St Nicholas. Further help came from Geoffrey Wheeler, Anne

xi

Acknowledgements

Easton, Philip Heritage, Andrew Player, Elfreda Powell, Jan Stadler and my agent Jeffrey Simmons. My friend Bren Newman has supported and educated me constantly in the world of computer technology; I cannot thank her enough for her advice and cooperation.

Finally, I would especially like to thank Jaqueline Mitchell, my commissioning editor at Sutton Publishing, and the other members of the team: Anne Bennett, Jane Entrican and the unsung heroes and heroines in the back office.

M.C.

Introduction

One day I wrote her name upon the strand,
But came the waves and washèd it away . . .
Edmund Spenser, Amoretti, 1595

Jane Shore was the mistress of King Edward IV of England for at least the last twelve years of his life, from 1471 or 1472 until his death in 1483, but if he lived all his life in the glare of publicity and had to fight for his throne twice over, she has remained in the shadows. There are at least two reasons for this: few women in the fifteenth century, apart from queens, certain aristocrats, and a few who were prominent within or near the Church, were able to enjoy any real independence; and the lives of others, if mentioned at all, with varying degrees of inaccuracy, were not usually recorded in detail. Jane Shore, unlike many royal mistresses, especially those in later centuries, did not seek fame or indeed rewards. As a result even her name, if considered worth including, has usually been relegated to footnotes or brief references in books about other people.

To revert to Edmund Spenser's imagery, the waves of time may have washed her name away briefly, but the tide of reputation unexpectedly soon came in again and magically restored it. No magic was involved: her survival in legend was due to the poets and dramatists who wrote about her, passing on her story and interpreting her past behaviour in the light of changing social conditions. They needed a real-life heroine, an icon. No new media ever ignored her, a successful eighteenth-century play was translated into French and German, leading to operas with French and Italian libretti, four films were made about her in the early days of cinema, aspects of her story have led to PhD dissertations in American universities and analytical essays in Britain.

During her lifetime she was described and condemned as a harlot, a word originally used to describe men but later restricted to women. She was not a prostitute, not a courtesan, for she came from the middle class and did not try to find favour by cultivating anyone who happened to be near the court. Yet without much effort – it was the king who sought her out – she found herself occupying the top job, the best job available to women at the time: she became the king's mistress, and she was the mistress he really wanted. He had usually had many of them in a quick-moving procession. Safety in numbers, his wife Elizabeth Woodville may have thought, and King Edward never deserted this beautiful widow whom he had married in secret against everyone's wishes. At the same time he annoyed her because he sacked all the other women but insisted on keeping Jane. Sir Thomas More, writing in the next century, explained why: 'but her he loved'. Sadly, the king died in 1483 and Jane was on her own.

There are frustrating gaps in the records of Jane's life but many of them can be filled from the evidence of her times, dominated from the start to the finish of her life by rebellion, war, violence, jealousy, sexual ambition, personal enmity, treason, murder, usurpation and ruthless social climbing.

Jane Shore was a name acquired in two stages by a young middle-class woman and in history and hearsay it has remained with her. Hers was not just a rags-to-riches story with secrets of some sort, but a story with undertones of family breakdown, romance and revenge which could only have happened during the later decades of the fifteenth century, when both royalty and middle-class society were changing fast, moving out of the Middle Ages towards the first decades of the Renaissance and the modern world. If Jane had not been so close to King Edward IV for twelve years or so her name would probably not have been known or remembered outside a few pages included in a much contested unfinished work by Sir Thomas More and a few cynical mentions in Shakespeare's tragedy *King Richard III*, admired by many, popular with the public but again much contested.

Today, in the early twenty-first century, many women see their names not in sand, as Spenser imagined, but in lights, usually over the entrance doors to theatres or cinemas or, at least, in heavy black type in newspaper headlines. The names may come and go, floating in and out on the tide of public opinion, which controls the headlines, or in photographic captions, theatre programmes or film souvenirs: these do not often last very long, they fade quickly or else they are carefully filed away in archives, sometimes rediscovered by posterity or sometimes even by accident. After the sudden death of Edward IV in 1483 Jane figured only in gossip about her later lovers, one of them the late king's lord chamberlain, his close friend. People as different as King Richard III and the chroniclers of her own time referred to her as a harlot, she was forced to walk in penance through the streets of London and spend two periods in prison. However, she married a second time and was partly rehabilitated in the sixteenth century by Sir Thomas More, even if his accuracy and his apparent support for her are still questioned today, and nobody can demolish the sympathetic humanism in the few readable and much quoted pages he wrote about her. It could be said that he saved her life, but it was in fact her life in legend.

'Fame,' says the proverb, 'is dangerous; good bringeth envy; bad, shame', and Jane Shore knew both experiences, she knew both the ups and downs of life, although until recently the basic facts of this life were incorrectly remembered or else recorded in such elusive ways that they might never have been discovered. However, in 1972 Nicolas Barker published in *Etoniana* the results of brilliant research, assisted by well-deserved good luck, that had been prompted by Jane's possible connection with Eton College, as will be seen later; at the same time Sir Robert Birley, Head Master of Eton from 1949 to 1963, explored most of her many appearances in literature, while others have explored further.

Yet many mysteries about Jane's existence remain, for even in the twenty-first century, some basic facts have remained elusive. Her date of birth has never been proved but it seems safe to assume that it was probably in or about 1450, eight years after that of Edward IV. It is known with reasonable certainty from the Latin original of More's unfinished work *The History of King Richard III* that she died in the eighteenth year of Henry VIII's reign (1527), implying that she was well into her seventies at the time, rare longevity for the early sixteenth century. However, More's phrase, 'for yet she liveth', meaning that she was still alive when he was writing, had a different kind of relevance after her death, as will be seen later, since after 1527 her name moved regularly in and out of headlines, appearing in the titles of poems, books and plays, reflecting the changing life of England and particularly of English women.

Introduction

In 1548 Edward Hall published his history of *The Two Noble and Illustrious Families of Lancaster and York* (a shortened version of a very long title) and dedicated it to Henry VIII's son Edward VI. It is known that Hall had access to information that was subsequently lost, but he carefully acknowledges all his published sources, including notably among the English writers Sir Thomas More and William Caxton, mercer and printer, the well-known chronicler Robert Fabyan and the document that he calls *The Chronicles of London*, now known as *The Great Chronicle of London*. Hall's one-word evocations of each reign that he described give a concise impression of the times through which Jane Shore lived (excluding the first two he listed, the reigns of Henry IV and Henry V). He chose his one-word descriptions with care and the results are evocative:

> The troublesome season of King Henry VI
> The prosperous reign of King Edward IV
> The pitiful reign of King Edward V
> The tragical doings of King Richard III
> The political government of King Henry VII
> The triumphant reign of King Henry VIII

Jane's life was to be longer than the lives of any one of these kings, even if Henry VI actually reigned for thirty-nine years, and died, murdered, in the Tower of London when he was fifty, but if her life remains more mysterious, it has lasted a long time indeed, in two modes. By examining her background, including much of the life of Edward IV, avoiding speculation as far as possible, and profiting from valuable twentieth-century research, as shown in the notes to the following text and the bibliography, much can be restored of the life and personality of the royal mistress who differed from most of those other concubines whose names have remained inseparable from those of their royal lovers. Jane was different because she was unambitious and sought no reward for the help she gave to others; she escaped from the loveless marriage arrangement made by her parents because it offered her no future and no children, which she wanted. Maybe she loved King Edward and possibly she unconsciously anticipated the time in the distant future when women hoped for, and finally won, not just a room of their own but a life of their own.

Introduction

As Simone de Beauvoir hinted in *The Second Sex* of 1949, during the centuries when so little was offered to women in the way of training and professionalism, the post of mistress was one of the few available to them.

Jane was one of the early figures who tried to escape from the conventions of current society which allowed women merely to exist, but prevented them from living. Very few women at this period escaped from convention. Jane broke the rules, as mistresses, royal or not, had done before her time and would continue to do so later. Her unconscious courage was acknowledged, not during her lifetime, but during the later centuries when her legend was never forgotten and is still remembered. Adapting famous lines by a twentieth-century writer, it could truthfully be said of her that in her end was her beginning.

Genealogical Table

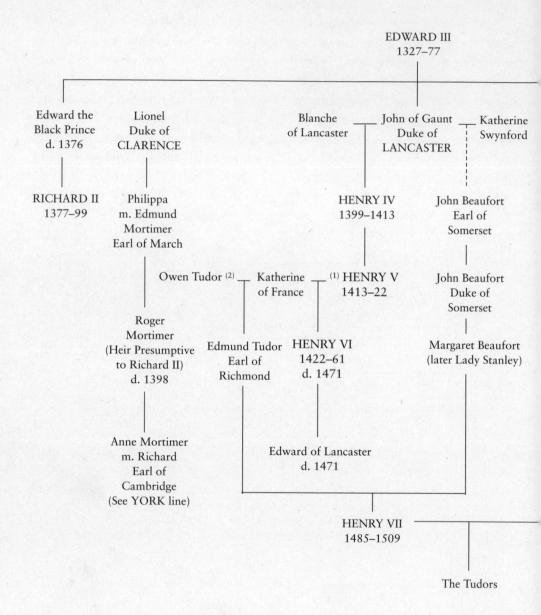

EDWARD III
1327–77

Edward the
Black Prince
d. 1376

Lionel
Duke of
CLARENCE

Blanche
of Lancaster

John of Gaunt
Duke of
LANCASTER

Katherine
Swynford

RICHARD II
1377–99

Philippa
m. Edmund
Mortimer
Earl of March

HENRY IV
1399–1413

John Beaufort
Earl of
Somerset

Owen Tudor (2)

Katherine
of France

(1) HENRY V
1413–22

John Beaufort
Duke of
Somerset

Roger
Mortimer
(Heir Presumptive
to Richard II)
d. 1398

Edmund Tudor
Earl of
Richmond

HENRY VI
1422–61
d. 1471

Margaret Beaufort
(later Lady Stanley)

Anne Mortimer
m. Richard
Earl of
Cambridge
(See YORK line)

Edward of Lancaster
d. 1471

HENRY VII
1485–1509

The Tudors

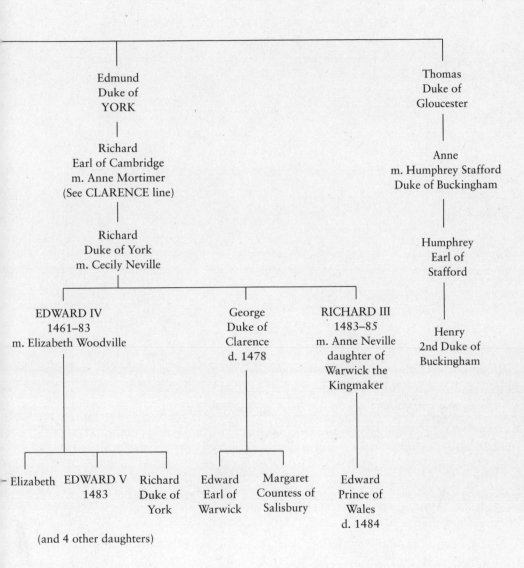

Edmund
Duke of
YORK

|

Richard
Earl of Cambridge
m. Anne Mortimer
(See CLARENCE line)

|

Richard
Duke of York
m. Cecily Neville

Thomas
Duke of
Gloucester

|

Anne
m. Humphrey Stafford
Duke of Buckingham

|

Humphrey
Earl of
Stafford

EDWARD IV
1461–83
m. Elizabeth Woodville

George
Duke of
Clarence
d. 1478

RICHARD III
1483–85
m. Anne Neville
daughter of
Warwick the
Kingmaker

Henry
2nd Duke of
Buckingham

Elizabeth EDWARD V
1483

Richard
Duke of
York

Edward
Earl of
Warwick

Margaret
Countess of
Salisbury

Edward
Prince of
Wales
d. 1484

(and 4 other daughters)

PART ONE

The Life

ONE

Early Days, Early Years

Surely no royal mistress in the not so distant past has been more mysterious than the young woman known later as 'Jane Shore'. There are no records of the crucial dates in her life: when and where she was born, or when and where she was first married and acquired the name of Shore. She had no Christian name in the writings that mention her until about 1599, when the playwright Thomas Heywood decided, in his two-part drama about King Edward IV, to call her Jane, as did both her husband and the king. The name she had received at birth, Elizabeth, was not discovered until 1972, along with confirmation of her second marriage, all of this clarified by her father's will, proved in 1487.[1] Throughout her long survival in legend and literature, which has been created by poets, dramatists, novelists, early film-makers, theatrical and television producers, in addition to biographers, she has always been known as Jane Shore.

Fortunately a good deal is now known about her father, who belonged to an important group of men in the late medieval city of London. These were the merchants, or mercers, who so impressed the Scottish poet William Dunbar in the late fifteenth or early sixteenth century; it was their continuous activity and success against all odds that had kept the country going through several decades of overseas fighting in the Hundred Years War and trouble at home. This included a rebellion which reached the city itself, plus a civil war which began in 1455 and lasted for thirty years in all, while throughout these upheavals there had been a constant shortage of able-bodied people caused by recurring outbreaks of plague. This was hardly a cheerful time in the history of England nor for the family in Cheapside where 'Jane Shore' was probably born.

The seemingly endless war between England and France, initiated in the previous century by King Edward III, was drawing painfully to a close and despite the victories of the former king, Henry V, notably of course at

3

Agincourt in 1415, France now seemed dangerously close to triumph. There had been an attempted two-year truce between the warring parties in 1444, while during the following year the province of Maine, still in English ownership, had been secretly promised to France by King Henry VI of England. In 1445, that same year, Henry, aged twenty-four, was married to the teenage Margaret of Anjou, daughter of René, Duke of Anjou, in the hope that such an alliance would help to bring the two countries together in peace. This it failed to do, and the new Queen Margaret, a girl of sixteen, did not even bring a useful dowry with her. The English king, who was more interested in spiritual life than personal ambition or political negotiation, likewise failed to satisfy anyone; the English were angry when the imminent loss of Maine became known and by 1449, when the French had regained the important province of Normandy, they were more angry still.

This situation was not likely to help the business activity of London, especially the export trade, mainly in woollen cloth and some home-produced silk, but the city merchants, responding to the challenge, continued to work with more concentration than ever, fortunately able to continue exports through Flanders, and there was little radical change in the way their personal lives were organised, for they remained constantly optimistic: they knew how much the country and the military leaders themselves depended on them. John Lambert, father of the girl who became known as Jane Shore, was one of the merchants, or mercers, admired by William Dunbar in his poem *In Honour of the City of London* and is assumed to have conducted his business in Cheapside. He had decided when he was about fifteen or so, the age when boys took up apprenticeships, that he would train to qualify as a mercer, hoping for a profitable career. It is worth noting that the Mercers' Company, which he aimed to join, was the most important of the many livery companies which controlled trade at the time and it still exists today as a charitable concern. John Lambert's period of apprenticeship had been shortened from the usual period of ten years to eight, possibly because he was a highly promising young man.

He had been born in about 1419 or 1420 and sometime in the 1440s he married Amy Marshall, whose father was a prominent member of the Grocers' Company, second only to the Mercers' in reputation and success. John Lambert, who had set up in business as soon as his apprenticeship was over, quickly won a good reputation, he was energetic and highly ambitious, essential qualities in the city. He soon took on apprentices of his own and before long he was taking part in the administration of the city. He was appointed as an alderman in 1460 and chosen as a sheriff for a year, when he acted as warden for the area known as Farringdon Within, an important part of the city which included St Paul's church as it was then known, and of course many other churches of varying importance. The boundaries and the area it included can be studied in detail in John Stow's *Survey of London* of 1598, which lists every street and important building in all of the twenty-four wards making up this proud old city, which had been first established in Roman times. (The twenty-fifth ward lay on the south side of the Thames.)

The aldermen were not only merchants, they acted as bankers, for the Italian banks were not yet fully established in London. Their duties in maintaining order were important and they had great powers which earned them much respect: they could act as local justices, pronounce sentences and determine punishments of all kinds – from the stocks to the pillory, from whipping to many other indignities that had to be suffered in public. They also ran Ludgate prison and supervised sentences of capital punishment: so they were indeed men to be respected, even feared.

'Jane', as she was later known, therefore, was to grow up in a family where the father was an important and for most of his life a responsible man. Probably John Lambert had ambitions to be chosen as mayor, which unfortunately did not happen, but like many other mercers and sheriffs he soon joined the bankers, lending money when he was satisfied that the debtors would pay him back and making more money as a result. It was well known that among those who constantly required finance were the kings of England, for parliament never voted them sufficient funds for court expenses and especially those needed for fighting a successful war.

If the Hundred Years War was at last approaching its end it was not yet over, and in the early days of 1450 nobody could tell what would happen next. Inevitably there would be heavy outstanding debts which had to be paid later, somehow: but how? Much depended on those 'merchants full of substance and of might' as Dunbar described them.

John Lambert was known to be a supporter of the Yorkists, and so cannot have approved the current rule of the Lancastrian King Henry VI, destined to be the last in a long series of Lancastrian kings of England. He in no way resembled his heroic father, Henry V, who had died young in 1422, when his son was only nine months old. The child was declared king of England that year while a month or so later, after the death of his maternal grandfather, Charles VI of France, he was in principle king of France too. He was declared of age in 1437, but as he grew up it became obvious that he possessed few, if any, qualities of kingship in the practical sense, for he preferred meditation and prayer to politics. His advisers soon saw that the future of the reign would be difficult, and they began to fear the representatives of the rival Plantagenet group, the ambitious Yorkists, who were likely to become dangerous opponents. The leaders of both groups were descended from Edward III, through the sons of his sons, and each of the rival claimants now had to prove his case, each demonstrating that his own descent was more direct than that of the other. The Duke of York was in fact descended directly from Edward III through both his parents.

If John Lambert made no secret of his support for the Yorkists, led by the ambitious and not too popular Duke of York, a view he shared with many Londoners, for the time being he concentrated on his business, his civic duties and the establishment of his family. The date of his marriage to Amy Marshall is not known; their first surviving child, christened Elizabeth, was probably born in 1450 or perhaps slightly earlier, in 1445 at the earliest, and if the Lambert parents had hoped for the essential son and heir – a daughter was of secondary importance – they were soon rewarded, for the family increased later by three sons, John, Robert and William.

Despite the uncertainty of life at this period John Lambert prospered. His wife Amy soon acquired high status on her own account and was so highly respected that she was referred to as 'Lady Lambert', seen as the outstanding wife of an outstanding man. Despite the difficulties of the merchants' work at the time there was still every hope of a good future for their children. Unfortunately, however, for the Lambert family and for all the citizens of London the year 1450 soon developed into a particularly dangerous and violent time which set the pattern of everyone's life for at least thirty years ahead, mostly dominated by fighting and uncertainty. Soon after that the unexpected 'usurpation' and tyrannical behaviour of the future Richard III caused the violence to recur, if briefly. It was difficult to imagine that peaceful times would ever follow and in 1450 the English had little to be proud of, especially after the loss of Normandy the previous year. The same year had seen the end of the unpopular Duke of Suffolk, Earl de la Pole, who appears to have been an incompetent leader, even if the decisions behind his attempt to counter-attack the French, the wrong decisions, had been taken by Henry VI, who was not qualified to direct military operations. Henry hoped to save Suffolk from public wrath by banishing him from England for five years but in May 1450 the duke was seized by his personal enemies and beheaded in a rowing boat (with a rusty sword) while attempting to cross the Channel. He was treated with ignominy, his body abandoned on the shore. Nobody was upset, nobody cared about Suffolk and most people welcomed his disappearance. Incidents of this kind reveal the brutal style of the late Middle Ages, when memories of chivalric romance seemed to be fading and those attractive images of tranquil pleasure accompanied by minstrels on harp and lute had to be forgotten, at least for the time being.

The year 1450, possibly that of their daughter's birth, could well have been a happy one for the Lambert parents, but in addition to the still unending war with France it was also the year of a short but violent rebellion against the English government led by a man from Kent, Jack Cade. In 1450 only very old people could possibly have lived through or even remembered the violence of the unsuccessful Peasants' Revolt of 1381, the sixth year of Richard II's reign, but the peasants' protests, which were largely ignored, and the death of their leader Wat Tyler, killed by the Lord Mayor of London in the presence of the king, had not been forgotten. Now, seventy years later, and during the final disastrous decade of the Hundred Years War, it was not merely peasants but responsible people of all classes, including the gentry and the clergy, who felt it was essential to protest about the misconduct of the war and the increased taxes they were now being asked to pay, both for many heavy military losses and for the upkeep of the court and the royal family. Queen Margaret of Anjou, who had first appeared to the Londoners in 1444 with a splendid escort of nineteen carriages filled with her attendants, had not concerned herself with economy.[2]

Relatively little seems to be known about Cade, although he had recently been tried for possible sorcery. In the proclamation for his arrest, in 1450,

7

he was accused not only of using books of magic but of having 'raised up the Devil in the semblance of a black dog' in his lodgings in Dartford.[3] Activities of this kind were anything but rare at the time, for many uneducated people, and even many who had had the benefit of better education, still believed that only magic or witchcraft could help them achieve their ambitions or get them out of trouble. Appropriately, as the leader of what turned out to be a strong, brief but disturbing rebellion, Cade was a violent, ambitious character, like so many men of those times. In an apparent attempt to attract the attention of another ambitious and potentially violent man, Richard, Duke of York, Cade called himself 'Mortimer', recalling the name of the duke's mother, for he knew that the duke intended to make a claim for the throne; this had not yet been openly put forward, but the duke's threat was becoming widely if unofficially better known and had begun to alarm the government. Its members feared that Cade could bring him useful support.

Cade and his band, joined by rebels from the east of the country, marched from Kent to Blackheath and submitted their complaints to the king, only to find themselves virtually ignored, in the hope that they would be discouraged and melt away. Cade was not a man to accept this kind of treatment and in the end, after various disturbing incidents, the rebels forced their way into the city, which suffered badly, despite Cade's early attempt to forbid any pillage. Very soon the rebels turned into an undisciplined mob, ignored their leader and decided among other opportunistic moves to attack the premises of a merchant named Philip Malpas, who was an alderman, very rich and apparently very unpopular: he must have been carefully chosen. He lost virtually everything and he was not the only one.[4] There are no accounts of an attack on the Lambert house, but all the aldermen naturally rallied to the defence of the city by preparing such weapons and armour as they possessed, most of it old and rusty, but the citizens had to do what they could to protect the capital and naturally took special care of their own homes.

The rebels may have begun their protest quietly enough but they knew how to terrify the city, and the situation worsened. Even the sheriff of Kent was beheaded in the Mile End area and another man suffered at Whitechapel. Worse still: Lord Say, 'Great Treasurer of England . . . was brought out of the Tower of London unto the Guildhall, and there he was of divers reasons examined' and finally executed at the Standard in Cheap.[5] The severed heads were nailed up on London Bridge, there was fighting and drowning, the bridge was set on fire, and Cade made certain of even more support by breaking open two prisons, the King's Bench and the Marshalsea, releasing all the prisoners and hoping of course that they would join his followers.

All this and more was recounted in documents of the time. The Lamberts, who presumably lived not far away from these scenes of violence, possibly in Cheapside itself, must have been alarmed, and the children would not have been allowed out of the house. However the aldermen in particular continued to oppose the Cade supporters, using whatever weapons they possessed, although there was nothing they could do to end the fighting. It is shocking to think that the garrison in the Tower of London actually fired on the London civilians, even killing women and children.

Finally, after more than two months, when nobody seemed capable of ending the struggle, Lord Scales, who was in charge of the official military defence, organised a meeting with three high dignitaries of the Church and as a result a general pardon was issued. But there was no happy ending: after a reward was promised for the capture of Cade he was hunted down in Sussex and killed. His corpse was brought back to London where his head was cut from his body and fixed to London Bridge; at the same time parts of his dismembered body were distributed round the country in order to deter any future rebels. It was a reminder of the ruthless behaviour of those earlier centuries. So ended the man who had almost subdued the city and had proudly gone to Cannon Street to touch London Stone with his sword. He is still remembered near the western boundary of Kent by a plaque in the Sussex village named after him: Cade Street. That may have been a long way from Cheapside, but the end of Cade is typical of the heartless and cruelty-ridden time which formed the framework to the early life of Elizabeth Lambert.

The Cade rebellion, although particularly destructive to London, was not an isolated incident, and was followed by other violence. In fifteenth-century English history it is hard to find more than a few weeks when there was no outbreak of anger, with the result that many young people, even children like Elizabeth Lambert, could have assumed that the whole of life was full of anger and violence like this. Soon after Cade's death the Bishop of Salisbury, after saying mass, was murdered and stripped bare by various parishioners from Erdington in Wiltshire, who were even proud of their wicked behaviour. The bishop had been carefully targeted, for it was he who had officiated at the marriage in 1445 of the unpopular and ineffective Henry VI to Margaret of Anjou at the Premonstratensian abbey[6] at Titchfield, also in Wiltshire. Edward Hall, in the edition by Grafton of his *Chronicle*, ended his account of this twenty-eighth year of Henry VI's reign with despairing words: 'and so from thenceforth daily succeeded murder, slaughter and dissension'.[7]

There was no good news during the rest of 1450: Caen was surrendered to the French, so was Cherbourg, and unsurprisingly morale in England fell to a low point. What would happen now?

Richard, Duke of York, had occupied two important posts in France, acting as the English king's Lieutenant there in 1436/7, and later becoming Governor of France and Normandy from 1440 to 1445. Returning to England after his years abroad, ending with the loss of Normandy, he had watched all political developments carefully, but everyone in royal circles also watched him, for his ambition was becoming clear. His ancestry meant that his claim to the throne was good, but his hopes were dashed when in October 1453 Margaret of Anjou, Henry VI's wife, gave birth to a son. This was so unexpected an event after nearly nine years of marriage that there was gossip: the child was surely not legitimate, claimed the Yorkists, especially since the king, suffering from an attack of mental instability, had apparently failed to show any interest in his son and did not even bless this new heir to the Lancastrian cause. During the king's illness the Duke of York was appointed Protector. He had hoped to return to France with some senior command but the suspicious Lancastrian court decided to make him Governor of Ireland instead. As Protector he had a valid excuse for delaying his departure to Ireland as long as he could. Fortunately, at least in some ways, the king had recovered from the upset to his health by the end of 1454, and the Duke of York had to give up his protectorate.

However, the country was still in the grip of violence even though the Hundred Years War had reached its dismal end in or about 1453 with defeat for the English at the battle of Castillon in Guyenne, in the south of France, and the loss of Bordeaux, the valuable port on the west coast.

There was no official peace treaty. England, which had previously owned almost half the area of France, was now left only with Calais and the Channel Islands, a miserable situation. Exports from England went through the Wool Staple at Calais, so at least this was saved, and the town retained an English Captain. Then, as though people could not imagine life without conflict, there came the immediate threat of a new and different war: 'the Wars of the White and Red Roses' were to follow with scarcely a break.

Henry VI seems to have had more health trouble, with the Duke of York again acting as Protector, but although the king recovered quickly and deprived him of his post, this time it was too late. Nothing, it seems, could pacify the restless duke, and he won the support of another ambitious man, his wife Cecily's powerful uncle, the Earl of Warwick. Already in 1455 the impatience of these men 'let slip the dogs of war' and years of fighting followed, years which were to be dominated by the career of the Duke of York's son and heir, the young man who in 1461 became Edward IV, king of England and some ten or twelve years later took Mistress Shore as his mistress. Their stories were parallel for many years, even if in some ways far apart.

The seemingly romantic title given to these wars is said to have been a phrase used casually by Sir Walter Scott four centuries later in his novel *Anne of Geierstein* (1829), a story set in England, France and Switzerland during the fifteenth century. In the twentieth and twenty-first centuries some British historians have disliked the use of this phrase to describe a bloody war which went on far too long, changing the course of English history itself, but after more than five hundred years it is too late now for any other memorable description to be adopted. More memorable, although presented with disguised violence, is the well-known painting by the Pre-Raphaelite Henry Payne, in which he recalled the fanciful scene in the Temple garden introduced by Shakespeare into *Henry VI Part I*, Act II, Scene 4. The possible contestants wear gowns, not armour, and they offer the famous roses, although their gestures are threatening.

The city mercers and their families might have been worried now, for a new war coming so soon might well threaten their business activity further. Yet they knew that indirectly they could make money out of the fighting, for without the capital they provided no army could be paid: coin is the sinews of war, as Rabelais had written. This fresh conflict, basically a civil

11

war, began soon enough in the early summer of 1455 with the first battle of St Albans and victory went to the Yorkists.

Assuming she had been born in 1450 at the latest the young Lambert daughter would be at least about five years old now and joined by one or two of her brothers. Her parents, like all the city merchants and their families, might have worried about the new war situation but they were not faint-hearted, they continued to work hard: they had no choice. Some took sides, but in the city the Yorkists, who included John Lambert, still predominated. Thanks to the aldermen, whose battles took place well away from the battlefields, a kind of peace returned to London, but it was not to last.

The Yorkist faction was now openly fighting for the throne of England. In the first stages of this conflict victory went sometimes to York, sometimes to Lancaster, but the Yorkist defeat at Wakefield in 1460 seemed to be a disaster, for the Duke of York himself was killed. Queen Margaret, now virtually in charge of the Lancastrian force, was triumphant and the Duke of York's severed head, adorned with a paper crown, was nailed up on the gates of York. The duke's younger son, Edmund, had been killed too.

However, the Lancastrians had temporarily forgotten the eldest son, Edward, known as the Earl of March, who was only eighteen in 1460.

The Lancastrian leaders underestimated the earl's determination to avenge his father's death; the young leader left the Welsh border, set off rapidly towards the north, and on his way, undeterred by any danger, fought and won the battle of Mortimer's Cross in Herefordshire, defeating an army of Welsh Lancastrians who had attempted to destroy the Yorkist army.

It was too early to assume that the Yorkist faction under their young leader was now ready to take control of the military or political situation. On 17 February the second battle of St Albans, fought under the command of the Earl of Warwick before Edward and his army arrived, was won by Queen Margaret's troops. The queen had realised that she would have to take command, for her husband was incapable of doing so: he still preferred praying to fighting. At St Albans she broke with military tradition: her forces attacked the enemy's flank and not the front, taking the Yorkists by surprise. The military historian A.H. Burne has imagined how the enemy might have reacted to this manoeuvre.[8] Was it a clever move by someone who might have been a feminist *avant la lettre*, an accident, or merely a desperate action? The queen had adopted a strategy that was 'unusual, brilliant and phenomenally successful. It must have made the leading soldiers of the time do a little quiet thinking'. In the past there had been a rule: 'armies should engage front to front; but here was an army engaging front to *flank*'. In this century women were regarded merely as marriage partners, they were not expected to take decisions about important problems and certainly not about the conduct of a battle. Was the queen poised to start a new kind of warfare?

In 1461 this was a very different Margaret from the sixteen-year-old bride who had come to London seventeen years earlier for her marriage 'with two steeds trapped all in white damask powdered with gold . . . and her hair combed down about her shoulders, with a coronal of gold, rich pearls and precious stones'.[9] Life had moved on; the queen could optimistically assume now that she would soon receive support from both Scotland and France, as she had been promised, and boldly came to London, not many miles south of St Albans. She was triumphant, but much more unpopular than she had realised. She sent messengers to the city gates, asking for admission. The mayor and some aldermen, hoping for negotiations, thought they should meet her, but the citizens would have none of her. Reluctantly she decided that her army must turn back, and as a result London was spared the chaos and bloodshed that would inevitably have followed. The Lancastrian troops had already acquired a bad reputation for pillage and robbery, and would have wrecked the city.

It was now, in the aftermath of this second battle of St Albans in 1461, lost by the so far heroic Earl of Warwick, that London became aware of a new military leader, potentially even more heroic, the tall and handsome Edward of York, known as the Earl of March, only nineteen and still intent on avenging his dead father. His basic tactics were simple: he believed in attack whereas Warwick tended to prefer defence. Now, however, Edward was forced to remember that this fighting had one aim: Henry VI must be defeated and then he himself would take his place on the throne.

The later and crucial stage was conducted in fact by Warwick, proving that he was not only an expert on battlefield defence but that he could deserve the name he was soon given, the Kingmaker. The *Great Chronicle of London*[10] described what happened: 'He [Warwick] mustered his people

13

in St John's Field where unto that host was proclaimed and showed certain articles and points that King Henry had offended in.' Did the crowd find him 'worthy to reign as king any longer or no. Whereupon the people cried hugely and said, Nay, Nay. And after it was asked of them whether they would have th'earl of March for their king and they cried with one voice Yea, Yea.'

This simplified decision, hardly a democratic vote or a plebiscite, was reported to Edward who was lodged at his mother's house in the city, Baynard's Castle. He modestly issued his thanks for the decision and added (of course) that he was not worthy to be king. However, he was soon accepted by dignitaries of Church and state, after an 'exhortation' by the Archbishop of Canterbury and other bishops present, in addition to 'other noble men', probably influenced by Cecily of York, Edward's mother. In principle, Edward was proclaimed king of England. Next day he rode to St Paul's 'and there had *Te deum* sungen with all solemnity.' Later he went to Westminster, his right to the throne was proved and he was proclaimed king. 'And thus,' according to the *Great Chronicle of London*, 'took this noble prince possession of the realm of England upon a Tuesday being the 4th day of March'.[11]

However, the young man, essentially a military leader at this period of his life, insisted on proving himself in a final battle. Politics and parliament were not yet real enough to him and he had not forgotten his father's death. After joining Warwick he led the Yorkist army north, where the Lancastrians had withdrawn. The queen and her military leaders were hoping for a strategic pause but Edward was determined they would have no such thing. He planned to attack them at once.

It was on Palm Sunday, 29 March 1461, in a snowstorm, that Edward and the Yorkist army defeated the Lancastrians at Towton in Yorkshire, about five miles from Tadcaster. This conflict, which lasted all day, engaged the two largest armies ever opposed to each other so far on an English battlefield and an estimated 20,000 men died. The battle ended the first stage of the fifteenth-century civil wars, it passed into folk memory and is remembered locally every year. A commemorative cross was erected and still stands. Later, the Duke of Gloucester is said to have asked for a small chapel to be built in memory of the men who had lost their lives, but if it ever existed it has now vanished without trace.

With Towton, history became entangled with legend. A.H. Burne has mentioned that on this site there grew, until recently, an unusual dwarf rose,[12] 'with white petals and a red spot', but after seven centuries this has vanished too. The site where it was observed is still known locally by the name it had earned in reality: Bloody Meadow. The citizens of London could only be selfishly thankful that the bloodshed had been so far away to the north. Queen Margaret, her husband and her son escaped to Newcastle, then Scotland. Edward IV was king of England.

These details give only a bare summary of the Wars of the Roses, but the ruthless fighting, which no one tried to prevent, formed the background to the early lives of both Edward IV and also, indirectly, the girl who was to be known as Jane Shore, later his favourite mistress. No two young people might have seemed more unlikely to meet, even though this is no simple rags-to-riches story.

The future Jane Shore, who would probably be about eleven or twelve years old during 1461, the year of Towton, would now learn more about Edward IV. Everyone wanted to see the new young king, and the girl, who would have been considered grown up at the time, might have had the chance, along with everyone in the city, to watch him riding in processions through the streets, on his way to Westminster or to any of the royal palaces in or near the city. These processions helped to inform people of what was going on and provided entertainment at the same time. The handsome young king, already attracting attention through his eye-catching clothes, which included expensive fur trimmings and brilliant jewellery, was an immediate star, the late medieval equivalent of a twenty-first-century celebrity. He had dismissed the unpopular Henry VI along with his increasingly aggressive queen, and changed the government of England. There was to be an uneasy kind of postscript to this story later, for Edward appeared to lose his grip in 1469, not recovering control until May 1471. With the death of Henry VI's son at the battle of Tewkesbury in 1471 and the quiet killing of Henry himself in the Tower of London a few weeks afterwards, the Lancastrian line of Plantagenet kings came to an end.

TWO

Growing Up

During these last six years, the first stage of the Wars of the Roses, Elizabeth Lambert had grown up into a girl of eleven or twelve, and was no longer a child; the former Earl of March had become the new king of England through battle, even if he had not won a serious political majority, despite a special service of thanksgiving in Westminster Abbey and a lavish coronation. However, he was still technically only a king in waiting since Henry VI, the anointed sovereign, was still alive at that time even though he was in hiding. Even in 1461, the ambitious Queen Margaret still hoped desperately that the wars were not over, for she had set her heart on winning them, and she was already embarking on serious pro-Lancastrian diplomatic moves in France.

In England however, the entire population and especially the city merchants, even if they had not known or cared a great deal for the late Duke of York, now understandably wanted to hear even more about his son Edward, newly confirmed as king. The public knew that the young Edward was a heroic military leader, but they wanted to know what he was like personally, not just that he was tall, dark and handsome; or was he fair, as the unsatisfactory portraits in London's National Portrait Gallery and even the Royal Collection seem to show? Unless they had actually watched him in a street procession nobody would even know what he looked like. Women and girls, who had heard about his good looks, were ready to get excited about him.

There was no secret about the way he had been brought up: the education of the young Earl of March at Ludlow Castle, the family home, had been carried out according to the rules of his class, the aristocracy, but his apparent inborn talent for leadership, especially in warfare, seems to have been innate, inherited. His father had had sufficient experience of military life and many contacts with political life, even if over-coloured by his own ambition, to direct the young man's practical studies, having first chosen suitable tutors to carry out all details of the varied instruction needed. Edward was not allowed to be idle, for moral, religious and historical teaching was rated as highly important, although naturally the young man could also indulge in hunting, jousting or any other sports during his leisure. Carefully chosen experts would supervise the book-learning, something which Edward seems to have enjoyed, even if he was never to develop into an intellectual. It was known that he learnt to read Latin and to speak tolerably good French, while later in life, especially after visiting Bruges, he collected some fine books, which are still preserved in the British Library in London,[1] but he seems to have preferred books that were objects of beauty in themselves with fine script, print or lettering and attractive illustrations. Scholarship as such was not his main interest: he seems to have appreciated the artistic value of the books he chose rather than the messages they were intended to carry to the reader. During mealtimes at Ludlow Castle he had to listen to readings from religious or highly moral works, a practice usual at the time and continued later, particularly in abbeys, convents and certain schools. Edward possessed through inheritance the practical qualities that would be essential in the early part of his life; the rest would be indeed the 'adjunct' to personality, as Shakespeare was to describe education in *Love's Labour's Lost*, the near-spontaneous development of those valuable inborn qualities, the indefinable extra that was to become paramount during his later years when he had finally stopped fighting, at least in England, and was able to concentrate on governing the country, carrying out many essential reforms in several spheres. But all that lay a long way ahead.

Elizabeth Lambert's parents in Cheapside would also follow the rules of education, again those relevant to her family circumstances, far removed of course from those of her future lover both because the education of girls was totally different from that given to boys of the merchant class and because the ambitions of her family and her class, although strong, were naturally different from those of the high-born York family. However, the future was to prove that the king would be permanently dependent on the merchant class of London, for he was always in need of money, while at the same time he soon developed a personal interest in trade. So Elizabeth, even if born into the middle class, was not as far away from the king as it might have seemed.

Amy Lambert in particular would be keen now to ensure that as her daughter grew up she would receive the best education available for girls at the time but as the family would have known only too well, the choice for girls was limited: they could attend the elementary schools as boys did but otherwise parents would have to employ private tutors. The girls themselves might decide they would like to enter the Church and if they did so they could benefit from the best education in England, although the conditions obviously would not suit everyone. Most private tutors would be retired teachers or priests, possibly even scriveners, who would be useful at least in teaching children how to write.

In 1949 Simone de Beauvoir (inescapable in any context touching on the education of women) when considering their situation during the Middle Ages, decided that women were so well protected, within the middle and upper classes at least, that many of them had little incentive or encouragement to think about anything that might allow them the independence of a career. In one sense, however, middle-class parents in the fifteenth century could offer girls a ready-made introduction to the world of commerce, for their children, who were expected to grow up quickly, would be encouraged to work closely with them even before the boys were apprenticed, usually of course outside the family, while the girls, after marriage, often worked with their husbands, who might depend on their help. The Lambert family would be ready to arrange all this in due course.

However, records have come to light showing that if given the chance, or if widowed, some women at this time were enthusiastically ready to develop an independent and rewarding career of their own. One particularly interesting group among the merchant class were the 'silkwomen', for the valuable trade in silk fabrics and embroidery was virtually in their hands alone. The career of one of these women, the twice-widowed Ellen Langwith, has been documented in detail[2] and proves that the women of the fifteenth century were certainly capable of creative and responsible work and soon commanded respect from everyone. However, hardly any girls remained unmarried, for parents and other relatives would search carefully for the right partner, who must first of all be useful to *them*, while the daughters themselves had little or no say in the matter. If the chosen man suited the prospective bride, if she liked the look of him, that was a bonus. No husband? Surely it was only a question of finding one. As Paul Murray Kendall remarked in his study of medieval life *The Yorkist Age*, the word 'spinster' could be used to describe someone who spun yarn: a word describing an unmarried girl or woman was hardly necessary in late medieval society, for such people were rare indeed.

Education must come first, however, marriage a little later, but not much later. Education was organised with one dominant aim: in the city, it must lead to progress in business and also, at the same time, to advancement in social life. After a boy had completed his apprenticeship it was usual for him to accept a placing and work his way up, but this would not necessarily be in the same trade or business that his father conducted. Girls must be groomed for a different type of success: it was assumed that every girl would marry, but she must marry well, she must accept a husband who was either well established or very soon likely to be, then, as a wife and mother, she in her turn could bring up a group of children who would also be well or even better educated, then make good marriages themselves or even hope to move closer to the gentry. This might often happen in the case of boys who had decided to take up a career in law, which was a popular choice. Marriage was inescapable, and just as much a business as anything else, determining social status and financial ease: it would determine the future and prove the truth of the old much-quoted saying: 'Marriage is destiny'. As in business, the result could be good or bad. On the whole young couples made the best of things, there would be respect and sometimes, perhaps, even love, although sentimentality and hopes of romance were not encouraged.

Parents, of course, and especially perhaps mothers, who felt personally responsible and were themselves experienced, were intent on a good future for their daughters, but education for girls remained complicated. In his detailed *Survey of London* John Stow referred to several schools and colleges for boys, some of them still well known today, but nowhere does he mention a single educational establishment exclusively available to girls. None of the charitably minded generous people, mainly men but some of them women, who endowed or maintained the schools apparently considered that girls needed any specially organised instruction – the only 'learning' of value to them would be mostly provided at home. However, there are often references in Stow's *Survey* to 'poor children' who had to be looked after in charitable establishments and presumably young girls were included among them. Sylvia Thrupp, in her authoritative study of 1948 *The Merchant Class of Mediaeval London*, mentions that elementary education was available to girls as well as boys, but emphasises that the former had no access to the higher education now available for their brothers, who could attend the grammar schools. Eton College had been founded by Henry VI in 1440 and there were many opportunities for boys to move out of the merchant class and take up other professions, notably law, as already mentioned. Latin was taught in the grammar schools and probably 40 per cent of Londoners could read it. This was a high proportion, for apparently only about one half of male Londoners (excluding priests) could read English, although by the mid-century it was used commonly in many documents. Better-off parents wanting higher education for a daughter could probably find it without too much trouble, although they would have to pay for it, but John Lambert could certainly have afforded it for his daughter, even though the family soon included at least three sons. One of them, William, later entered the priesthood.

It is clear at least that many girls received an excellent practical education at home, essential to them for the reasons already mentioned, starting with the management of the home itself and also an understanding of the family trade or business, much of which, except for trades such as bulk warehouse storage, was arranged and conducted in the family home. It was assumed without question that a well-educated girl with some knowledge or even experience of business was better equipped not just for her own personal life, but for the all-important good marriage. Girls were married early, and widows did not stay unmarried for long: they were always in demand as partners, because in many cases at least it was assumed that for one generation at least they and their new husband would have access to the inheritance left by the first.

But what can be assumed about the education given to Elizabeth Lambert? It is known that she learnt to read and write, even if no letter or other document written by her has yet been found. It is not difficult to imagine, without too much speculation, what she read, although her parents' home in Cheapside would not contain a library as such. It was not yet possible to buy printed books as we know them, for William Caxton, who incidentally was also a mercer, did not start printing in Westminster until later in the century, probably about 1476. However, there was no shortage of parchment copies of books, and it is possible that John Lambert, whose business sometimes took him to the continent, might bring back books from places like Bruges or from Germany, where printing began earlier. However, nearly all the early printed books were in Latin, which the Lambert sons may have learnt to read, but not their parents nor their sister. To borrow a phrase from Professor E.F. Jacob in his 1961 study *The Fifteenth Century, 1389–1485*, the Lambert household might have been described as 'literate but not literary'. There was probably a small private chapel in the house which would contain simple devotional tracts and works such as *The Golden Legend*, also devotional, including many lives of saints and a long-standing favourite, becoming later one of Caxton's most successful printed books. Chaucer, who had died in 1400, would be known about, but it seems unlikely that the merchants and their families had the time or inclination to read the most famous poet of the Middle Ages or that moving earlier classic *The Visions of Piers Plowman*. The writers who succeeded them, at least those who are remembered or even studied today, would be probably various imitators of Chaucer or else too sophisticated for this essentially practical household; the meetings and ceremonies of varied kinds that John Lambert would have to attend, sometimes accompanied by his wife, plus the domestic and other work that she had to organise, would leave them little time for reading, quite apart from the essential business accountancy and trading details that both parents would need to supervise. There would be no time for the more sophisticated fourteenth-century writers like Hoccleve or John Lydgate who earn occasional mentions today. The voyages described by the mysterious Sir John Mandeville might have been read out of curiosity at least, although whether the travels he described were mere adaptations of continental works is unknown.

The early teaching that Elizabeth received would be mainly oral: counting songs, nursery rhymes, fairy tales, ballads and riddles, while she would surely have been encouraged to sing and dance. The range of ballads was wide, and even if many of them had not yet been written down, some of the adults or the older servants would know them by heart and pass them on to the children. The favourite ballads would probably include some from the classic group about Robin Hood, Maid Marion and the sheriff of Nottingham, still popular in Hollywood five or even six centuries later. The long-lasting ballads included dramatic memorable stories such as the well-known *Clerk Saunders* and *Edward, Edward*, which came from Scotland. Since prose fiction as such was not yet being written in England, and the classic work that recalled the splendid days of chivalry, Malory's *Morte d'Arthur* was not printed until about 1485, the young Elizabeth probably did not have the chance to read it. However, when she was growing up, she would certainly be told legends, often set in early English history, while some crude romantic stories which had nothing to do with literature and have not survived may have been available to her, if her parents allowed them into the house.

It seems unlikely that she ever had the chance to read or even hear about that delightful earlier work *The Owl and the Nightingale* with its sophisticated discussions on morals, love and marriage. Instead, perhaps, as she grew up, she would find and enjoy the stories recounted in poems such as 'The Nut-brown Maid', that subtle and delightful classic telling how a lover, in disguise, tested the devotion of the girl who said she loved him. Perhaps, as she began to see more of her own city, she may have heard that famous and colourful poem 'London Lickpenny',[3] thought earlier to have been written by Lydgate but now rated as anonymous. Nothing is more evocative of commercial London life in the early or mid-fifteenth century. The speaker recounts his experiences in coming to the city from Kent and this monologue-poem expresses all the day-to-day liveliness of the busy, bustling city where everyone was trying to sell something to everyone else: for instance there were Flemish merchants offering 'Fine felt hats, spectacles for to read', and of course there was plenty of food:

> Cooks to me, they took good intent,
> Called me near, for to dine,
> And proffered me good bread, ale, and wine;
> A fair cloth they began to spread,
> Ribs of beef both fat and fine.
> But for lack of money I might not speed.

That was the speaker's problem, he had no money, but all the same he spent the day having a good look round, reminding his readers or listeners of all that was available in this actively cheerful series of markets: he was offered 'hot peascods', strawberries, and 'some spice', popular, in fact essential in those days to disguise the taste of meat that could be more than high, often just bad:

> Pepper and saffron they gan me bede,
> Cloves, grains, and flour of rice.

Again, with no money, he could not buy anything, but he wandered on through different markets:

> Then into Cheap I gan me drawn
> Where I saw stand much people.

It was here that some of the goods handled by mercers were being offered by stallholders, probably at cut prices or in small quantities:

> fine cloth of lawn,
> Paris thread, cotton and umple [possibly remnants].

Even if everything sold here was cheap this poor man still could not afford to buy anything, not even 'hot sheep's feet', while in East Cheap he was offered 'ribs of beef and many a pie'. This lively poem even evokes the sound of the market:

> Pewter pots they clattered in a heap;
> There was harp, pipe and sawtry [psaltery].

It was all noisy good fun but the speaker truly 'lacked a penny', he drank a pint of wine but was left very hungry and never found the hood he had 'lost in Westminster among the throng', for no man of law would help him unless he could be paid, and the poor man couldn't do that. He went back to Kent, saying 'Jesus save London that in Bethlehem was borne'. In London you had to have money or nobody took any notice of you. That situation has not changed.

The Lamberts and their fellow mercers knew all about money and the need to have it; as a class mercers were far from poor, they worked hard and were usually able to lend money, as already mentioned, which earned them interest. They could do that even when normal business was not brisk. When Elizabeth was taken out shopping in the big markets she would learn the value of money and how bargains were concluded. She and her mother – for she would not often be allowed out alone, and the two of them might be accompanied by a servant, indicating that 'Lady' Lambert was a superior mercer's wife – would have to buy food nearly every day because of course it could not be preserved for very long. The Lamberts would employ at least one cook and various kitchen staff, usually male, for strong arms were needed to deal with the animal carcasses supplied by the butchers and poulterers. Because no offal of any sort was discarded meat preparation was complicated and often hard work.

Visitors from abroad were impressed by the display of wealth in English middle-class houses, particularly silver plate, which was not merely ornamental but used at table every day; however it has to be admitted that many foreigners had a low opinion of English cooking – and unfortunately there is nothing unusual about that. Yet visitors found Englishwomen welcoming and warm-hearted, ready to greet any stranger who happened to come into a tavern not with handshakes or curtsies but with friendly kisses.[4] These women were not prostitutes: the latter could easily be found if wanted.

The basis of Elizabeth's upbringing would certainly be practical and surely affectionate, but as she grew older she would be taught more seriously about the importance of religion, for the Church still had great power, and details from the recent history of England would be explained to her as well. She would learn at least the names of some kings and queens who had occupied the throne before Henry VI and Margaret of Anjou, who had been married not long before she herself had been born; she would learn about the 'official' king's father, Henry V, the military hero, and perhaps, further back still, she might have been told about Henry IV, the usurper who had forced Richard II to abdicate and finally let him die in prison, probably poisoned.

As the young Elizabeth grew up – encouraged like all children of the time to grow up quickly – she would hear about her father's Yorkist views on the monarchy, and it would not have occurred to her to think he might be wrong or that the new young king people were talking about might have to deal with opposition; she, like the whole family would accept the unrest and violence that took place in the 1450s and after: it was the background to her life, to everyone's life, especially if they lived in London. In the country there was unrest too but of a different nature, usually quarrels about ownership of land, while relationships between the owners and their tenants, the problem of finding labour to replace the losses caused by the plague, all made things more difficult. In addition destructive battles had been fought over many fields in the Midlands and the north and if the soldiers were not paid they pillaged the countryside for food. There was no standing army and there were of course no accessible newspapers; news travelled slowly, although gossip and rumour circulated easily, usually with very little accuracy.

At the same time the girl in Cheapside would soon learn about the more pleasant side of life; she would be taught to appreciate the high-class textiles which her father bought and sold, and she would learn about the fabrics and fashions in vogue, much loved by medieval people who liked to show off the rich colours and texture of velvet, the variety of furs, the gold filigree, the embroideries and lace, in addition to other splendours. The work of the tailors and cutters, who were represented by their own livery companies, was very much admired. Most men in the better-off classes paid great attention to their clothes and often owned more finery than their wives, especially if, like John Lambert, they had to attend formal gatherings and feasts as part of their duty. Jewellery was popular, worn equally by men and women, for in a world without banks and banking, money, apart from commercial arrangements, had to be invested somehow and English goldsmiths, who created the jewellery, were skilled and popular.

Since the Lamberts were essentially an ambitious family – the energetic 'Lady' Lambert was presumably as ambitious socially as her husband was in business – they would probably find time to consult the reading material that was becoming very popular about good manners, which were considered very important. Boys especially, when they took up apprenticeships, were taught early that they must be responsible and polite, that was the way to success; in no circumstances must they pick their nose or allow themselves noisy farting. As for Elizabeth, she soon developed into a pretty girl with fair hair, the colouring that had always been admired and later received a special mention from Robert Burton in his *Anatomy of Melancholy*;[5] so her parents were surely pleased. There is no record of her childhood years, but the colour of her hair was mentioned later by at least one sixteenth-century poet who wrote about her, Michael Drayton; while the chronicle writers, also later, mentioned the thrill of 'gay apparel' as one of the reasons for the abrupt change she made to her life later, probably in the early 1470s.

It has to be remembered too that medieval people had to make their own entertainment in most ways; they could not go to any theatre to find colour and gaiety, although the miracle plays on biblical themes were popular, if limited in scope. At least everyone knew the characters and the plots, and the characters identified themselves when they first appeared. Elizabeth, remembered later for her charitable work, may well have seen that moving early play *Everyman*, and she may have remembered – for who could forget it – how all his so-called friends desert Everyman, except 'Good-Deeds', the one helpful figure who stays at his side when death approaches. Just as people created the richness of life for themselves by wearing dramatic clothes and costly jewellery, they never tired of watching street processions; they also made certain that their homes were well furnished, although the bedrooms in particular seem to have been very small and the furniture was hardly comfortable. The walls were often hung with decorative items such as painted wall-hangings and there are some rare survivals of paintings actually on wall surfaces. Portraits were rare too, limited to royal and aristocratic personages and rarely hung on the walls. Many people mentioned in this story have remained invisible, their appearance only known through engravings produced in the following century, probably based either on distant memories or on documents that had disappeared years before. What did John and Amy Lambert look like? Unfortunately we can only guess.

One aspect of Elizabeth Lambert's education deserves a mention: who were her 'role models', to use a popular phrase of today? The Virgin Mary and the saints were never forgotten, but the Middle Ages themselves did not include a great number of outstanding women who might impress young girls, probably because nobody saw any reason for recording their lives. Yet there were three who can still attract attention centuries later, all belonging to the world of religion and inevitably talked about. The earliest of these was the seventh-century Abbess Hilda of Whitby who lived *c.* 614–80 and had developed double religious houses for both men and women working seriously in the areas of devotion and education. The important Council of AD 664, which confirmed the acceptance of Christianity in Northumbria, took place during her tenure as abbess. The Venerable Bede admired her, and through priests Elizabeth might well have known about her. She was followed several centuries later by Julian (Juliana) of Norwich whose shrine at Walsingham in Norfolk still has a great following in the twenty-first century. Her dates are uncertain but she is known to have died sometime about 1443 and her enduringly famous mystical work *Revelations of Divine Love* is still a classic today.

Among the many visitors who found their way to her presence in Walsingham was another woman who made a name for herself at this time. This was the surely eccentric Margery Kempe, daughter of the mayor of Lynn (later King's Lynn), again in Norfolk. After marriage and the births of fourteen children the incredibly energetic Margery ran a small business of her own for a short time but then decided to devote her energies to God, went on pilgrimages round Europe and unconsciously invented a new literary genre – the autobiography. Since she could not read or write she dictated to a scribe all her travel adventures and religious and mystical experiences, which took her about two years. Some people were able to read the transcription, which was made by a long-suffering monk under the author's watchful eye and constant tearful interruptions. She would often burst into ecstatic tears for no particular reason. Some contemporaries, possibly in the 1460s, had had the chance to learn about Margery Kempe's unusual personality and wonder why there was so much weeping. Unfortunately it cannot be known whether Elizabeth Lambert had heard of this book, although it is unlikely that she had the chance to read it; late in the century the only copy available of the work mysteriously disappeared from circulation and was not seen again until 1934, when, according to her biographer Louise Collis, it was rediscovered in a Yorkshire country house and eventually published by the Early English Text Society. Margery, however, was known and gossiped about in her own century and although people hearing about her probably thought she must have been mad, they surely paid attention. If the young Elizabeth heard about her she would not have been tempted to follow her example. Margery was unique.

Would Elizabeth have heard or even read of any other outstanding women of early centuries? Not too many seem to have been remembered during the Middle Ages, unless the early chronicles were known in the Lambert household, but she might have heard something about Boudicca, heroine of the Roman occupation. On the whole, however, women would have had scanty mention in the records. In the early history of England there were a few others about whom not a great deal is known but their lives were surely of value, if only for a time, but at least people would have talked about them and Elizabeth might have heard this talk. One such was the mother of William the Conqueror, known in France as William the Bastard. She was not Count Robert's wife but a girl called Arlève, or Arletta, daughter of a tanner, who happened to attract his father, the Duke of Normandy, one day when he was riding by and saw her hanging out the washing. She was soon summoned to the palace. William always maintained that his status of 'bastard' made him all the more determined to stand up for himself and win, which he did. Nothing more was heard of his mother, although it is known that she was, of course, married off. There were no magazines or scandal sheets at the time, but obviously there was scandal which entertained women in particular. Young Elizabeth would have listened to gossip whenever she had the chance, since there were few other sources of entertainment at the time.

Another woman of interest in those early years was Edith of the Swan Neck, the long-standing mistress of Harold of England, who was defeated by William in 1066. There was such carnage at the battle of Hastings that Harold's body could not be identified by anyone, except by one woman, Edith. She was summoned to the corpse-strewn field after the battle, and her previous intimate life with Harold enabled her to point out the so-far unrecognisable dead body. There is also a mystery about Aelfgifu of Northampton who bore sons to King Cnut; he then married Emma and his previous mistress appears to have been left on her own. However, Cnut made use of her by sending her to Scandinavia to supervise his old territories on his behalf.

There were a few more important women in history whom Elizabeth might have heard of and she might well have been warned against any involvement in such strange experiences: surely somebody would have told her about Eleanor of Aquitaine, who lived from about 1122 to 1204; she was a historical figure who sounds legendary, due to her marriages, her possible lovers, her journeys to the crusades and her extraordinary behaviour in general. Would Elizabeth have heard of the romantic legend about 'Fair Rosamond', the long-term mistress of Eleanor's second husband, Henry II of England? This legend may have been an invention but it had great appeal to later painters and poets, notably among the Pre-Raphaelites. She was reputed to be Rosamond Clifford, a member of the well-known family, and it was said that she had several children by the king. Was it true that the king had built a special house for her and did the jealous Queen Eleanor find out about it? The entrance was supposed to be through a maze with complications only known to the king but in the end, of course, the Queen discovered the secret and took her revenge; there are many versions of how she is supposed to have killed Fair Rosamond. Did she arrange for her to fall into a concealed pit or did she somehow administer poison? Rosamond is said to have been buried in a church at Godstow in Oxfordshire until a visiting cleric, the Bishop of Lincoln, ordered the tomb of this wicked woman, this 'harlot', to be removed, and Rosamond was reburied in the neighbouring chapter house. If Elizabeth had heard this story or even read some of the ballads written round it, would she have thought about it later? It had originally been told by Ranulf Higben, the fourteenth-century chronicler, and later retold by John Stow and others but it seems to have been recounted for children as a cautionary tale, for it is known to have fascinated them and even encouraged them to read.[6] This was one of the stories that supplied the equivalent of romantic fiction, which had not yet been invented. Years later, several poets, including Samuel Daniel and Michael Drayton, found it natural to link the name of Jane Shore with that of Rosamond. Their names were also to be linked in many anonymous ballads, but the young Elizabeth Lambert would only have been told about Rosamond as an example of how she, a respectable member of a respectable family, should not behave.

Then there was that impressively wicked queen, Isabella, again a historical, not a legendary figure, who came from France and was said to have been incredibly beautiful. She was married to Edward II but took one of his enemies, Roger Mortimer, as her lover; together they succeeded in removing her husband from the throne. Isabella, known later as the 'She-Wolf of France,' and Mortimer then ruled the country as regents, having arranged for her young son to occupy the throne and be King Edward III at least in name. Eventually Edward, although little more than a child, got the better of his aggressive mother and sent her to a convent. Mortimer was executed. Isabella was a woman whose conduct set a scandalous example of how *not* to behave.

If Elizabeth's family ever gave her news from France, she may have learnt that in 1450, the beloved mistress of the French king Charles VII, Agnès Sorel, *la dame de beauté*, as he called her, had suddenly died, possibly from poison, and that the king's heart was broken. It might have struck the young English girl that any woman, apart from the queen herself, should somehow manage not to be too close to a king, it seemed to lead to trouble. She might also have noticed that queens did not always have a very interesting life: they had been virtually sold by their families as a mere clause in a treaty, they were there, as everybody knew, to produce heirs to the throne and that was almost all, so the king would find a mistress, even a succession of them. Women like Queen Isabella, who fiercely took matters into their own hands, sometimes came to a bad end. A mistress would often be better remembered than a queen, but she often led a dangerous life; Elizabeth would be surely conditioned by some of these stories about women, many of them true, and none of them comforting. But they implied drama, melodrama, excitement of some sort. And young girls would have listened to them.

These were a few individual women, some good, some bad, who were not forgotten in early English history, but it is hard to find many records of individuals in the city of London generally who can be remembered now as possible icons for an adolescent girl in the mid-fifteenth century. In his absorbing 'biography' of London Peter Ackroyd writes of the 'feminine principle',[7] but the women he describes were all members of anonymous groups: he does not see them as individuals, for presumably none of them emerged far enough from the crowd to be remembered on her own. Later in life 'Jane Shore' herself was destined to act as a woman on her own, but it is not easy to think of many predecessors whose behaviour might have influenced her. In the meantime her 'education', in the double sense of upbringing and learning, was soon over. She had acquired some learning, it became that 'adjunct' to herself, but it was certainly not all book-learning; some of it was legend, and legends, which always seem to have involved women, were more easily memorable than history, especially perhaps to a girl. It was still too early in history for any woman outside the Church or the aristocracy to be given a systematic education. Even in nineteenth-century France, Stendhal, who appreciated women but never lost his irony about them, noted this problem. 'Women,' he wrote in *De l'amour* of 1822, 'only know what we [i.e. men] don't care to teach them, what they read for themselves in the book of life.' He was not wrong about that. The young Elizabeth would watch and listen to the grown-ups, and would be learning in the same way, while probably never forgetting the old legends or even the achievements of a few women in history.

It was time now to think of the next stage in her life, the most important stage in any girl's existence in those earlier centuries, and she would not have long to wait: marriage.

THREE

Marriage is Destiny

It has to be repeated: Elizabeth Lambert's destiny was at first that of all girls born in the city of London in about 1450 towards the end of the Hundred Years War. She was born in or close to a year of violence and destined never to escape from it throughout her childhood and adolescence. Then possibly in the early 1470s she herself acted with a different kind of violence, breaking away totally from her earlier life; a different life overwhelmed her personally, and she would surely have been influenced by those chaotic, uncertain times. Soon the Wars of the Roses had gathered momentum and as battle followed battle few people in England had been able to escape the invasive cruelty they engendered: it affected most households in the land, although some parts of the countryside escaped. Much of this violence involved, directly or indirectly, the man who was to change Elizabeth's life later. However, it was *his* life that was now about to change, his personal life, and the way it happened cannot be omitted from this story.

Edward, known as the Earl of March when young, was about eight years older than Elizabeth Lambert and had been born in Rouen in 1442 when it was still in English hands. He was the eldest surviving son, as already described, of the Duke of York and his wife Cecily, who was a member of the Neville family. Edward's younger brother, the second son, Edmund, was followed by George and finally the youngest son, Richard, was born in 1452, in England. Altogether Cecily gave birth to ten surviving children, five of them sons. Then, in 1464, Cecily announced, to everyone's amazement, that she had been unfaithful to her husband before Edward's birth and as a result the young king had been born illegitimate.

Why did she say this, and was it true? Maybe it *was* true, and in the twenty-first century there is still argument about it, started or at least developed in 2000 by Michael K. Jones, who claimed to have found the

32

evidence among the archives of Rouen cathedral.[1] The truly interesting point is why she risked making this shocking announcement, but the reason in fact was simple: she had to think of something, anything in fact that might influence her son Edward because he, unsurprisingly now that he was king, was thinking about marriage, and as far as Cecily was concerned, he had acted in an unpardonable, irresponsible way: he had chosen someone for his queen, but he had chosen the wrong woman. The trouble was, now that he was king of England, he had to acquire a suitable consort, and was this woman, in Cecily's eyes at least, suitable? No, far from it. As the king's mother, Cecily had an importance of her own and when she made statements about important events, those who were close to her listened.

As a teenage boy Edward had already displayed a natural talent for military activities and all that implied. When he was only twelve or so he was reported to be leading an army, although of course there would be experienced soldiers at his side. Children in the fifteenth century were not allowed to have a long childhood for they might easily lose their parents early, and had to be equipped for self-reliance. This is why Edward's younger brother Edmund is said to have attended important council meetings in Westminster when he was only ten, and it would not be long before the York parents, especially Cecily, would begin to think well in advance about a useful, even prestigious marriage for her eldest son. After her husband's death at Wakefield in 1460 she was on her own, although fortunately the Neville family was there to support her if necessary. But Cecily, as will be seen later, was a strong-minded woman quite capable of managing her own and her young son's lives. Her second son, Edmund of York, had died with his father at Wakefield and Edward surely now received more attention than ever.

For the last few years his life had been dedicated to his military conquests, but now that he was king he would have to strengthen his position as a royal person as far as he could. The 1548 version of Edward Hall's *Chronicle*, edited by Richard Grafton, and known as *The Union of the Two Noble and Illustre Famelies of Lancastre & Yorke*, referred to the third year of King Edward IV's reign[2] by quoting the useful proverb 'Marriage is destiny': and this destiny, everyone believed at the time, would form the new and crucial development in the young man's life. The king was no longer merely a brilliant teenage boy who had avenged his father's death and had then won the decisive battle of Towton, thus temporarily at least defeating the Lancastrian hopes of retaining the throne. Henry VI was still in name king of England, but Edward assumed he had dismissed him and therefore in principle the country was now his own. However, the status of the new king had to be confirmed seriously as soon as possible, even if he had already been given two coronations, one secular, one religious.

It had to be admitted that the vote of approval for his accession had been a somewhat haphazard affair, and his advisers began to think about how his position could be strengthened and enhanced. There was one obvious way in which this could be done fairly quickly: he must acquire a suitable wife to be his queen who would provide him with legitimate heirs to inherit the kingdom. The new monarchy, it was assumed, would surely then be safe. Everyone in the country, not only the nobles, but the entire population (except of course the fervent Lancastrians, who had not yet lost all hope of recovery) assumed now that the king's advisers would find a suitable young foreign princess quickly and negotiate an advantageous marriage settlement. It was the normal way to proceed.

In the meantime the hard-working middle classes, especially in the city of London, continued to advance their business, for they knew that when the king married he would need extra money to pay for the upkeep and staffing of his future household, meaning that he would come to them for even more loans. There was still no other way of raising additional funds beyond those allocated regularly by parliament and these were never enough. John Lambert would naturally be more than pleased that the country now had a Yorkist king, for the house of York appealed to him; perhaps they seemed more enterprising on all fronts, and enterprise was something that John Lambert and the city merchants understood and appreciated.

In fact the Earl of Warwick, the 'Kingmaker', as he had been named, had not wasted any time: he was already at work, making diplomatic overtures to various royal families in Europe. On Edward's behalf he naturally aimed high, visiting France in the hope that the French king's daughter would be available as the future queen of England. King Louis XI thought she was too young, but this shrewdly intelligent monarch was never short of ideas: in the hope of maintaining good relations with Edward and England he suggested that his wife's sister might be suitable instead.

The French queen's sister, Bona of Savoy, was an attractive girl, and sister-in-law to the king of France, but Warwick came to realise that she would not be a suitable queen of England, as her status was not high enough, and as a result the negotiations seemed to stall. Before they ended, however, Warwick, still in France, heard devastating news from home; to his horror he learnt that the young king in England had let him down: he had admitted that he was married already. As a result Warwick was made to look a fool and this thoughtless behaviour by the king was something he resented for the rest of his life. Bona herself and the French royal family were naturally more than disappointed: they felt they had been badly treated, insulted in fact, and later it fell to Shakespeare, in *Henry VI, Part III*, Act III, Scene 3, to give the young girl a chance to express her feelings, for she did not enjoy her status as a failed wife-to-be and failed queen of England. Either she had quickly become vindictive or else she sarcastically dismissed the whole incident as a waste of time for herself and especially for the French court. She instructed Warwick:

> Tell him, in hope he'll prove a widower shortly,
> I'll wear the willow garland for his sake.

She did not believe in polite regrets. It should be added here that fairly soon after the possible alliance with England had come to nothing Bona embarked upon a successful marriage to the Duke of Milan, so nobody had to feel distressed on her behalf. An earlier attempt by Warwick to find a suitable wife for Edward had led to even more trouble because he had been asked to approach the Spanish royal family and suggest that Isabella of Castile might be a good choice. Unfortunately however this too came to nothing and the young princess subsequently married the King of Portugal, a step which led without much delay to the union of that country with Spain. Later in life Isabella remembered her rejection by the English king and announced coldly that it had made her 'turn away' from England.[3]

It was later that Edward then surprised and disappointed everybody in England and abroad: he confirmed what had happened, admitting to his shocked advisers and the members of his family that he was in fact married already. A few months earlier he had made a totally unexpected choice, consulting nobody, as far is known, and then kept the secret for as long as he could.

There are many versions of this story; but Edward Hall and his editor Grafton told it to the *Chronicle* in various instalments.[4] One day in April in 1463 the king was out hunting in Wychwood Forest near Stony Stratford in Northamptonshire and paid a visit to the Manor of Grafton, home of Jacquetta, former Duchess of Bedford, who was now married to her second husband, Sir Richard Woodville, Lord Rivers. Staying in the house at the time was one of her daughters by her earlier marriage, Dame Elizabeth Grey, a young widow whose husband, the Lancastrian supporter Sir John Grey, had been killed at the first battle of St Albans in 1455. Unfortunately for this Lancastrian family the battle had been won by Edward's Yorkist forces and as a result Elizabeth, the widow, had lost much of her income. Now she hoped for the chance to plead with the new king for some improvement to her life, especially since she had two young sons to bring up.

According to legend she met the king as he rode through the forest, and, holding the two boys by their hands, she knelt down in front of him. Had it all been carefully planned? Most people, after all, knew that Edward was highly susceptible to attractive women, and Elizabeth Grey was certainly attractive, even if she was in difficulties.

She 'found such grace in the King's eyes', the Hall-Grafton *Chronicle* continued, 'that he not only favoured her suit but much more fantasised about her person, for she was a woman more of formal countenance, than of excellent beauty, but yet of such beauty and favour, that with her sober demeanour, lovely expression, and with a feminine smile, (neither too wanton nor too humble) besides, her tongue was so eloquent, and her wit so pregnant, she was able . . . to allure and make subject to her, the heart of so great a king.'

Before this meeting in the wood, legendary or not, Dame Elizabeth Grey may have had nothing more in mind than the restitution of what she had lost through her husband's death, for after all Edward was clearly responsible, if indirectly, for that death. However, the young man found the widow infinitely more interesting than she had expected and looked her over with an experienced eye: 'After that King Edward had well considered all the lineaments of her body, and the wise and womanly demeanour that he saw in her, he determined first to attempt if he might provoke her farther, if she would be his sovereign lady, promising her many gifts and fair rewards, affirming farther, that if she would thereunto condescend, she might, after being his paramour and concubine, be changed to his wife and lawful bedfellow: which demand she so wisely, and with such covert speech answered and impugned, affirming that she was for his honour far unable to be his spouse and bedfellow: So for her own poor honour, she was too good to be either his concubine or sovereign lady.' Edward had not expected this response, for in the past his invitations, if that is the word, had hardly ever been refused. The chronicler continued: 'that where he was a little before heated with the dart of Cupid, he was now set all on a hot burning fire, thanks to the confidence that he had in her perfect constancy and the trust that he had in her total chastity, and without any further deliberation he determined with him self clearly to marry with her . . .'

If the young king had first thought of asking advice he must soon have realised that everybody would attempt to make him change his mind. Although Edward was inclined to fancy any presentable woman he met and was already well experienced in the techniques of seduction, he was not used to rejection. According to later gossip he had actually threatened Elizabeth Grey with a dagger and was even more impressed when she continued to resist him.

So what was he to do? The answer was simple as far as he was concerned: he made up his mind that he *would* marry the woman who had had the courage to resist him, but he would marry her in secret. Which he did on 1 May 1463 in the presence of a very few people including her mother Jacquetta, the former Duchess of Bedford, who was presumably surprised but inevitably pleased by this match, which was now legal. In order to keep the secret no banns had been published and it is not clear where the ceremony took place: it could have been in Grafton Regis, perhaps in the Bedford family chapel, but it was not in a church. Other chroniclers wrote that the marriage was conducted by a priest and Fabyan added one picturesque detail, there was also present a boy 'to help the priest sing'. Naturally, after this ceremony, the couple spent several nights together, still in secrecy, presumbly in the Bedford manor house. Edward, who explained his absence to his attendants by saying that he had been out hunting, seemed to be behaving like an adolescent boy, but he must surely have realised that moves were afoot at court to find him a suitable wife who would take her place as a suitable queen. He still seemed to think he could manage the situation somehow. In fact he succeeded in doing so for the entire summer of 1464. Then there was a Council meeting in September, held in Reading, and on that day there was no escape for the young king, since his future marriage was on the agenda. There was some discussion and eventually Edward was forced to admit that he was married already. Nobody was pleased, in fact everyone was horrified: the king of England simply had no right to act in such an irresponsible way.

'When this marriage was bruited abroad,' wrote the chronicler further, 'foreign kings and princes marvelled and mused about it: noble men detested and disdained it: the common people grudged and murmured at it and all with one voice said that his inadvisable hasty wooing and speedy marriage, were neither meet for him being a king, nor consonant with the honour of so high an estate.'

It is worth remembering here that Shakespeare thought this story so entertaining that he used it in *Henry VI Part III*, Act III, Scene 2, transposing it into a London palace and inventing a rapid dialogue between the two parties, but still following the story that had by then become common knowledge; he also introduced Edward's two younger brothers, George and Richard, who listened carefully to most of this dialogue as they stood apart, presumably in a corner; they found the whole thing something of a joke, and before they left the scene Clarence remarked, 'he is the bluntest wooer in Christendom'. George, Duke of Clarence, was about thirteen years old at the time and his brother Richard was eleven.

Shakespeare presumably introduced this scene before he evoked Warwick's efforts in France in order to emphasise that Edward had consciously deceived the man to whom he owed his kingship. The story was soon known all over Europe and gossip from Italy made it even more dramatic: it was said that Elizabeth had had a dagger of her own and used it to intimidate the king. So there was a choice for those who retailed the story – who took the defensive action and who was aggressive? In the end it did not matter, Elizabeth Grey had her way: if Edward wanted her in his bed, he must marry her.

Various efforts were made to change Edward's mind but of course it was far too late. His new wife's mother, Jacquetta, daughter of Pierre, the Count of St-Pol, was not of royal blood but her father had been one of the most powerful magnates in France, so she could not be dismissed as a woman with no aristocratic family behind her, as many people had complained. Edward's mother, Cecily of York, had several arguments in addition to the astonishing statement of her own infidelity: she became even more furious and reminded her son that he had once entered into an arrangement, a kind of betrothal or pre-contract, with a certain Lady Elizabeth Lucy who had also borne one of his children, but Edward, undismayed, thought this to be a good sign: he could produce children (he had had at least two by this date, normal among the aristocracy of the time), his new wife already had some and so they would surely have some more together.

In desperation Cecily arranged an interview with Elizabeth Lucy who admitted that she had had sexual relations with Edward but there had been no betrothal. Her description of how her son was conceived, relayed by Sir Thomas More, gives an amusing indication of Edward's charm. No woman could resist him: 'Whereupon Dame Elizabeth Lucy was sent for. And albeit that she was by the king's mother and many other put in good comfort to affirm that she was ensured unto the king, yet when she was solemnly sworn to say the truth, she confessed that they were never ensured' (i.e. engaged).[5]

She then gave her own description of how the king had seduced her: 'Howbeit,' she said, 'His Grace spoke so loving words unto her that she verily hoped he would have married her, and if it had not been for such kind words she would never have showed such kindness to him to let him so kindly [i.e. naturally] get her with child.' Edward, well before his marriage, had already had years of practice in seducing young women and knew exactly how to approach Elizabeth Lucy. At the time a betrothal or engagement could in fact have been legally binding. Sir Thomas More adds, 'This examination solemnly taken, when it was clearly perceived that there was none impediment, the king, with great feast and honourable solemnity married Dame Elizabeth Grey . . .'. As More's editor adds, 'More seems to describe Elizabeth's coronation in 1465, not her secret marriage in 1464.'[6] Fortunately, Elizabeth Lucy's love-child, Arthur, was well brought up by the Lisle family, later ennobled by Henry VIII and lived until he was at least sixty.

By now of course even Cecily of York had more or less given up her protests but after Edward's death another attempt was made to prove that he had been as good as married already when he secretly wed Elizabeth Grey. This refers to the possibility that he had been engaged to a Lady Eleanor Talbot, although there is no definite proof of this. However, an unexpected, surprising genealogical table was published in *The Ricardian* vol. XIV of 2004[7] in which this lady was listed as having made two marriages. Lady Eleanor was a daughter of John Talbot, 1st Earl of Shrewsbury, by his second wife, Margaret Beauchamp of Warwick, and had been born in about 1436, one of five children. She married in 1449 or 1450 Thomas Butler of Sudeley but – according to the table on p. 90 – in 1461, she was widowed, upon which she acquired a second husband: Edward IV. This fact was mentioned after Edward's death and used by the Duke of Gloucester, expecting to become Richard III, as one further alleged proof that Edward had been illegally married to Dame Elizabeth Grey and therefore his children could not legally succeed to the throne. However, in the meantime Eleanor had died, in 1468.

This is why Edward's mother, Cecily, who could think of no other reason for urging her son against the marriage, had confessed, in her efforts to discourage him, that she herself, who had been pregnant so often, had experienced an adulterous relationship before Edward's birth. Edward probably did not believe her and had silenced his mother's complaints by the one statement that could not be contradicted: 'I am king,' he said. And it could have been argued that whether he was desperately in love or not he felt that now was the time to make it clear that he was thoroughly grown up and that nobody could tell him what to do.

It was later assumed that the Earl of Warwick, who had been made to look ridiculous when trying to find a wife for a king who was secretly married already, concealed his resentment for the time being. He swallowed his pride sufficiently when he was asked in 1465 to accompany Elizabeth to Reading Abbey where she was honoured as Queen, implying that the legality of the marriage had been accepted. Even stranger perhaps was the presence there also of Edward's younger brother the Duke of Clarence who later, as is well known, disapproved of most things that Edward did and was to develop into an obvious enemy of the queen. However, it also became clear that these two men soon began to have a secret understanding which was totally anti-Edward and developed eventually into serious hostility.

Surely no romantic novelist could have invented a better story than King Edward's marriage, and for a time few people seriously questioned what lay behind it. It was certainly not as romantic as it might have seemed and several aspects of it were challenged by J.R. Lander in his interesting essay on marriage and politics in *Crown and Nobility 1450–1509* of 1976. He explained how the Woodvilles had not suddenly invented social progress through advantageous marriages; their relatives, the powerful Neville family, which included the Earl of Warwick, had achieved great success through this system over a long period. After all, the marriage contract, which had survived ever since the Christian Church had existed in England, was a well-known method of rising in the world for people who had no career, something true of virtually all women, and even of some men, among the aristocracy. How far there had been a secret plot to offer Elizabeth Grey, née Woodville, to the 22-year-old king can obviously never be known. At the same time it was wrong to dismiss her mother, Jacquetta, as a woman without class. She was, as noted earlier, the daughter of a French count while her brother John and her uncle, the Bishop of Thérouanne, had both played important roles during the reign of Henry V. In her way, she too had lived through a dramatic story with a romantic ending. She had married a middle-aged man and was soon left a young widow, which was precisely her daughter's situation later. After the death of her second husband her dowry had been returned to her provided that she did not remarry without the king's consent, but she disobeyed and did so, with the result that 'their temerity had cost the couple the enormous fine of £1,000 which Cardinal Beaufort characteristically raised for them in return for the duchess's life interest in various manors in Somerset, Dorset and Wiltshire'.[8] Like mother, like daughter. There was even a rumour in France later that Cecily of York had been unfaithful to her husband with an English archer named Blaybourne, which may have been a joke, but at least it amused the French court.

In the meantime Jacquetta could have regretted whatever secret arrangements had been going on because she was later accused by one Thomas Wake of having secretly made plans herself to bring about the marriage through witchcraft.[9] Wake was said to have taken to court a leaden image 'made like a Man of Arms, containing the length of a man's finger, and broken in the middle and made fast with a wire'. This was an example of the popular 'image magic' often used, or at least attempted, at the time, in the hope of clarifying difficult situations or resolving unpleasant ones which had seemed intolerable. It was thought that this could be the only explanation for young King Edward's strange and unexpected behaviour, while the accusations became serious, so much so that the king felt he must take some action himself. The case came to court before the Bishop of Carlisle on 22 January 1470 with further allegations that the Duchess of Bedford had also made 'two other images, one representing Edward IV and another Elizabeth Grey', but the man who might have testified that these allegations were true, John Daunger, refused to do so. As a result the case collapsed. No doubt enemies of the Woodvilles and the Nevilles had been hoping that memories of the famous earlier accusations against Eleanor Cobham, Duchess of Gloucester, would be strong enough to help the case: the duchess had been condemned to public penance, prison and lifelong exile to the Isle of Man on what seemed like sound evidence: she was accused of enlisting a well-known magician or witch with the aim of harming an enemy and promoting her husband's interest. She maintained that she was merely using the image-magic devices in a way that would help her to conceive a child, but nobody believed her; she was so ambitious, it was said, that she wanted to be queen.

In the end Elizabeth had been crowned in Westminster Abbey in 1464, her husband having insisted on a lavish ceremony. In accordance with tradition, since he had already been crowned, he did not attend himself, unless he watched the proceedings from a secret hiding place. However, most of those who had complained about the marriage were certainly in the Abbey, and even played some part in the ceremony, having realised that mere complaints would not change the situation. John Lambert also might well have attended the coronation service himself and his daughter, now grown up, may have been taken out to watch the queen on her way to or from Westminster Abbey. Was she enough of a daydreamer to start thinking about her own marriage?

Amidst the condemnations of this unpopular royal marriage and all that followed it in the way of favours for the Woodville family, Edward might have noticed that his wife, Elizabeth, had seven unmarried sisters who, unsurprisingly, did not stay unmarried very long. Many other arranged and profitable marriages took place among endless criticism, especially one union between John Woodville, a young man of about twenty, to a wealthy widowed lady, the Dowager Duchess of Norfolk, Katherine Neville; who was close to seventy and had already been married three times. Some critics even said she was eighty but this has been disproved. The Woodvilles did not invent the system of advantageous marriage but they obviously carried on the tradition with enthusiasm and it cost them nothing for Edward, presumably, paid most or all the expenses and allotted useful appointments to practically any of his wife's relatives who needed them. Had he been desperately in love or had he optimistically hoped that he could deal with any difficult situation that might arise? He was a brilliant strategist on the battlefield but he must have realised by now that the social scene was infinitely more difficult to manage.

Edward was probably faithful to his wife for at least a short time and it should be remembered that they had in all ten children (of whom three died in infancy). Unfortunately in one sense for her, the queen gave birth to three daughters before England gained two princes, Edward and Richard, but she could at least feel that she had been the dutiful royal wife and mother.

Edward was the Don Juan of medieval monarchs: he could never resist attractive girls or older women, but it is not clear how soon he acquired new mistresses at this stage of his life. Probably he did not wait very long but did not bring them to any palace where the queen was in residence; he probably arranged some small nearby house where he could visit them easily and secretly. Dominic Mancini later gave a memorable description of Edward's way of dealing with the women he fancied: 'He was licentious in the extreme: moreover it was said that he had been most insolent to numerous women after he had seduced them, for, as soon as he grew weary of dalliance, he gave up the ladies much against their will to the other courtiers. . . . He overcame all by money and promises and having conquered [the women] he dismissed them. Although he had many promoters and companions of his vices, the more important and especial were three relatives of the Queen, her two sons and one of her brothers.'[10] How could anyone have imagined that not too many years were to pass before one of these sons, the Marquess of Dorset, was believed to be the lover of Jane Shore, the former Elizabeth Lambert, either sharing her with the king when the latter reached his early middle age, or inheriting her after the death of Lord Hastings?

In the meantime, what was happening in the life of the young Elizabeth Lambert? Her parents, like everyone else, would have been watching all these developments at King Edward's court with fascination. As for Elizabeth, she was probably not old enough to understand all the complex political problems raised by the king's choice of a queen, but she might have enjoyed the romantic story of the secret marriage.

Now however it was her own marriage that was to preoccupy the Lambert family, for in 1465 she would be at least fifteen, and that was very grown up. In fact, given the tantalising lack of records about her life, there is even a faint possibility that she might have been married already.

FOUR

A Civil Contract

So King Edward had acquired a wife, lovesome, to use a word favoured by the poet William Dunbar, at least to him, if this indeed was a love-match, and if, in the private marriage ceremony which consecrated it, he undertook that he was forsaking all other. He had at least frustrated the official wife-seeking manoeuvres, serious but tiresome, which had been made on his behalf; and as a Christian he had conveniently forgotten – if he had ever known them – all those dire restrictive pronouncements from the fathers of the Church; St Augustine for instance had said that 'there is nothing that degrades the manly spirit more than the attractiveness of females and contact with their bodies'. The sexual act, thought the Church dignitaries, existed only for the propagation of the human race, while St Jerome unfairly said that 'he who is too ardently amorous of his wife is also an adulterer'. He believed that 'nothing is more vile than to love a wife like a mistress' and suggested that 'the wise man must love his wife with judgement, not with passion': a pronouncement which seems to anticipate the conveniently rational attitude of the eighteenth century. A wife was for domesticity and rightful heirs, a mistress was for romance, love, even passion. However, for the most part, the population of late medieval England accepted the Church-controlled arrangements for marriage without too much complaint, while some brave couples, like the young Margery Paston and the family bailiff, Richard Calle, married each other defiantly through the old-established 'holdfast' system, exchanged their vows privately in a church, and then lived happily until Margery's death, despite the unforgiving attitude of the class-conscious Paston parents towards the girl's choice: how dare their daughter want to spend her life with a man from a lower class? But Margery loved him; she was not interested in a marriage that would have taken her into and even beyond the gentry, perhaps nearer to the aristocracy. Marriage was destiny, at all levels and in different ways.

William Dunbar, writing about London merchants in the late Middle Ages and in the earlier years of the sixteenth century, mentioned their wives as 'lovesome, white and small'; he was not concerned with the wisdom of the early Christians, but was celebrating every aspect of life in the city of London, and describing the attractive women from the comfortably off middle-class merchant families whom he would have seen every day in the streets, usually escorted by servants and sometimes on their own. These young women whom he admired and wrote about were aware they were eligible now for the marriage market, and realised that their parents might have already begun thinking ahead, not so much on any daughters' behalf as on their own. The selection of a suitable son-in-law was an important matter for the middle classes, unfortunately even more important to the parents than to the prospective bride: it was an aspect of business life, commercial, financial business. At the same time it was also the normal 'business' of life itself, especially as girls and women saw marriage at the time, for it meant the perpetuation of the family with the arrival of a new generation. There was no sentimentality about it, and little or no romance. The lawyer Sir John Selden's much-quoted definition in his *Table Talk* of the next century – 'marriage is nothing but a civil contract' – was to be relevant for a long time.[1]

In the fifteenth century girls were married very young but usually not younger than the supposedly legal age of twelve, although in exceptional circumstances, particularly among the aristocracy where the inheritance of land, titles and money was a crucially important matter, little or no attention was paid to this restriction. The average age of marriage for middle-class girls seems to have been from thirteen to fifteen or seventeen at the latest, but as is well known, the carefully organised alliances by marriage among royalty were often planned while the future spouses were still infants, well in advance of the official betrothal and the marriage proper, which took place later, usually when the girls reached puberty.

Late in his reign, in 1478, King Edward himself, who would do almost anything to bring in funds or the promise of a useful inheritance, was keen to marry his second son Richard to the heiress of John Mowbray, Duke of Norfolk and Earl Marshal of England. Richard, Duke of York, was four years old at the time and little Anne Mowbray, who would eventually succeed to one of the most valuable inheritances in England, was six. The marriage, not regarded as particularly strange, took place in St Stephen's chapel at Westminster on 15 January 1478; unfortunately it did not bring about the expected result, for sadly, just before her tenth birthday, the little 'duchess' died. The king, not to be outdone, had to resort to legislation in order to preserve the inheritance; he arranged that it should go to young Richard for life and if necessary to himself. The rights of others in the Mowbray family were set aside.[2] The four-year-old bridegroom, as everybody knows, faded from history not long afterwards when he disappeared, along with his elder brother, in the Tower of London at some unknown date in the last years of the century.

As for the supposedly happy time of courtship, it hardly seems to have existed for many young people at this date, or else it was instantaneous, limited to a kind of physical inspection, as Sir Thomas More later described it in his *Utopia* of 1516.[3] He set out, through one of the supposed residents of the imaginary island, how the careful Utopians would not allow girls to marry before the age of eighteen, and boys had to wait until they were twenty-two. Pre-marital sex was strictly forbidden and anyone found guilty of it was in deep trouble. The procedure to be followed before marriage was strict: 'The prospective bride, no matter whether she's a spinster or a widow, is exhibited stark naked to the prospective bridegroom by a respectable married woman, and a suitable male chaperone shows the bridegroom naked to the bride.'

When the visitors to Utopia laughed at all this they were at once reminded that anyone buying a horse looks it over carefully and 'when you're choosing a wife, an article that for better or worse has got to last you a lifetime, you're unbelievably careless . . . You judge a whole woman from a few square inches of face, which is all you can see of her, and then proceed to marry her – at the risk of finding her most disagreeable, when you see what she's really like . . .'.

A similar system was retold later in a much-quoted anecdote passed on by Sir John Aubrey[4] about how More's own future son-in-law chose his bride. When the young William Roper visited More's house to make his choice he was shown two little girls asleep in a truckle bed. The father led him 'into the chamber and takes the sheet by the corner and suddenly whips it off. They lay on their backs, and their smocks up as high as their armpits. This awakened them, and immediately they turned on their bellies.

Quoth Roper, I have seen both sides, and so gave a pat on the buttock he made choice of saying, Thou art mine. Here was all the trouble of the wooing.' Perhaps the author of *Utopia* was only following general practice, unless this system was his own invention or one of the jokes that he was known to enjoy.

Early marriage often brought its problems: the unfortunate Richard II of England, having lost his beloved young wife Anne of Bohemia in childbirth in 1394, later married a young French princess, Isabelle, who was a mere seven years old; he chose a child, he said, because he hoped that her youth would enable him to form her into the ideal queen he felt he needed. Among several unusual cases of early marriage in the fifteenth century one in particular led to unexpected, important, dramatic events later: Lady Margaret Beaufort, daughter of the Duke of Somerset, born in 1443, was married as a child to John de la Pole as part of a hoped-for dynastic arrangement, but the marriage was dissolved. She was next married in 1455, when she was eleven or twelve, to the son of Owen Tudor who was the presumed second husband of Katherine de Valois, widow of King Henry V. This son was Edmund Tudor, later known as the Earl of Richmond. He believed that the marriage should be consummated early, which meant that Margaret gave birth to a son at the age of twelve and was left a widow at thirteen, her husband having died of the plague while in prison. Later she married twice more but could not have any further children, such was the physical damage she had suffered through early childbirth. Significantly, in 1485, after the battle of Bosworth Field, when Richard III was killed, it was Margaret's only son, then aged twenty-eight, the second Earl of Richmond, who became king of England as Henry VII, the first ruler of the Tudor dynasty. There was nobody else in the direct Lancastrian line to take over the throne from the defeated Yorkists. Without this son, born of an early marriage, it is not clear who might have become king of England in that important year. His mother had quietly worked on his behalf all his life, and it was sad that he died shortly before her. Marriage is destiny.

If the monarchy and the aristocracy hoped to profit from early marriage, so did the middle classes. For them the 'profit' would be sound business improvement and at least some family advancement rather than great riches and titles. Eileen Power, whose *Medieval People* of 1924 has long been a classic, described in detail the life and marriage of Thomas Betson, the fifteenth-century Merchant of the Staple, operating the valuable wool trade through Calais. He had been attracted to a young girl named Katherine Swynford, to whom he wrote affectionate letters, although she was not much of a letter-writer herself. However, she married him when she was fifteen and they enjoyed seven years of married life, during which she nursed him through a severe illness and had five children. After his death she soon married again, for widows rarely stayed on their own.

Eileen Power also described the sad case of the little boy of nine who was told he would be spending the night with his 'bride'. He cried and said he wanted to go home. Another girl was said to have tempted a boy into marriage by offering him two apples. The medieval marriage scene had its comical side, and the word marriage was not easily associated with romance until several centuries later. But fortunately some couples, unmarried or married, did fall in love. Some of Eileen Power's descriptions have recently been challenged[5] but the salient points of her essays remain valid.

It must have been about the year 1460, when Elizabeth Lambert was presumably ten or twelve years old, that her parents began to look about them seriously with the intention of finding a possible husband for their daughter. This was the start of a crucial and crowded decade in the history of England. It included the battle of Northampton, the death of the Duke of York at Wakefield and then, soon after, the second battle of St Albans, the deposition of Henry VI, the Yorkist victory of Towton, and the coronation of Edward IV in 1461; this event was followed by an outbreak of plague, then finally the young king's marriage in 1464. Five years later, in 1469, would come an abrupt if temporary change in Yorkist fortunes (to be described later). Some observant and no doubt sceptical people may have foreseen that Edward's occupation of the throne was far from secure, for the highly ambitious Earl of Warwick, who had done so much to promote Edward's kingship, felt that he deserved more honour and more rewards, and although he was an extremely rich landowner he still wanted additional status. At the same time Edward's younger brother George, Duke of Clarence, a restless young man, constantly jealous of his brother, longed for power of some sort and moved closer to Warwick. The future, or indeed the present, was far from settled for anyone.

By 1461 however, when Elizabeth Lambert would be at least eleven, marriage could not be too far ahead. Her parents would certainly have begun thinking about it.

John and Amy Lambert might have felt relieved that they had managed to survive a particularly turbulent decade, sometimes good for business, sometimes not, but a challenge to all the mercers who had found the strength and industry to carry on. Now they wanted to forget the upheavals of the recent past, think of the future and, as far as possible, devise ways in which they could continue to strengthen their personal position. Alderman John Lambert – he had been very proud of his 'promotion' in 1460, although he was to lose it only too soon – had realised that he could still profit from any future war or rebellion by lending money to the king who would constantly need it for his family or his soldiers. Since there was no standing army, recruitment might be needed at short notice any time and funding arrangements would have to be in place. John Lambert had also been able to satisfy one ambition: he had come into possession of some land, given to him by the king, who was perpetually in need of loans and ready to offer land in exchange or in gratitude. Edward had acquired land which had previously belonged to Lancastrian owners and so he could afford to be generous. John Lambert's new possessions were in the West Country and in 1461 he was appointed Collector of Customs in Southampton. He was surely proud of all this advancement and therefore a suitable marriage for Elizabeth would be particularly appropriate now, for a son-in-law who was already conducting a successful business himself – and no other man would be acceptable – would help to extend the improved social status and financial situation of the Lambert family even further while taking over responsibility for their daughter at the same time.

If many aspects of Elizabeth's life remain mysterious, at least something is known about the circumstances of her marriage – her first marriage, as it was to be – and something about the husband who was found for her. Her parents would be looking for a man who had established a good business or joined a profession, and he would preferably be a little older than their daughter. It is unlikely that John and Amy Lambert would need to employ a marriage-broker to help them find a suitable son-in-law, as some parents did, for they were well known by now and nobody could possibly have complained that their daughter might not be a good match.

At the same time it is essential to add here that for unknown reasons there were in a sense two marriages, one legendary and one real. The legend of how Elizabeth Lambert became Mistress Shore, married to a goldsmith, persisted well into twentieth-century reference books. It was believed in medieval times that 'Matthew Shore's' goldsmith's shop was situated at the north side corner of Lombard Street and Gracechurch Street, a belief that was to prove of great interest later to Barclays Bank plc, for the original James Barclay had himself married the daughter of a goldsmith, John Freame. The latter's shop, trading at the Sign of the Black Eagle, originally stood on the site which until May 2005 was still the location of the Barclays Bank head office at 54 Lombard Street, while the black eagle has been retained ever since in the arms and motif used by the bank. Freame may perhaps have been confused with the mythical Matthew Shore, even if the names are not similar. The bank liked to link Jane Shore with the legend of a goldsmith associated with Lombard Street, and she figured later in a series of curved metal screens installed in the 1960s in the entrance corridor to the former head office, remaining there until the redesign of the building in 1985 before being transferred to Old Broad Street until its closure two years later. Later they were put into storage.[6]

When by the command of Richard III in 1483 the Bishop of London ordered Mistress Shore to do public penance in the area, it probably meant walking along Lombard Street. So she may have walked past no. 54, carrying a candle and wearing only her kirtle. Her ghost has not been forgotten there, but it is unlikely that any memories of her have migrated along with the Barclays Bank relocation to Churchill Place, near Canary Wharf, in May 2005.

For unexplained reasons the rumour had spread and persisted for centuries that Miss Lambert became Mistress Shore when she was married to an unidentified goldsmith named Shore, whose Christian name was usually given as Matthew. The reason for this misconception is not clear but there may be some partial explanation for it: at this period the London goldsmiths had a high reputation in England and Europe, so in principle the Lamberts might not have objected to a goldsmith husband for their daughter, provided suitable financial arrangements could be made. The chosen husband would have to be successful and his future prospects would have to be excellent. The houses in Goldsmith's Row – which still exists today – were greatly admired by visiting foreigners in the fifteenth century. There were apparently 250 goldsmiths' shops in the city where visitors could admire the gold and silver jewellery, plate and ornaments which were so highly valued during the Middle Ages. Gold was the most precious of all metals and since at that period there was no system for investing money, many people preferred to buy gold instead and display it in all possible ways. The mercers and goldsmiths were known to be close business associates but although both groups held each other in high esteem Elizabeth's parents did not choose a goldsmith for their son-in-law and her marriage to one of them was non-existent.

However, now to the real marriage. In his work as warden of Farringdon Within, John Lambert may have heard of or even met a younger man who was one of the wardens responsible for the Coleman Street section of the city, a large area unfortunately remembered for the earlier persecutions of the Jews under Edward II. However, it contained some fine houses and at least one which had previously been the synagogue. This young man was William Shore, whose name often occurs in the Acts of Court of the Mercers' Company although much less frequently than that of John Lambert. However, he suited the Lamberts, for he came of a good family and his achievements so far proved that he was a sound businessman.

Thanks to the detailed research of Dr Anne Sutton,[7] a considerable amount is known about Shore, in fact more than about his wife. He was born in Derby sometime between 1435 and 1437, the son of a successful man who was well connected both in Derbyshire and the Duchy of Lancaster. He also had business relations in Suffolk and Flanders. There is no doubt that William Shore was well brought up in an atmosphere of devotion to the Church. His parents were obviously close to the parish of All Hallows in Derby, described as 'a fine and wealthy Collegiate Church'. It had a 'Trinity Guild, a Chapel of the Virgin Mary, altars to the Trinity, the Passion and St Catherine, with vestments, books, jewels and ornaments including painted cloths showing the "old" and the "new" law hanging above the choir stalls.' Much more detail is available about this church, all of which guarantees the respectability of William Shore, for his family were generous supporters of it through donations of all kinds. As for William, who had one sister, he was apprenticed in 1451 or 1452, not long after the assumed birth of Elizabeth, and this brought him to London where his master was John Rankyn, also a mercer. This apprentice training was highly comprehensive and included time spent in Flanders. Shore was admitted to the Mercers' Company in 1458 or 1459 and after receiving his livery five or so years later he set up in business on his own. The Company also chose him as one of their representatives sent to greet the king when he returned to London after the battle of Towton.

This may have been the time when Shore lived in the city and owned a 'tenement in the Parishes of St Mary le Bow and St Mary Aldermary', numbers 104/21–22. There were shops on the ground floor in this locality, seven of them altogether and living quarters on the floors above. Its situation was good, near the area where mercers tended to congregate. It seems that William Shore vacated the properties in 1472 when they were then leased to another mercer named William Gowle. The latter found that the premises needed many repairs; so it can be assumed that Shore would not have brought a young wife to a house in poor condition, but that his many journeys abroad probably meant that he had had no time to organise the upkeep of the premises. When the couple married it's likely that they lived somewhere in the city area, although it is not known exactly where.

The merchants of the London middle class, who were growing more prosperous throughout this century, are known to have regarded their daughters as a form of merchandise too, for the girls did not choose their husbands; when the parents chose them on their behalf they presumably hoped that their choice would earn approval from the prospective bride. By the standards of the time William Shore was virtually a middle-aged man, busy and successful. Dr Sutton has assumed that the marriage took place in the late 1460s, when Elizabeth would be in her teens and her husband in his thirties, probably about fifteen years older than his bride. The proposed match sounded safe and reasonable, but it was not romantic.

Had Elizabeth had daydreams about the man who might one day be her husband? Or had her parents first considered a goldsmith as a son-in-law but failed to obtain the conditions they or the possible husband wanted for this business arrangement? It is not known, but since Elizabeth had been taught to read, she may have been impressed by stories or legends about earlier women, as already mentioned, most of them romantic and including that crucial element of love which was not given much place in contemporary marriage arrangements. Love remained an essential ingredient of legend but it had little to do with real life.

Perhaps, while she waited to meet the man who was to become her husband, Elizabeth may have heard about some of the women who had had love affairs with kings and were much talked about. The only problem was that in so many cases there was plenty of sex, but possibly no shared love. One of the most unpopular royal mistresses in early English history, Alice Perrers, was said to have belonged to a good Hertfordshire family, came to court as a lady-in-waiting to Queen Philippa of Hainault, and became mistress of King Edward III before his wife died. Alice dominated the king completely for the last years of his life and is remembered in particular as one of the most grasping mistresses ever known among the women who saw this post as the best way of gaining personal power. She did everything she could to acquire money and property although she was neither alone nor poor, being the wife of William de Windsor, who became Lieutenant of Ireland. It is said that when the king was dying she tried to pull the rings off his fingers before rigor mortis set in. However, she had made the best of her situation and in Stow's *Survey of London* there is a description of her leading a cheerful company of knights and ladies in procession from the Tower of London through the city. It seemed to be an enjoyable entertainment for everyone, and of course no royal personage was present.[8] Later the Good Parliament in 1376 asked for her to be impeached, such was the disapproval of her behaviour by the general public. The story of Alice is by no means romantic, but its ending is instructive. Alice remained married to William de Windsor, who persuaded a later parliament to reverse the previous harsh judgement. This was one of the real-life stories that the young Elizabeth may have heard, proving that marriage did not necessarily produce stability, sex had little if anything to do with love, and some husbands used their wives to improve their own prospects, either directing their behaviour or condoning it. Unfortunately for her reputation, Alice is said to have been the model for the grasping Lady Meed introduced by the unknown author into *The Visions of Piers Plowman* in the late fourteenth or early fifteenth century. This was hardly a suitable story for respectable young girls to hear, but it was the kind of tale they enjoyed.

As for Elizabeth's marriage, she behaved like the dutiful daughter her parents assumed her to be. They had surely brought her up carefully with marriage in mind, union to a respectable man, and now it had happened. It is not known when and where the marriage took place, or where precisely the couple lived. If she had not chosen William she had presumably not objected to the choice, for in the 1460s most girls did not do so. She did not respond to him and he does not seem to have attracted her in any way, although his social and financial status obviously pleased her parents. She knew she had virtually no say in the matter and perhaps she assumed at first that the two of them might grow closer into a friendly partnership: it might even develop into love. She could only hope for the best.

William Shore's social background was impeccable and his sister, whose Christian name was never mentioned, had married into the Agard family, who belonged to the local gentry, a fact which would have impressed the socially ambitious John Lambert. There is no sign however that the new Mistress Shore was ever taken to Derby to meet her husband's family or that she met any of them in London. She had been brought up to think of marriage as little more than a change of living arrangements, just an expected and normal change in her way of life. She knew, of course, that a husband would take her virginity and then there would be babies. When eventually she petitioned for divorce it was stated as part of her case that she had looked forward to having children but it had soon become clear that the marriage was not developing well.

Sir Thomas More partially explained the situation later. 'This woman was born in London,' he wrote, 'worshipfully friended, honestly brought up and very well married (saving somewhat too soon), her husband an honest citizen, young and goodly and of good substance.' He did not name him or mention his age. More gave a short and simple explanation of what had happened: 'But forasmuch as they were coupled ere she were well ripe, she not very fervently loved for whom she never longed.'[9] They were too young, even William Shore himself had had no experience of women, for reasons that were to become obvious. More added no other details about William but probably, when he was writing the *History of Richard III* and chose to digress about 'Mistress Shore' he and all his contemporaries may have known or suspected what the problem had been: William was impotent, neither emotional nor sexual love existed between the couple, the marriage was not real, it was no fun. So Mistress Shore – her Christian name was never mentioned in the chronicles that appeared in Elizabethan times – was dissatisfied with her existence. Presumably too her husband continued to expand his business activities which included travel to the continent and if he was away for long periods at a time, leaving his wife on her own, it seems possible that Mistress Shore felt life was passing her by; she may even have begun to look at other men.

It is not easy, six centuries later, to imagine life without easily available visual images of most people deserving of mention and since portraits at this time were limited to highly placed figures, almost exclusively royal, one can only wonder how Mistress Shore saw the men she might have admired from a distance; they would have had to be men she could actually see. In the end, like almost every other woman in London, she must have admired the king and she would at least have seen him on the many occasions when he rode in procession through the streets, always dressed in the most elegant of clothes. Yet not even a daydreaming lonely young wife would have considered pursuing him: it was out of the question, especially since she was a mere middle-class girl and Edward's reputation as a high-handed womaniser was not to his credit. It is interesting here to remember what Francis Bacon wrote in the next century in his essay *On Beauty*. He did not see beauty in isolation, thinking of virtue at the same time; he believed that 'Virtue is like a rich stone best plain set; and surely', he went on, 'virtue is best in a body that is comely'. He also wondered if 'very beautiful persons are otherwise of great virtue'; they could 'prove accomplished but not of great spirit, and study rather behaviour than virtue'. However, he pointed out that 'this holds not always; for Augustus Caesar, Titus Vespasianus, Philip le Bel of France, Edward IV of England, Alcibiades of Athens, Ismael the sophy of Persia, were all high and great spirits, and yet the most beautiful men of their times'. It is worthwhile noting that both Philip le Bel and Ismael the 'sophy' were contemporaries of the writer. Bacon was inclined to believe that 'persons in years seem many times more amiable' but things could be different for young people. 'Beauty is as summer-fruits, which are easy to corrupt, and cannot last, and, for the most part, it makes a dissolute youth, and an age a little out of countenance; but yet certainly again, if it light well, it maketh virtue shine, and vices blush.'

In this essay Bacon referred only to men, not women, and mentioned that 'the principal part of beauty is in decent motion'. Nobody ever remarked that Mistress Shore walked or danced well, but she had surely been taught to do so. Long before Bacon wrote or published this, presumably in 1597, her outstanding beauty, according to the early Elizabethan poets, had apparently been noticed and talked about. Proverbs about women and marriage, usually cynical and derogatory, have always been popular, but one that is different in tone remains valid and seems relevant in the case of Elizabeth Lambert, now Mistress Shore: 'She who is born beautiful is half-married'. If her beauty *was* talked about, her parents would naturally have been anxious for several reasons to find a suitable and hopefully protective husband for her as soon as they could, and would never have imagined that the carefully planned marriage might go wrong. They had been too much concerned with the financial settlement, and if there had been any truth in the rumour that a mercer had been in competition with a goldsmith, the mercer would have won, since his prospects would have been brighter, unlimited in fact. As things turned out, the two young people involved in this arrangement were unlucky; it suited neither of them and at this period Mistress Shore may have begun to think for herself. Perhaps, after all, parents were not right all the time, although most girls would never have dared to say so.

It is just possible that William Shore had heard of the Merchant's Tale that Chaucer had included in his *Canterbury Tales*. The merchant was very unhappily married and his actual tale included an old man with a young wife: they were known as 'January' and 'May'. This youthful wife cleverly managed a sexual encounter with her aspiring young lover at the top of a tree. However, unlike May, Elizabeth does not seem to have been pursued by a lovesick Damian.

FIVE

Marriage, Divorce and Love

There is no hint that during this blank, presumably unhappy, unsettling period of her late adolescence or early womanhood, Jane, as it is convenient if still not correct to name her, decided to take a lover and give up any pretence of being a faithful wife. If her marriage was a failure in its essentials she had at least discovered something about sexual and married life despite finding it difficult to accept what was half a marriage; however, she had gained the social aspect of married life: to the outside world at least she was a respectable wife who presumably lived in a comfortable house somewhere in the city. But she had no personal, physical or emotional satisfaction, no sexual fun and no hope of any children, at least for the time being. She surely had women friends and it is to be hoped that she found the courage to discuss her difficulties with them for she would certainly not be the only one with marital problems. How much she said about the situation to her mother, 'Lady' Lambert, can never be learnt, for nothing is known about the latter's opinion of her daughter's conduct; and it can be taken for granted that in any difficult situation, especially in this one, which concerned the non-virility of their son-in-law she, like most other wives and mothers, would not find it easy to talk about it with her strong-minded argumentative husband.

When John Lambert was finally told about the situation, which would soon have been unavoidable, he would have been disappointed and angry about the apparently failing marriage but probably hoped, with masculine optimism, that the problem might somehow resolve itself. John had presumably gone to a great deal of trouble to find a suitable, even ideal, young man ready to join the family and the two men had surely been convinced they had come to a useful financial arrangement; John Lambert would have paid a dowry and if they had signed any other contract together, possibly dealing only with trade, the situation might have been

58

difficult to unravel, and neither of them would have welcomed that. If the worst came to the worst, the dowry would have to be repaid. So there was probably stalemate and nobody worried too much about Jane's wish to have children, or in fact about Jane generally. There was nothing unusual about that, for throughout the fifteenth century most women, including those in the middle class, were still treated as second-class citizens and young women in particular were not expected to break ranks in the hope of achieving an independent life of their own. Fortunately some of them, who have remained anonymous, did carry on a minor trade in goods of principal interest to women, such as haberdashery, jewellery, confectionery and also spices, for these latter were essential ingredients in cookery at the time; 'silkwomen' have been mentioned earlier.[1]

Mistress Shore does not seem to have been interested in becoming a trader – she had left that aspect of life to her father and her husband. However, she wanted her unsatisfactory situation to be resolved somehow; she was still young and determined that she was not going to spend the rest of her life as a married woman who was not, technically at least, really married. She began to think about possible legal separation or divorce, although how long she waited before taking any practical steps is not clear, and she would have known that nothing was likely to happen quickly. Jane may have inherited something from all that her parents had experienced in the way of practical action and somehow, eventually, she learnt that in certain circumstances a marriage could be legally dissolved. As a result she, or perhaps lawyers acting on her behalf, approached the ecclesiastical body that dealt with such matters, the Court of Arches. Possibly her father might have suggested this course or even insisted on it and might have been ready to help. If not, then Jane was already learning the value of independence. The court was situated locally, in Cheapside, and the sessions took place in the crypt below the nearby church of St Mary-le-Bow. Jane's case was heard but quickly dismissed, for she was made to understand that these ecclesiastics were not much concerned with the non-consummation of a marriage: they dealt almost exclusively with problems of consanguinity, blood relationship; for instance they would consider the case of a couple who wished to marry but might be too closely related and needed clarification as to whether their marriage would be considered legal.

Apparently Jane's plea was heard more than once, possibly in the hope that the members of the court might re-think their attitude or that a change in the judges appointed might lead to a different decision. However, these representatives of ecclesiastical law remained adamant, the marriage could not be dissolved, even though the couple had certainly been cohabiting for at least the regulation three years and beyond without achieving consummation, and time was passing. Was any appeal possible? In theory, yes, but the expense was known to be prohibitive and there could be no guarantee of a satisfactory outcome. Jane, or her advisers, finally decided to take the risk and applied to the appropriate court of the Apostolic See in Rome. Perhaps, they hoped, some Maecenas would appear, ready to pay the heavy costs involved. Jane may have been already close to the king, although there is no clear evidence on the subject, but if that was the situation he might have quietly directed the whole procedure.

To everyone's surprise and relief, Jane's problem won the understanding of Pope Sixtus IV and his advisers, and in order to help her he arranged for another English court to hear the case. He sent a special mandate to the Bishops of Hereford, Sidon and Ross, authorising them to proceed. They did so, learning that Jane and her husband had cohabited for the regulation number of three years or more but that the marriage remained unconsummated. In the end, without any defence or appearance by William Shore, Jane was granted a divorce on 1 March 1476. If Dr Sutton was correct in deciding that the marriage had taken place sometime in the late 1460s, it had taken a long time to come to an end, but Jane had had to wait between her early attempts to pursue the case and then wait still further for the king to intervene somehow or other, if indeed he did, and in any case he was often away. The legal costs were paid, although it is not known how. Desmond Seward, writing about the situation in 1995, asked the straightforward question: 'Did the king pay?'[2] In any case it is known that the Bishop of Hereford, John Millington, had been helpful to Edward in the past and since he was now helpful to Mistress Shore it seems likely that the king was close to her; she may well have become his mistress already, although his own political problems might have delayed the start of their relationship, as will be shown later. It is interesting to note that about this time the king also took a helpful interest in William Shore who, on leaving the country soon after the divorce, received letters of protection for his 'lands, goods, servants and possessions', as Desmond Seward states; and the London records include no mention of him until after 1484, when Richard III was king.[3]

Although no direct intervention from Edward can be proved he might have advised Jane about what to do, for like Louis XV of France many years later the English king enjoyed hearing gossipy stories about trouble between couples, married or unmarried; even in the eighteenth century the gazettes did not print all the intriguing details relating to such cases. Louis XV was also kept informed by his chief of police. In Edward IV's time there were no official police informers and there was no printing in London until late in the century. There was of course plenty of gossip; Edward's own self-indulgent interest in women was well known both in England and in continental Europe. His subjects did not complain too much, they accepted the situation – after all there had been many royal mistresses in the past. These women had usually been regarded as harmless (with the exception of Edward III's mistress, Alice Perrers) and even as a source of entertainment, attracting either admiration or cynical abuse from the public. In the past the births of several illegitimate children (Henry I, who reigned from 1100 to 1135, was said to have had twenty) were often regarded as a sign of royal virility, while many other kings had acknowledged their illegitimate offspring, some of whom appeared at court; suitable husbands were found for the daughters and some of their half-brothers were given posts in the army. Since Edward's marriage to Elizabeth Woodville produced ten children in less than twenty years (although sadly some of them died very young) he could not be accused of neglecting his wife. Whether he still loved the beautiful widow who in 1464 had 'bewitched' him – if not literally – is not clear, but she had been forced to accept the non-stop procession of his casual mistresses which seems to have continued, although less intensively, after his marriage. In one sense their existence was the price the queen had to pay for the generous treatment that her own large family received from the king.

However, she did not approve of the way her husband and his friends, including his lord chamberlain William Hastings and her own son by her first marriage, the Marquess of Dorset, would behave like schoolboys in their pursuit of women, for the two latter would even inherit the king's temporary mistresses when he tired of them. Queen Elizabeth Woodville must have believed that this was not suitable 'royal' behaviour: the women should have been pensioned off, found a suitable husband, if necessary, but not allowed to lurk anywhere near the court with the king's close friends or his relatives by marriage.

As already mentioned Shore left the country soon after the divorce, which is understandable. When he died in 1495 he was buried in an alabaster tomb in the church of St Paul in Scropton, Derbyshire, where it can be admired today. Affixed to it is the portrait in brass of a tall, dignified, sad-eyed man wearing a long tunic trimmed with fur, the formal dress of a senior merchant, with his merchant's mark well in evidence. It is thought that he may have died during a visit to the Agard family who owned property in Scropton. His will shows that even if he had no children he was not short of family and friends who were to benefit from the extensive possessions and property he had accumulated during his lifetime. The orientation of his existence had remained his business, which he continually expanded, his life in Derby, where he had always kept in touch with his family and friends, and his devotion to the Church. The will also shows that he made many bequests in the area of religion.[4]

Queen Elizabeth Woodville had affected to ignore the existence of her husband's mistresses, and the king showed no inclination to desert his wife: in any case, the latter, and her family, would never have allowed any such thing to happen. Even the bold Edward would not have dared to mention it and he certainly did not want it: he enjoyed being king of England and so far had managed a semi-bigamous private life very well. However, when one mistress to whom her husband had become too attached became officially unmarried in 1476, that mistress became hard to ignore and her presence irritated the queen intensely. This was of course Jane Shore, and according to More, the queen could not persuade Edward to give her up, in fact she was the one 'of all women she most hated'.[5]

After her divorce, Jane was now in principle a woman ready and free to act on her own. Her independent status allowed her to become a Freewoman of London, thanks to a law passed in the previous century, which meant that she could, if she wished, earn money and, more importantly perhaps, buy land. It is to be hoped that William Shore would not have expected Jane to support herself, despite the end of the marriage; he had been chosen as an honourable man and a potentially good husband

and obviously nobody had ever contemplated that the marriage would go wrong in the way it did. No details are available about any financial settlement that might have been approved by the Court of Arches. However, if Jane was now a kept woman, kept by the king, then William had no further responsibility and in a practical but gentlemanly way, as soon as he knew about her lover, at some unknown date, he made no more attempt to share her person and her bed with the king. Whether one or other of the partners, or both, moved house and at what stage of the marriage break-up, is not known.

One important question always asked in any account of Jane Shore's life is hard to answer: how and where had she met the lover with whom her name would always be associated, King Edward IV? There has been continuous guesswork about this. It is not clear whether she encountered him first at some court entertainment which she might have attended during or before her marriage, accompanied by family or friends, or even with her husband, but it is intriguing to note that it was probably the amount of vague and inaccurate information about her that had led to the picturesque and long-lasting legends, starting with the supposed marriage to the goldsmith, as described earlier.

Edward in fact was credited later by at least one illustrator with having possibly some acquaintance with the 'legendary' husband. 'Matthew Shore', the goldsmith, obviously kept a shop, and in one surviving image, probably engraved in the sixteenth century, the king, wearing his crown, is shown visiting the premises and being served by a young woman, clearly meant to represent Jane. Of course it was not Jane because there was no goldsmith's shop. If this mercantile and would-be democratic king had learnt in reality about Jane's existence he could have called at the Shore or even the Lambert home on some matter of business, alleged or genuine, for he himself was involved in trade, especially the woollen-cloth trade. Obviously he did not walk about the city wearing his crown and if he had wanted to choose and buy anything from a goldsmith or any other shopkeeper the owner of the business would have been summoned to his presence in one of his many palaces.

One description of the imagined first meeting between Edward and Jane was given by a romantic novelist in the early nineteenth century whose explanation was different, hardly credible and merely amusing. Mrs Mary

Bennett, the author in question, writer of many successful novels throughout the nineteenth century, published *The Goldsmith's Wife* in about 1839 and described how the king would wander round the city streets in disguise or fancy dress looking at the women: and that is how, she suggested, he found Jane. It was typical of the legends that persisted for a long time about the start of this relationship. The same novelist also invented another fact, unwelcome this time, that Jane and her father had quarrelled bitterly about the marriage that was said to have been forced on her. Although there is a lack of evidence about the family atmosphere for many years that followed, the contents of John Lambert's will, discovered in 1972[6] show that by the end of his life, at least in the 1480s, the family seems to have been closely united.

From the early 1470s both Jane and the king lived through an uncomfortable time, for their personal situations before and during the divorce proceedings remained complicated, especially, in fact, for him. If her difficulties had been marital his were political, and even such an experienced seducer would not have found it easy just then to start and pursue a new relationship which seems for once to have involved him emotionally. His coronation in 1461 and his marriage three years later had barely allowed him to 'settle down' either as king or as a married man. There were Lancastrian plots and rebellions against him, plus the growing hostility of Warwick. It seems unlikely that Edward and Jane could even have met or seen much of each other before the divorce proceedings began, for Edward had to live through the difficult and complicated six months known as the 'Readeption', a period lasting from 6 October 1470 to 11 April 1471, when to the surprise of everyone except fervent supporters of the deposed King Henry VI and the ambitious Earl of Warwick, Edward himself was deposed.

The Readeption period was crucial in the life of Edward IV. It had been anticipated much earlier than the dates quoted; it was due in the first place to the jealous ambition of the Earl of Warwick and the unexpected route by which this apparently staunch Yorkist supporter came to ally himself with the equally jealous and ambitious Duke of Clarence, Edward's younger brother. As Warwick's ambition grew stronger and this apparently unlikely alliance deepened, the so-called 'kingmaker', incredibly enough, became a turncoat, a Lancastrian supporter no less, and was even later reconciled, following some assistance from the French king, Louis XI, with the deposed Queen Margaret of Anjou. He met her finally in Angers, for long and painful discussions, and in the end they became allies. The whole episode could be described as a 'damned near-run thing', as Wellington was to say of Waterloo in 1815. These three unlikely people might have failed to establish any workable cooperation, but somehow in the end they came to an agreement. As a result Edward's position as king was clearly unsafe, even if eight or nine years had passed since his triumphant coronation in 1461. The king had not realised how far Warwick had gradually become more resentful during that time, until in the end resentment became first rivalry and finally treachery. The 'kingmaker' may have thought that he himself would make a better king than Edward, and the Duke of Clarence, his unexpected ally, had the same ideas about his own fitness for kingship. The shallow and unreliable Clarence believed that his good looks at least would help him gain admiration from the public, but he lacked any true firmness of purpose – his jealousy of Edward was not enough.

In brief, Warwick, the ally turned enemy, defeated Edward at the battle of Edgecote in late July 1469, two weeks after he had skilfully married his elder daughter, Isabel, to the Duke of Clarence in the hope of strengthening his closeness to the royal family. Incredibly perhaps, in the following August, Warwick succeeded in imprisoning Edward himself at Middleham Castle, his Yorkshire home at the time. Credibly perhaps on this occasion, Edward's charm is said to have influenced his guards: either he escaped from his imprisonment or he was released and then briefly reconciled with Warwick. But Edward could not be idle, or think about a rendezvous with Jane, for he immediately had to suppress a rebellion in Lincolnshire against tax-gatherers working on his behalf; then almost without a pause he defeated Warwick's supporters at the battle of Empingham, fought five miles west of Stamford. This was named the battle of Losecote Field because the losers, as they ran away, dared not linger on the battlefield long enough even to fasten their clothing. However, it was at this point, in mid-1470, that Warwick and Clarence fled to France, their journey leading to the reconciliation of Warwick and Queen Margaret at Angers. The two traitors – there can be no other way to describe them – quickly returned to England, succeeded somehow in deposing Edward and in arranging a second coronation for Henry VI. As for Edward, he became briefly a royal refugee; by luck and daring he was just able to escape to Flanders via Lynn (later known as King's Lynn) in Norfolk. It was unlike him to take flight, but in this tense situation there was no alternative. His younger brother Richard, his lord chamberlain William Hastings and a few other supporters went with him.

If Jane had met Edward shortly before the start of this troubled period, although there is no proof that she had, it looked as though she was still destined to an existence which had to be lived out from day to day against the disturbed background of war, rebellion and political argument. It would not have been easy for the king to be with her, even if, while hoping for or even planning her divorce, he had already supplied her with a love-nest house close perhaps to the palace of Westminster. Once Edward had arrived in Flanders the Flemish-born diplomat Philippe de Commynes, whose highly readable historical memoirs were completed at the end of the century, inevitably took notice of him and wrote down his impressions. Commynes, who had served in Burgundy, already knew something of Edward IV, for the latter's sister Margaret had been married to Charles the Bold of Burgundy in 1468. The observant diplomat did not express great enthusiasm for the king of England, although he admired his appearance: he saw him as 'not an outstanding man but a very handsome prince, more handsome in fact than any other I ever saw at that time, and he was very courageous'.[7] Edward of course was hoping for help from his brother-in-law, but Commynes thought that he had not taken the danger from Warwick seriously enough, and it had been brewing for a long time. The Flemish diplomat seems to have been the only historian of this complicated situation to mention one mysterious incident: an unnamed woman came from England, ostensibly to visit Clarence's wife in France, with a secret mission: to deliver an offer from Edward of peace talks; but her even more secret plan was to persuade the Duke of Clarence, through his wife, that he must not support Warwick but return to Edward, his own brother, after all. Commynes admired the success of this amateur diplomat and one is left wondering who this woman was. Obviously she was not Jane, and obviously too Edward would not have found many opportunities to send messages to the young woman he had presumably begun to fancy somewhat seriously.

The watchful Commynes was not impressed by Edward: he thought he was too much accustomed to 'more luxuries and pleasures than any prince of his day because he thought of nothing else but women (far more than is reasonable), hunting and looking after himself. During the hunting season he would have several tents brought along for the ladies.' Commynes added that 'he had made a great show of this and also he had a personality as well suited to these pursuits as any I have ever seen. He was young and more handsome than any man then alive.'[8] The writer could not resist adding that after this 'adventure', that is, his request for help from his brother-in-law, and his return to England, 'he later became very fat' and therefore less glamorous, less fascinating to women. In the end Charles the Bold gave some support to Edward, although he was not exactly keen to do so and kept most of it secret. He also gave him some money and this enabled the refugee to return to England, where he landed at Ravenspur in Yorkshire. He had been away for only six months.

Warwick however might have appeared to be on the way to dangerous success; at the end of September 1470 Henry VI had been released from the Tower and crowned for the second time. However only one month after Edward's return, in April 1471, Warwick himself was killed as he fled from the battle of Barnet; this conflict was won by Edward after the unreliable Clarence had at last decided to give support to his brother: perhaps the unknown woman who had come from England had been sufficiently persuasive in the end. Edward had tried, but narrowly failed, to save his old friend's life. It was still too early for anyone to relax, for this display of Lancastrian hostility was not yet all over: Margaret of Anjou, accompanied by her son, Edward, Prince of Wales, who had grown into a belligerent eighteen-year-old, reached England too. On 4 May 1471 Edward defeated her at the battle of Tewkesbury. More importantly still, he also destroyed her interest in life, for her son, the only direct Lancastrian heir, was killed; it looked now as though the help Edward IV had received in Burgundy and Flanders had been decisive. It also looked as though this had brought an end to the second stage of the Wars of the Roses.

Yet if Edward thought he was now a free man who could keep company with any woman he chose, especially perhaps Jane, this was not yet the moment. He was reunited with his wife, who had retired into sanctuary at Westminster when her husband had been forced to leave the country. This provided the queen with a period of security (of at least forty days) within a consecrated building. On Edward's return she greeted him with good news, for she had given birth, while still in sanctuary, to a son, their fourth child, who, confusingly perhaps, was christened Edward. At last, after the birth of three daughters, the king now had a son, an heir to the throne, and the succession was safe.

But Edward still had little time for that additional extra-marital private life that he always needed; in mid-April 1471, according to Commynes, he had been able to spend only two days in London before encountering Warwick at Barnet. The Flemish diplomat did however record one interesting detail: Edward could not forget the 'great debts he owed in the city, which made his merchant creditors support him'; along with 'several noblemen and wives of rich citizens with whom he had been closely and secretly acquainted' and had 'won over their husbands and relatives to his cause'. It is hard not to think that John Lambert was one of the 'rich citizens' involved, and there might have been a possible chance for Jane and Edward to meet, although surely not for the first time. Before the end of May 1471, Edward had to deal with an attack on London that was potentially dangerous, led by the bastard son of William Neville, Lord Fauconberg. The rebels reached the city, as the Cade rebels had done some twenty years earlier, and this new threat might have been dangerous. However, Edward successfully drove the aggressive invaders away – he had not lost his military skill.

Then he had to attend to an act that seems to most people of the twenty-first century to be nothing short of cruel, but in the fifteenth century, and in Edward's eyes, it was essential and it was logical. In May 1471 that most unfortunate of kings, Henry VI, aged fifty, was quietly murdered in the Tower of London, obviously by Edward's command, as no one else could have taken that decision. Margaret of Anjou, widowed and childless, was left for some time in the Tower, but not imprisoned, and then sent back to France, ransomed by the French king; she lived for a few more miserable years in one of her late father's châteaux, near Dampierre, supported in meagre fashion by Louis XI and dying in 1482, eleven years after her husband. The Lancastrian dynasty had ended, and in an attempt to convince the population of this fact the corpse of Henry VI was displayed for a time outside St Paul's church before being taken to Chertsey Abbey in

Surrey by the monks. There seemed to be some evidence that the long-suffering ex-king had been murdered and had not died a natural death from melancholy and depression, as the public had been told. For a time miracles were said to have occurred at the site of his tomb; later Richard III ordered his reburial in St George's Chapel, Windsor.[9]

Edward now hoped he could stay in England, in control of his own country; he needed some years to carry out various projects that he had had in mind for a long time, and he was more than occupied. He wanted to work on many important administrative innovations, such as the reform of the coinage, for all such reform had been neglected during the early years of Henry VI and forcibly postponed during the ensuing wars. The complex legal system had suffered in the same way and needed an overhaul. The king had other problems too, personal ones. He had been out of his own country for no more than six months but he may have been forced to live through that time without the company of women, a disaster for him. Since his son had been born in May 1471 he had obviously been living with his queen in the late summer or early autumn of the previous year, but he had never made any attempt to be monogamous. Even if a military king could in principle order women to be brought to him when he required, it is hard to imagine Jane as a kind of camp-follower, and Edward might have had difficulty in going to London or anywhere else to be with her. The early meetings of these lovers remain mysterious, like so much of Jane's own life and so many episodes in that of Edward. In telling her story it has always been necessary to tell his at the same time, for the circumstances of both separated them for so long. But in the end separation does not seem to have changed their feelings for each other.

Francis Bacon, writing in Elizabethan times, did in fact speculate about the problem of long separation when war governed people's lives, a situation that unfortunately has never been out of date; in his essay *On Love* he mused on the well-known need for love – although the term sex-life would be more straightforward for later readers – among military men: 'I know not how,' he wrote, 'but martial men are given to love: I think it is, but [i.e. just] as they are given to wine, for perils commonly ask to be paid in pleasures.' In the same essay he included that much-quoted phrase, 'therefore it was well said "That it is impossible to love and be wise".' His remarks would fit the case of the young Edward fairly well, but when he came closer to Jane he seems gradually to have grown out of his over-prolonged adolescent attitude towards attractive women.

It has to be assumed that after his return to England in 1471 and his restoration to the throne the king could now resume the kind of private life that he enjoyed, part of it shared with his queen and the family court circle, part of it shared with his chosen mistress of the time, his last mistress in fact. Jane was more or less established in his life about this period, and even though she would not be living in any of the royal palaces, Edward's closeness to her and his obvious need for her infuriated the queen.

It is possible that the king had installed Jane in a kind of private retreat, a little house within easy reach of the nearest palace. In the nineteenth century there was a rumour[10] that Jane had lived in a 'moated house in Tallhampton-court' but exhaustive research has discovered no mention of such a locality and certainly no mention of the items said to have been preserved there, even including furniture, such as Jane's dining-table. Other equally unsuccessful attempts have been made to identify the location of the house where Jane now lived – could it have been in Hackney, could it have been in Ludgate, in or near to the vanished Flower-de-Luce Court? Unfortunately all the properties mentioned in this context[11] no longer existed even by the eighteenth century or earlier and any attempted link with Shoreditch has always been denied, for that name was much older and used long before Jane's time.

Sir Thomas More was to give a simple explanation of the relationship between Jane and the king: 'For many he had, but her he loved . . .'.[12] At the risk of sounding sentimental this seems to have been the key to their relationship, even if More tried to be fair in his *History of King Richard III*, and not be carried away by Jane's reputation. Even men like Edward, who have spent their youth in idle sexual adventures, sometimes change as their physical prowess weakens. The whole of More's unfinished essay, much edited in the sixteenth century, has been attacked by modern historians for its inaccuracies, its bias and even its authorship, but Dr Alison Hanham, in her *Richard III and his early historians, 1483–1535*, refers to the few pages about Jane as 'charming'. Unfortunately for many historians, these pages also constitute virtually the only source so far known which presents contemporary personal information about Jane and some explanation of the ways in which she was 'different', at least from King Edward's point of view. She was clearly not ambitious for power or personally rapacious, as Alice Perrers had been and as many royal mistresses were to be in future. Among the many kept later by Charles II, the cat-fights between them were to become only too well known, providing entertainment for the population. As for Jane, somehow, either through her upbringing, her unhappy marriage experience, or simply through her own nature, she seems to have developed into a kind of modest private diplomat, helping the king resolve the problems caused by the many difficult situations he could not easily avoid: 'where the king took displeasure, she would mitigate and appease his mind; where men were out of favour, she would bring them in his grace; for many that highly offended, she obtained pardon. Of great forfeitures she got men remission. And finally, in many weighty suits, she stood many men in good stead'; More also mentioned that she did not expect to become a grand and rich lady: she received 'none or very small rewards, and those rather gay than rich, either for that she was content with the deed self well done', or perhaps he gave a hint of Jane's pride in her status of royal mistress and the power she had gained: 'or for that she delighted to be sued unto and to show what she was able to do with the king; or for that wanton women and wealthy be not always covetous'.[13]

Jane's behaviour was certainly rare among the so-called 'wanton women', a term which seems to imply a condemnation of anyone not a member of respectable society. The coldness between Jane and her husband, described by More and later defined as due to Shore's impotence, had been the start of her unhappiness and her vulnerable state: 'Which was haply the thing that the more easily made her incline unto the king's appetite when he required her'. She could not resist what he offered: 'the hope of gay apparel, ease, pleasure, and other wanton wealth was soon able to pierce a soft, tender heart'. So Jane had all those despised feminine longings after all, she was not given to austerity: she had been admired in the past for her beauty and it would seem that her husband had not overwhelmed her with generous gifts.

More's biographical notes do not stop there, and although he does not say outright that he had met her in her old age he may have done so, or else he may have known people who knew her well. She had been good-looking, known to have had very white skin and sparkling eyes. 'Proper she was and fair', rather short in stature, not exactly a beauty when young, but attractive, then very much wrinkled and bony when in her seventies; it was rare at the time for anyone to live so long. However, the young Jane's charm was obviously not limited to her physical appearance. 'Yet delighted not men so much in her beauty as in her pleasant behaviour.' Her conversation seems to have formed a great part of her appeal: 'For a proper wit had she', she was 'merry in company' – surely different from the queen, who would be too coldly dignified for merriment – 'ready and quick of answer, neither mute nor full of babble, sometimes taunting without displeasure and not without disport [merriment]'. More refers discreetly, without naming them, to some of her possible predecessors (no doubt Elizabeth Lucy, mentioned earlier, and Eleanor Butler, who had died in 1468): the king would say that he had three concubines who had different talents, one was the 'wiliest', another the 'holiest', 'but the merriest was this Shore's wife, in whom the king took special pleasure'. No wonder the queen hated her. How Jane had learnt her merriment is not clear, but it was probably due in part to memories of the early, cheerful and extrovert social life of Cheapside, unless she was 'merry' now because she had survived her loveless marriage while appreciating deeply the king's devotion to her – and she might even have loved him in return. Two centuries later Robert Burton, in his *Anatomy of Melancholy*, mentioned her pleasant voice,[14] for he listed this possession as one of the 'allurements' of love: 'It was Cleopatra's sweet voice and pleasant speech which inveigled Anthony,' he wrote. 'Roxolana bewitched Solyman the Magnificent, and Shore's wife by this engine overcame Edward the Fourth: *Omnibus una omnes surripuit Veneres* . . . [this one charm replaces all others].'

The years between 1471 or 1472 and 1483 were for Jane the happiest time of her life. Presumably she at last had all the 'gay apparel' she wanted, jewellery too, that can be seen in many of the later engravings and assumed portraits of her that are still accessible. She also had her own house and she would accompany the king whenever the circumstances were right. Perhaps he was able to take her to Eltham Palace and show her the splendid hammerbeam roof his carpenters had built over the Great Hall. Was she even concealed among the crowd of over two thousand guests when the king held a feast there in 1481? We do not know, yet a picture emerges of an attractive and modest young woman with an unfashionable readiness to help everyone, including women and children especially.

More interrupted his 'history' of Richard III to write about her, seeing her behaviour as outstanding among that of the 'average' royal mistresses for her unselfish attitude and the care she expressed for people who needed help, something not forgotten later by ballad-writers and poets. More had taken the opportunity to write about the virtues of a middle-class woman, something that was never done in Jane's time and only touched on later in More's own time. A queen, an abbess or a future saint could be remembered and written about, but not the daughter of a city alderman, a still-young woman who had emerged from a failed marriage, and now was just the favourite mistress of a licentious king known to be perpetually hungry for women: superficially at least she was not a suitable subject for a serious essayist. Jane remained unambitious and More insisted that she deserved to be known and appreciated simply for what she was and for the unselfish things she did, although he had to justify himself: 'I doubt not some shall think this woman too slight a thing to be written of and set among the remembrances of great matters . . .'. He contrasted her with those people, namely men, 'famous only by the infamy of their ill deeds'. These deeds are described 'in marble', wrote More, 'and whoso doth us a good turn, we write it in dust'.[15] Jane Shore, he concluded, was the living example of this, for despite having helped so many, according to the later ballad-writers at least, she was soon to be forced into poverty and neglect. More inferred that Jane, unlike Richard III, had carried out many good deeds, and if the ballad-writers and others often mentioned that she helped women and children, no details were ever given. As far as one can tell, Jane, unlike other royal mistresses, never wanted publicity in any way. Was there no protection or help for the woman who was so soon to be abandoned by everyone and left on her own? Apparently not, unless she had for some reason refused it. Feminism seems to have entered More's unconscious mind, but the word had not yet been invented, while social welfare, not mere charity, which Jane was to need so badly, was still limited to personal generosity and not regulated. More himself, writing a piece of prose planned as an attack on Richard III from start to finish, or at least to the end of this unfinished fragment, needed to set against him a figure as different as possible, and he chose Jane. He wrote in the first place as a humanist, and there have been endless attacks on More's motives and bias in writing this so-called 'history'; however, in 1981 the historian Charles

Ross mentioned a fact too easily forgotten: these few pages about Jane form 'the first pen-portrait of a living woman ever written in England'.[16] The crucial pages are only part of her story, but they form one of the parts that inevitably still fascinate the readers of today. More's description of a royal mistress reveals Jane as different from most of those who attained this position: these women had almost always been in search of mere personal power. For once, in the case of Jane, a mistress could have infinitely more value than a mere wanton woman or a harlot. Oddly perhaps the word 'harlot' had earlier been used to describe only men, and men of no value. It would be interesting to examine the reasons behind this change in the word's usage.

The 'great matters' to which More referred were those that now, in April 1483, began two years of tragedy for the house of York.

SIX

Loss, Punishment and Penance

To everyone's surprise and dismay King Edward died on 9 April 1483 after a short and mysterious illness. The visiting Italian historian Dominic Mancini gave his version of what might have happened: 'one day he was taken in a small boat, with those whom he had bidden go fishing, and watched their sport too eagerly. He there contracted the illness from which he never recovered although it did not long afflict him'.[1] He was said to have caught a chill which developed into a fever because the fishing trip took place along the Thames in misty and changeable spring weather. Many tentative suggestions for the cause of his death have been put forward: poison, for instance, which was always suspected in medieval times when a king became ill or died, perhaps a slight stroke, or even, as suggested later by Sir Winston Churchill, appendicitis.

Why did Edward die so quickly, so suddenly? He was still only forty – a few weeks later he would have been forty-one – but he had lived a self-chosen exhausting life for over twenty years, constantly leading or partaking in battles, perpetually indulging in rich food and drink, always involved in love affairs with a strong sexual content, some presumably more intensive, while all the time assuming that his youth and buoyant good health would protect him from illness and allow him time for the business of governing England and conducting some sort of foreign policy. It never occurred to him that he might give up some of his entertainments, including part of the courtly socialising demanded by his married life, as well as his unmarried life with temporary mistresses, followed by the more settled relationship with Jane. He could have simplified some of the more formal life without effort but it was all too important to him – he was determined to go on living a personal life that was as ceremonial and glamorous as he could make it.

He had risked a good portion of this life on endless battlefields, but the finality of death, especially an inglorious death in his own bed, was something he had presumably never thought about, despite regular observance of Christian practice. Some kings, including his exact contemporary, Louis XI of France, became obsessed with death, but Edward had chosen to ignore it. He had done nothing to preserve himself from the onset of middle age, but had assumed that he would remain young and healthy for ever. His activity in military, political and sexual life, all of which had begun before he was twenty, had obviously aged him prematurely; and as he inevitably grew fatter and less active in his mid-thirties he had probably lost his resistance to minor health problems and possible infections. He had another problem too which few physicians of the time were likely to solve: he had been used to constant victory in both military and diplomatic life, but now he saw himself outwitted by European rulers and diplomats who were more astute and richer than he was, notably the unavoidable, unattractive but clever Louis XI, who was known as the 'universal spider'. Edward also felt he had let down his old friends the Flemings, who were now estranged from him through the latest political entanglements with Burgundy and France. 'On this account,' wrote Dominic Mancini,[2] 'Edward fell into the greatest melancholy.' He was not a winner any longer, and since he had never been in that situation before, other than his enforced brief escape to the continent during the Readeption, he now encountered a greater danger: he became gradually more and more depressed and could not come to terms with a condition that he and his friends could not diagnose. His physicians might suspect it but could not treat it, for depression is deeper and more insidious than mere 'melancholy' and regret.

If Jane was close to the king as a comforting friend, her presence or advice could only soothe his unhappiness; she could not do anything to help him through his depressed state.

Edward had led a hero's life and had forgotten or refused to admit that in pursuing his father's claim to the throne he had been in fact a usurper, like Henry IV and others before him; he had fought his way to his kingship, in his case twice over. He had also insisted on the so-called romantic marriage that he wanted, despite opposition from his own family, his political advisers and from most of the country. He had suppressed several minor rebellions, some of them threatening, and in the mid-1470s he had developed a grandiose plan to invade France, the country that had once been subject to English rule; in the end however he had accepted a pension from Louis XI, a helpful solution for a king who was always short of money and had become very cautious about spending it, but not a very courageous option. After seriously preparing for more war he had now been bought off, he had given in to a form of bribery, and it seemed a feeble denouement. His ideas for promoting useful alliances by marriage were not realised either; he had hoped to marry his eldest daughter Elizabeth to Louis XI's son, the dauphin of France, but this plan failed, and so did several others. Edward had become a near-forgotten king, and if much of his life is duly chronicled in historical works of all kinds he was clearly becoming infinitely less interesting and controversial than his youngest brother, Richard, who eventually followed him, having removed his nephew, Edward's son and heir, from the succession to the throne. Edward surely could never have suspected that such a state of affairs could possibly happen, despite the troubled history of his family.

He in fact suffered painful disagreements within this family about possible political issues, including the succession, and does not seem to have put his mind to protecting his heir against possible dangers. Neither had he found the strength to deal with aggressive behaviour by various factions in Scotland in 1480 and afterwards, leaving the necessary action there to his brother Richard, who had been living more or less permanently in the north – mainly in order to avoid the Woodvilles – and had advised war against Scotland. Edward knew he could rely on military support from Richard, who had often accompanied him in the past, as he was experienced and trustworthy, although obviously Edward, if he had not been sinking into depression, would probably have had to give the basic orders.

To make matters worse, his other brother, George, Duke of Clarence, caused him immense trouble, perpetually complaining about the treatment he received from Edward, alleging that he himself was undervalued and unappreciated. He was also aware of the rumours about Edward's possibly illegitimate birth – their mother, Cecily of York, had alleged this when she had been trying to dissuade Edward from his planned marriage – and taunted his brother about it when he could. In fact Clarence was so jealous that in 1477 he had begun to behave in a strange, irrational way, especially when he accused a woman who had served his late wife, the duchess, of actually poisoning her. He even forced a jury in Warwick to condemn this woman, Ankarette Twynho, as guilty of murder and she was hanged, although there had been no evidence against her. As though that were not enough Clarence went further: his brother the king, he alleged, was not above using the devices of magic himself to run the country and at the same time was aiming to murder him. After he had accused others, some of them eminent, of using the well-known image-magic practices for dire purposes it was discovered that Clarence himself was ready to follow the same methods.[3]

Edward patiently tolerated these angry jealous scenes in public and private but in the end, realising that he had to stop his brother's tedious behaviour somehow, ordered him to face trial. It sounds a harsh decision, as though family ties did not count any longer, but in 1478 the court reached a decision that was harsher still: Clarence was arrested, tried, found guilty of treachery, committed to the Tower and sentenced to death. He was killed, either first stunned or stabbed and his body then immersed in a barrel of wine, or else he was simply drowned in the legendary butt of Malmsey. The odd and tragic end to this story is only too well known in English history and certainly many people at the time approved of what happened. Not everyone though: according to rumour, it was even said by some that Richard, Duke of Gloucester had pleaded with Edward on his brother's behalf. But Richard was too much of a realist and this supposed reaction was more than unlikely.[4] News about the royal family always began a trail of gossip, usually inaccurate or exaggerated. Later, but too late, Edward himself apparently felt remorse, although that rumour too is contested. Centuries later still, the Victorian writer George Henry Lewes was to suggest in his *Physiology of Common Life* of 1879 'that murder, like talent, sometimes seems to run in families' and in 1478 the Yorkist branch of the Plantagenet dynasty seemed to merit that description. It was not long since Edward had arranged at least one other murder, that of his enemy the saintly Lancastrian Henry VI. But the battle of Tewkesbury was in the past, the Lancastrian heir Prince Edward had been killed. So in principle Edward IV no longer had any rivals. If the end of Henry VI was one of the last deeds in a near-final act of the Wars of the Roses, does a respected king, after what was hopefully not an unfair trial, order the killing of his own brother, even if the latter had behaved in an exasperating way? Edward of York, like his brothers, was a man of his times. He seems to have been only dimly aware that he was nothing less than a murderer in the case of Clarence, and the murdered man was his own younger brother. Henry VI had been an enemy, while Margaret of Anjou, Henry's widow, escaped violent death because the Plantagenet kings did not kill women.

Much of Jane's story cannot be separated from that of the king: all through both their lives there was a constant interaction between their different but sometimes related experiences. So perhaps she was not too shocked by all these developments as she had grown up through scenes of violence, bloodshed, distant battles and nearby street-fighting, so that death as such presumably no longer took her by surprise. If she had tried to dissuade Edward from these killings, she would hardly have been successful; however, she may have been at least partly responsible for the king's alleged, if delayed remorse concerning the death of Clarence.

These incidents belong presumably to the period evoked by Sir Thomas More when he described how Jane Shore would help to resolve the endless problems that beset the king during the second part of his reign. She was aware of being close to a complicated family, and she realised her own insecurity, but she probably concentrated on listening to Edward's problems and it seems unlikely that she seriously attempted to influence the king in this type of situation: it would have been too dangerous, and a solution to this problem could only be left to the king and his queen. The latter had never forgotten her hostility towards her brother-in-law Clarence; it was part of her intense pro-Woodville ambitions. She had been afraid that if her husband should die early Clarence might be declared king or at least protector until her elder son attained his majority. Clarence would even have been capable, Elizabeth Woodville suspected, of seizing the throne by any means available to him. There is no confirmation of this, but given the queen's general attitude, by which the members of her own family were hoping to become ever closer to overall power, it cannot be forgotten. Jane's role, important in the circumstances, would presumably as usual be the one she fulfilled so well, that of sympathetic listener. It is hard to think of anything more different from the combative attitude of the queen, who remained more devoted to the interests of the Woodville family and her sons than to anything else.

All these far from happy events filled the last years of Edward's life. The only happier ones had come earlier, the birth of his second son Richard in

1473 and of his three younger daughters. A last son, George, was born in 1477 but died in infancy. The truly 'happier' event might have been the mere presence of Jane, who had drawn him into a kind of undemanding, semi-domestic, almost cosy situation where virtually nothing happened, and that was something pleasantly different from all that had happened to either of them earlier.

It was during this relatively quiet period however that Edward at least found time to deal with one problem which seems to have been on his mind for a long time, and if he had not listened to advice he might have acted too hastily. This was the existence of Eton College, situated near Windsor, the Berkshire town with its many royal connections. The College was a fairly recent foundation, and the founder in 1440 had been the last Lancastrian king, Henry VI, so Edward could not have been expected to value it greatly. According to Nicolas Barker, writing in *Etoniana* in 1972,[5] Edward had contemplated at least a change in its status even before his own acceptance as king, and later came into conflict with Pope Pius II by whose decision Eton was to be united with St George's in Windsor. Later, when Edward had become king, complicated and slow-moving negotiations continued, and it was not until 1470 that Eton was finally restored to its former status. Then in 1474 Edward seemed ready to change his attitude again and once more Eton might have returned to the control of St George's.

The date is important here, for by this time Jane was the accepted royal mistress and according to one legend it was she who persuaded the king to leave things as they were and not to remove any more property or rights from the College, which Edward had gradually been doing. It later became generally acknowledged, though without any reliable evidence, that if Jane had not persuaded Edward to stop his interference in the affairs of the College – there was no question of it being closed down – then it would have lost its true independence. It so happened that the Provost of Eton at the time, Pierre Bost, was also Jane's confessor, and he might have influenced her attitude. This possible influence may have accounted for the presence at Eton of her portrait, or what has been assumed to be her portrait, perhaps a copy of some later work that was 'doctored' until it looked vaguely like her; it is still in the College and has always attracted attention. Was it presented in gratitude by some unknown admirer of the College and/or of Jane herself? A similar portrait exists also in Queens'

College, Cambridge, but exactly why they have both been preserved, or who painted them, is not known. These questions have never been answered, although the portraits have led to surprising comments, especially the one mentioned by Nicolas Barker, that an eighteenth-century description of the College included no other fact, merely the existence of Jane's portrait.

Much of this is speculation, and there has always been speculation about that crucial time in the history of Eton, for there was another rumour – that it was the queen, and not Jane, who persuaded the king not to interfere in College affairs any longer. Elizabeth Woodville and her rival Jane, both possibly influenced by Bost, may have talked separately to Edward on the same topic, and what man could have ignored simultaneous advice or attempted persuasion, even gentle nagging, from two women on the same topic? So the king probably gave in to them both and both have received the necessary credit, though not of course for any joint effort, which would have been unlikely.

Edward had other problems which he would have dearly liked to resolve, but realised perhaps how difficult it would be, if not impossible. When he became ill he must have been aware that if he died now, one difficult situation both within and outside the family might cause deep, even insoluble problems. Over the years that had passed since his marriage two distinct factions had developed among those close to the throne: the first consisted of his own blood relations – Richard, constantly faithful, while sometimes even the fickle Clarence had been on his elder brother's side too – plus a few personal friends who were important to him, particularly his loyal lord chamberlain William, Lord Hastings; while the second faction, more or less in opposition, consisted of the entire Woodville family and their hangers-on. Several senior members of the second group had been given important posts, especially Anthony Woodville, Earl Rivers, the queen's highly educated brother, respected as a creative writer and also for his very different skill in jousting: he had been entrusted with the important work of tutor to Prince Edward, heir to the throne. Rivers himself was not a difficult or highly ambitious man, but there was deep hostility between these two groups and Edward had set himself the near-impossible task of trying to reconcile them.

When the king took to his bed and realised that he might be dying he still found the strength to make one last effort towards solving, or at least improving, this seemingly unsolvable situation. He summoned members of each group to his bedside, did not include the queen and explained his urgent wish for reconciliation. These men realised what they must do – they must at least listen, they must pretend, they must appear to renounce their differences and accept reconciliation. They shook hands, each of them repeated that they were no longer enemies. According to hearsay, the king, apparently satisfied by this, turned over on his pillows and died. Whether he had seriously believed these promises to be sincere is not known. Jane would probably not have been allowed to see him when he became ill.

A codicil had been added to Edward's will whereby, if necessary, his only surviving brother, Richard, would act as protector for the young Prince Edward, if the latter should be too young to occupy the throne immediately after his father's death. This amended will however was not executed; the Woodvilles set it aside, intent on hoping to arrange that someone in *their* family should be Protector. There was still open but silent warfare between the Woodvilles and Edward's surviving brother, Richard, Duke of Gloucester, who was supported at least for a time by a few men the late king had valued, notably Lord Hastings.

The date of the king's death, as already mentioned, was 9 April 1483 and the court began the period of ritual mourning, starting with Edward's lavish, costly funeral and his burial in St George's Chapel, Windsor, a building on which he had bestowed a great amount of care. For Jane, as it is simpler, if still incorrect, to name her, the situation was disastrous. The death of a king had always brought one essential and immediate follow-up: his current mistress immediately became a non-person, even if she had been accepted by the public and had established a kind of independent life for herself. The more civilised behaviour later of the Renaissance, although on its way to England, did not bring any rapid improvement to this situation. A few dates are significant here: it should not be forgotten that in 1559, about eighty years ahead, the celebrated Diane de Poitiers, who had been for twenty years the official, accepted mistress of Henri II of France, was not allowed to come near him, see him or speak to him when he was dying of a wound sustained by accident in a tournament. His widow, Catherine de' Medici, assumed what she saw as the correct civilised attitude, declaring that 'a dying king belongs to the queen'. At least Diane could retire to her own Château d'Anet in the Ile de France. Jane Shore, who was no aristocrat like Diane, had not been respected in the same way for she had made no attempt to attract public attention, preferring private life, and after all was barely tolerated, with disapproval, by the queen. At least she had her own house, at least her parents were still living and presumably could be helpful if she needed them. But the king was dead, and she herself no longer existed.

According to legend the best-known and most popular mistress of Charles II, two centuries later, was more fortunate: if the dying king did not actually say, 'Don't let poor Nellie starve,' she didn't, although sadly Nell Gwynn died not long afterwards, probably aged about thirty-five, in 1685. Edward, it seems, had carelessly neglected to make any arrangements that might have helped Jane, just as he had not carefully worked out valid details about his successor. Perhaps, if he had idly thought about any problems which his death might bring to Jane, he might have assumed in an equally careless way that since she had her own house and the many possessions he had given her, she would not be deprived of everything. It had obviously never occurred to Jane that he would die so young: she had just assumed that he would always be there. During her years close to Edward she had probably lost any sense of reality, life was comfortable and enjoyable, that was enough.

Fortunately for her however, a powerful protector appeared immediately and decided to take up residence in her house. This was comforting for her, perhaps, but it was soon seen to have been a mistake. This protector was none other than Lord Hastings, lord chamberlain to the late king and one of his closest friends. Apparently Hastings had always found Jane attractive, but, according to Sir Thomas More, he had behaved honourably, even during the earlier mistress-swapping in which Edward and his comrades had indulged. Hastings, said More, had 'somewhat doted' on her, but 'that while forbare her of reverence toward his king, or else of a certain kind of reverence to his friend', and Jane, who must surely have been in shock, feeling miserable and anxious, did not discourage him. She must have known earlier that he was attracted to her.[6]

There is no need to describe here how Richard, Duke of Gloucester, virtually kidnapped his nephew from the Woodville family and brought him to London, causing the dowager queen to retire into sanctuary in Westminster, along with her six daughters, her younger son Richard and her older son by her previous marriage, the Marquess of Dorset. The latter however soon decided to leave sanctuary and disappeared, thought to have gone to France. Gloucester then spent a few weeks calculating how he could make his own position more secure – for he knew, despite all his attempts to prove how he was potentially a more suitable king of England than his brother had been, that Edward himself had probably been a usurper. Richard and his supporters emphasised that he was unquestionably a legitimate son of the Duke and Duchess of York, while Edward had been a bastard. Cecily's angry confession at the time of his marriage had not been forgotten. Also, he himself had been born in England, at Fotheringhay, whereas Edward had been born in Rouen. Despite all the propaganda that he organised, Richard still did not have enough supporters round him to make him feel safe. He developed neurotic tics, noticed by observers: he was seen to be constantly biting his lip and fingering his dagger, all signs of his insecurity.

He had indeed few friends but compensated for this by finding many victims, and notably one of them was Jane. For instance he was intent on searching for Dorset, for all the Woodville family must be under his control, and he began at once to attack Jane for she was known to have been close to the missing man. One question about Jane's behaviour will never be answered: had she, when the king was still alive, accepted Dorset as a lover? Perhaps. In any case, he, along with the queen, as already mentioned, had gone into sanctuary at Westminster soon after Edward's death, but then managed to leave it in secrecy, to the annoyance of Richard, who had soon been accepted, to the dismay of the Woodvilles, as protector of the king-in-waiting. This was Edward V, aged twelve and now living in the Tower of London, soon to be joined by his younger brother whom the queen had reluctantly allowed to leave sanctuary.

Richard thought it essential at least to locate all the Woodvilles, as they were a threat, and he seemed ready to annihilate them if he could, although the dowager queen would be spared. Dorset still could not be found. Richard was convinced that Jane was secretly harbouring him and when once established as king in July 1483, he made a determined effort to blame her for this and force her to disclose where he was. On 23 October that year[7] the new king apparently issued a proclamation in Leicester, offering a reward of 1,000 marks in money, or 100 a year in land for taking 'Thomas late marquis of Dorset,' who, 'not having the fear of God, nor the salvation of his own soul, before his eyes, has damnably debauched and defiled many maids, widows, and wives, and *lived in actual adultery with the wife of Shore*'. Richard had planned to accuse him of treason, assuming that he might be still somewhere in England, possibly with the Duke of Buckingham, one of his early supporters, but he was not; so Richard concentrated in a puritanical way on Dorset's supposedly immoral cohabitation with Jane, who was a harlot, he insisted. Historians have argued over the order in which Jane's two admirers, Hastings and Dorset, loved Jane and/or lived with her, a problem unlikely to be solved and perhaps not of great importance, unless Jane's fidelity to Edward needs to be questioned. It has been assumed that as Edward reached the early mid-life crisis of his late thirties his relationship with his mistress had developed into a deep and steady friendship, the excitement of their sexual partnership becoming just a memory. Dorset was not found as a result of the proclamation.

The two and a half years of Richard III's reign formed one of the most dramatic and controversial periods in the history of England, under-standably receiving a great deal of attention from historians, biographers and novelists expressing all possible shades of opinion. There were a few, but principally two, leading players in the 'great matters' making up this drama, or rather melodrama: King Richard, the usurper, soon to be killed in battle in 1485, and his victim, Jane Shore, who in the end outlived all the tragic events of his reign, including the rebellion and death of a third player, his former ally the Duke of Buckingham. She was to survive Richard by over thirty years, through the reign of two more kings, Henry VII and Edward VI, then through some sixteen years of a third, Henry VIII, the grandson of her former lover Edward IV.

In late 1483, now that he was king – if still insecure – Richard needed someone to blame for all his problems, many his own fault, some real, some imagined. Although surrounded by men he had known and worked with for a long time, whom could he trust? And how could he explain what had happened to the two young princes, seen earlier 'shooting and playing' in the Tower of London gardens but then seen no more? Mancini recorded that before he himself left England in 1483 people were already enquiring, sometimes tearfully, about their disappearance, suspecting that it was not temporary but final. Richard was and still is suspected of having ordered their deaths, but no proof of yet another murder within the family has ever been established. As soon as it become obvious that he could trust nobody, Richard looked for somebody whom he could attack, for he needed some form of self-expression without any fear of reprisals. He soon realised that if he attacked Jane, as he now chose to do, she could not respond, could not cause him any harm; he knew he could treat her as a woman of no importance and use her existence to emphasise that his late brother had known and relied on worthless people, like this 'harlot'.

Much of Richard's behaviour at this crucial time cannot easily be explained even centuries later. He could have taken some action against the dowager queen, but had the tact not to do so. However, he accused her of acting in league with Jane and of practising sorcery, the allegation always suggested at this period in any unsolvable situation; the accusation was expected, but could not be proved. Jane however was particularly vulnerable and available for punishment and so Richard chose to be particularly aggressive towards her.

In the meantime dramatic events had taken place in the Tower, which involved her indirectly; she was not of course summoned there, not being grand enough, but the Protector had begun early to use her existence and her reputation as a means of demonstrating his authority. He had called two meetings on 13 June, one of them in the Tower, one in Westminster, and he appeared to conduct the former in two parts. He entered the appointed room, apparently in a good mood, and asked the Bishop of Ely if he could have some strawberries from his garden. Then he left the room but soon returned in a quite different mood, angry, destructive and bent on ambitious revenge. For this he chose vulnerable subjects, the queen and her unlikely associate, Jane. It was their sorcery, he alleged, that had caused his arm to wither, although everyone knew that it had always been in its present state. With hostile questioning skill he then succeeded in making Lord Hastings look like a traitor. In his *History of King Richard III*, More described what ensued: 'So was he [Hastings] brought forth into the green beside the chapel within the Tower, and his head laid down upon a long log of timber, and there stricken off, and afterwards his body with the head interred at Windsor beside the body of King Edward, whose both souls our Lord pardon.'[8] Shakespeare gave a brutal account of this death in Act III of *Richard III*, scenes 4 and 5.

It looked as though the Protector had temporarily lost his reason, for he also despatched to Pontefract in Yorkshire four leading Woodville supporters, including Earl Rivers himself. They were housed in the prison there and later executed. Rivers, while awaiting execution, spent some time writing a poem; although not a very good one: at least he found the mental strength to compose it, expressing his stoicism in the face of death. It has been described as owing much to Chaucer,[9] and consists of five stanzas of eight lines each. The last stanza, as 'translated' and edited by P.M. Kendall reads:

> My life was lent
> Me to one intent,
> It is nigh spent.
> > Welcome Fortune!
> But I ne went [never thought]
> Thus to be shent [ruined],
> But she it meant:
> > Such is her wont.

It was discovered after his death that the urbane but stoical Anthony Rivers had been wearing a hair shirt which, according to Kendall, was then 'hung up in a church in Doncaster as a holy object'. Rivers, the most civilised member of the Woodville family, is remembered as the author, or rather translator, of the first book in English printed and dated by Caxton in 1478, *The Dictes or Sayings of the Philosophers*. But in June 1483 Richard III saw him only as a potentially dangerous Woodville, and he had to die.

Richard's shock tactics were explained to the public by a proclamation alleging that a murderous plot had been discovered and had to be dealt with at once. It is hardly surprising that this summertime drama in the warm days of mid-June remained a legend in England and eventually supplied Shakespeare with a melodrama, although other little-known writers were to use the story earlier. Only More's account includes a mention of Jane in this context; the two Italian historians who described these scenes, Polydore Vergil and Dominic Mancini, clearly considered her of no importance: the latter in fact, when introducing his short Latin history, written in the next century, referred to King Edward's daughters and added 'but they do not concern us'.[10] How could women, apart from queens or rich and marriageable princesses, be of any use or interest? Mancini could not have anticipated that in 1486, Elizabeth, the eldest daughter, was to become queen of England, when her marriage to Henry VII united the two factions of Lancaster and York.

The Protector however, according to More, was much concerned with one woman, Jane, for he was intent on punishing someone whose intimacy with his late brother could be used to discredit him. Richard accused her of every misdemeanour he could think of: after failing to have her convicted as a witch and failing to make her confess to harbouring Dorset he had to find some other means of attacking her. Having heard that the traitor Hastings had moved into her house after the death of Edward IV, Richard ordered that all her possessions should be removed from it and that she herself be sent to prison. Unlikely though it sounds, there was now a rumour that she had unexpectedly come closer to the queen – who was still in sanctuary in Westminster – and had acted as a messenger for her in an earlier attempt to keep in touch with Hastings and possibly foil some of Richard's plans. The story seems unlikely but obviously the queen was desperate. So Richard took action and sent Jane to prison.

The news soon spread; Simon Stallworthe, who served the Lord Chancellor, wrote a letter to his friend in the country telling him, along with the other news of the day, 'Mistress Shore is in prison, what shall happen to her I know not'.[11] Jane had obviously attracted public attention. She no longer had anyone to defend her, and had to obey Richard, but she was still a Freewoman of London and therefore able to choose her prison. She chose Ludgate, for that was where anyone possessing the freedom of the city went, and she could rely on friends living nearby to bring her food and other requirements.

Had she perhaps heard the legend of how this famous and picturesque prison was said to have been founded originally by the mythical King Lud? Stow, in his *Survey of London*, wrote that 'In the year 1260 the gate was beautified with images of Lud and other kings but these images did not last: in the reign of Edward VI [they had] their heads smitten off . . . Queen Mary did set new heads upon their old bodies again and Queen Elizabeth rebuilt the entire gate beautifully with images of Lud and others, as before'.[12] The prison was said to have been built with stones from the ruined houses of persecuted Jews, and always attracted attention. In 1454 the Lord Mayor of London had been Sir Stephen Forster, of the Fishmongers' Company, but as a young man he had been in trouble, reduced to begging at the prison gate. He had been noticed by a rich widow who took him into her service and later married him. Forster, grown rich and famous, later wanted to commemorate his rescue and did so by enlarging the prison for the 'ease' of the prisoners there, and building a chapel. This was the place to which Jane went after her committal by Richard, and she would surely have known something of this story. But all she could do now was wait until the revengeful king decided to free her.

In the meantime Richard continued his efforts to discredit his dead brother, remembering their mother's complaints about her son Edward's marriage and her threat to make public her own adultery at the crucial time before Edward was born. It had been alleged by her and later by Richard's supporters that Edward had married illegally, for in addition to his so-called betrothal to Elizabeth Lucy he had also been betrothed to Lady Eleanor Butler.[13] If there had been any proof of this betrothal, which was considered binding at the time, he could have remarried Elizabeth Woodville, for Lady Butler had died in 1468, but if Edward had thought about such a possibility, which he surely didn't, he took no action. Richard tried to insist on all these facts because in addition to supporting his own claim it was a way of denigrating the unfortunate Jane: she could no longer boast that she had been the mistress of a king, since she was not only a harlot, but had merely been intimate with a man who had been born a bastard and later married illegally.

What could Jane do now? Her lover was dead, her short-term protector, Hastings, was dead, Dorset could not be found, although perhaps she did not want him to be found, for if so he would have suffered the same fate as the rest of his family. Richard was certain that Jane knew where he was. In any case she must have felt utterly deserted. After the king had released her from prison – it is not clear when precisely he did so – and he had earlier arranged the seizure of her possessions, there was yet another punishment in store for her, since her continued existence in freedom seems to have obsessed him. He wanted to annihilate her. He ordered the Bishop of London to condemn her to the performance of public penance, namely she must walk round the city or at least round St Paul's Cross on a Sunday, carrying a large lighted candle and draped in a sheet. Richard probably thought that this Church-controlled punishment – already inflicted in the past on King Henry II, and on the unfortunate Duchess of Gloucester, suspected of using witchcraft – would condemn Jane forever to the world's worst reputation a woman could suffer, for this was the punishment given to any common harlot. But Richard did not get his way. Jane obeyed the bishop but the effects on the crowds watching in the streets were unexpected: 'she went in countenance and pace so womanly,' wrote More, 'and albeit she were out of all array save her kirtle only, yet when she so fair and lovely, namely while the wondering of the people cast a comely rud [blush] in her cheeks (of which she before had most miss), that her great shame won her much praise among those that were more amorous of her body than curious of her soul.'[14]

In other words, Richard had been once again frustrated in his attempts to punish her and through her to punish his late brother who had obviously been unfit to govern the country; 'and many good folk also, that hated her living and glad were to see sin corrected, yet pitied they more her penance than rejoiced therein, when they considered that the Protector procured it more of a current intent than any virtuous affection'. In writing this More was obviously expressing what he thought of Richard III, occasioning one of the many complaints by Richard's latter-day supporters that this unfortunate king has been deeply misunderstood from the time of Edward's death until his own and ever afterwards.

What could Richard do now in order to destroy any remaining affection for Jane? There was not much choice. So it was back to prison for her, since her enemy did not give up easily. Was he perhaps unconsciously attracted to Jane, even 'amorous of her body'? By controlling her life, possessing her in this indirect way, he was in one sense getting even with his dead brother. She seemed to hold a strange fascination for Richard. Perhaps he was curious to learn the secret of her appeal, for he was more drawn to women than has been assumed. He had had two illegitimate children before his marriage to Anne Neville, who were now grown up and he later appointed his bastard son to the post of Captain of Calais. There could have been other children who were not acknowledged. The two best known of Richard's portraits show him as a serious, dignified man, surely reliable, a man who would not have displeased women, while the portraits of Edward presumably do him no justice, for the man who was said to be so handsome must either have been suffering from a hangover or else did not give the painter time to finish his work.

When some remaining Yorkist supporters heard about the treatment of Jane, they became worried, like Stallworthe. What these gentlemen did not know is that somehow, in spite of everything, something of Jane's mysterious charm apparently remained undimmed even during her second stay in Ludgate prison. Many 'official' visitors came there, either making regular checks on administrative matters or perhaps investigating individual cases. One of these visitors was so deeply impressed by Jane that all at once a new chapter opened in her life.

SEVEN

Last Years

This unexpected visitor to Ludgate jail would know all about Jane – he might even have gone there specially to see her – for she was a subject of London gossip now, well known at least by name, notorious in fact; but she probably knew nothing about him.

Five or six centuries after they lived there is still as much mystery about Thomas Lynam as there is about Jane Shore, perhaps even more. He was certainly a northerner, born in Sutton-upon-Derwent to the south-east of York, probably about 1440 or so, making him a little older than Jane. Richard, as is well known, liked northerners, finding them more trust-worthy and less hypocritical than the average southerner. The latter group included of course all the ambitious people who had found their way to court, sometimes deservedly so, but often through sycophancy, bribery or personal favouritism. Such people lurked near the king and queen, looking always for advancement, which many hoped to achieve without taking too much responsibility or carrying out too much work. Members of the Woodville family believed they did not need to do anything, convinced that even a distant relationship to the queen was enough for them to achieve preferment. Richard's attitude had been influenced ever since his brother's marriage by the scheming of this ambitious family, led by Queen Elizabeth Woodville. She was regarded by her brother-in-law as a snob who after all came from what he regarded as a class lower than his own: her first husband had been a mere knight and, even worse, a Lancastrian, while she herself had earlier been a lady-in-waiting to Queen Margaret of Anjou. Richard avoided Edward's queen and stayed away from London as much as he could. He was much happier when surrounded by people in the north who were not necessarily less ambitious but were ready to work hard and honestly in order to rise in the world. This of course is a simplified, idealised picture of the people that the new king liked to have around him –

although northerners might still believe today that little has changed since Richard III's time.

Thomas Lynam had extra qualities likely to please his employer, for whom he had worked earlier when the present king was still Duke of Gloucester. Lynam was a member of the Inner Temple, presumably well trained and experienced before Richard became king and his expertise in handling land deals was particularly valuable, so much so that the king brought him to London especially to supervise this aspect of legal activity. Richard, always eager to increase his personal power and the security of his reign, saw this work as a first priority, and assumed that if he could legally control the activities and land ownership of both the aristocracy and the gentry then his own position would be stronger and the danger of rebellion, constantly in his mind, would be reduced. He never forgot that he was a usurper, and he knew that others never forgot it either. The trouble stirred up by his former supporter, the Duke of Buckingham, had alarmed him seriously, but fortunately for Richard the rebellion of 1483 had been badly organised, suffered bad luck in various ways, especially from the weather, and failed.

The records of Lynam's activities that have been preserved[1] show the kind of problems he had to deal with, including the follow-up to the Duke of Buckingham's rebellion which entailed an investigation for possible treason. The king rewarded his lawyer regularly by giving him land and various manors in addition to his regular salary. Lynam was also chosen for responsible assignments, including for instance the checking and certification of arrangements made by Lord Powis as he led a thousand archers into Brittany. In fact Lynam obviously became invaluable to his employer, so much so that Richard made him King's Solicitor, presumably late in 1483, a post that was virtually equivalent to the modern post of Solicitor General, and he was also a member of the King's Council.

These details concern Lynam's activities in late 1483 and during the following year. But soon after his arrival in London, also presumably in 1483, the invaluable legal expert announced something that his employer could hardly believe: he had met a young woman in Ludgate prison and had chosen to make her an offer of marriage. Richard had punished her severely more than once, sending her to prison twice – this was her second stay in Ludgate – and arranging for her to do public penance to atone for her behaviour as a harlot; so why did Lynam make such a choice and how was his employer to respond? The young woman was of course Jane Shore, whom Lynam had met during what was presumably an official visit to the jail. If Richard had at first reacted with fury, by the time he wrote to Bishop Russell of Lincoln, his chancellor, he was apparently trying to prove how understanding and merciful he could be when necessary, although he had to admit that Lynam's plan did not please him at all.

'Signifying unto you,' he wrote to the bishop, presumably from York and presumably in 1483, although the letter is undated, 'that it is showed unto us that our servant and solicitor Thomas Lynam, marvellously blinded and abused with the late [wife] of William Shore, now being in Ludgate by our commandment, hath made contract of matrimony with her, as it is said, and intendeth, to our full great marvel, to proceed to effect the same. We for many causes would be sorry that he should be so disposed. Pray you therefore to send for him, and in that you goodly may, exhort and stir him to the contrary. . . .'[2]

Richard may have indicated that he could hardly believe the news but he obviously did not want to sack his solicitor, who had been so trustworthy until now, and there would have been no point in sending him back to the north, for he was presumably irreplaceable. If Richard had been angry on first hearing the news – he was away from London at the time – he may have thought it over; perhaps, after all, nothing could be done about the situation: 'And if,' he went on, 'you find him utterly set for to marry her and none other will be advertised, if it may stand with the Law of the Church, we be content, the time of the marriage being deferred to our coming next to London, that on sufficient surety being found of her good bearing, ye do send for her keeper and discharge him of Our said commandment, by warrant of these committing her to the rule and guiding of her father or any other by your direction in the mean season. Given &c.'

Whether Jane's father was officially requested to supervise his wayward daughter is not known, but in any case Richard, no doubt unwillingly, had realised he had to accept the inevitable. Lynam married Jane – precisely when and where remains unknown – although the marriage surely took place quickly in case the king changed his mind and before any unexpected political events could upset the lives of the betrothed couple or even that of Lynam's employer, the man who disapproved but felt he had to tolerate this unexpected development, despite trying in general to present an image of high personal morality in himself.

Since there is no record of when and where Lynam married Jane, P.M. Kendall for one had believed it never happened. It is possible that nothing would ever have been known of this marriage if the will of John Lambert, made in 1485, two years before he died, had not been discovered and carefully examined in 1972.[3] Thomas Lynam, remembered in this informative document, had been executor, along with the eldest Lambert son, Jane's brother John. Lynam was obviously by then part of the Lambert extended family and when his mother-in-law Amy died the following year he was included in the list of her sons who, along with Jane, were to divide her property equally among themselves. Lynam had evidently been a most welcome addition to the family.

By John Lambert's will Thomas Lynam, 'Gentilman' – he apparently liked to be known this way – received 'xxs' (20 shillings) and Julian Lynam, presumably Jane's little daughter, received 'xls' (40 shillings). John Lambert also remembered Thomas Lynam's servant, Isabel Thomson, who received a 'violet gown'. The most interesting bequest was made to 'Elizabeth Lynam, my daughter, a bed of arras with the velour tester and curtains [and] a stained cloth of Mary Magdalene'. When mentioning this in 1995 Desmond Seward[4] could not resist referring to Jane's earlier adulterous life, and wondered if her father's bequest implied a criticism, a joke or a sign of his forgiveness. John Lambert must have been pleased by Jane's second marriage and the birth of his granddaughter. At last his own daughter was respectable.

John Lambert had made his will not long before he died, as though reluctantly accepting that his life as a merchant adventurer was nearing its end. Despite all his valuable work as a mercer and his loans to the late king he had had some bad luck: various lands in the West Country that had been given to him had to be returned to their original owners because of changes in the political system. Later still he was actually sued by the Goldsmiths' Company.[5] How could such a thing have happened? It appears that in 1472 he had rented a house they owned in Wood Street and when he left it he was alleged to have been something of a thief, accused of taking away some window panes (glass was still a valuable commodity), iron bars, shutters, even the panelling in the chapel and at least one even more valuable item, a pewter 'laver' which had stood in the hall of the house and had been used by any men who entered for washing their hands. He did not simply take this vessel home with him, but sold it to the well-known Edmund Shaa who was a goldsmith himself and later became Mayor of London, in 1482. If these allegations were true, why did John Lambert behave like a common thief? Had he been worried at the time about his daughter's first unsatisfactory marriage or had the Readeption and the king's flight from England upset him? However, his general good reputation must have helped him because in the end he was not penalised too heavily; he had to return all he had taken, naturally, pay for the repairs following the damage he had caused and arrange for the laver to be returned from Shaa. That must have been very shaming for him. This happened two years after he had lost the title of Alderman in 1470,[6] which probably happened because he had been carried away by Yorkist sympathies during some argument in public; this was too close to the dangerous period of the Readeption, not a suitable time to indulge in political propaganda. But John Lambert had to express what he believed: he was obviously that sort of man, forthright and full of energy which he sometimes could not control.

The will of 1485 gives the impression of a united family when the Lamberts were living in Hinxworth in the north of Hertfordshire; John had bought a house there in 1484, perhaps at first for a summer residence. Perhaps too the Lynam family were regular visitors, taking time away from London, unless they were thinking ahead, in a mercenary way, about John Lambert's possibly imminent death and the inheritance they might receive.

There were family gatherings here, which included presumably Thomas Lynam, Gent, whose status, even if self-appointed, must surely have pleased his father-in-law, always keen for his family to move into the social class above his own. No more details are available about any members of the Lambert or Lynam family at this time, although it is thought locally that the present Hinxworth Place, not far from the church of St Nicholas, is the house that John bought, called at that period Pulters Manor.

Sadly there are major gaps too in the later history of Jane, her husband and her daughter. Confusingly the name 'Julian', or Julyan, was usually invariable at the time and could have been used to designate a boy, but the memorial brasses later installed on the family tomb (of which more in due course) include the figure of a little girl, although she is not mentioned anywhere outside her grandfather's will. Did she die young? Possibly, for children in those days were vulnerable, as they did not have the resistance to recover from child health problems and the Black Death constantly lurked about.

It is strange and sad also that there are so few reliable details about the later life of Thomas Lynam. He and his wife would have had a disturbed time during 1485 because Richard III was in serious trouble, and as everyone knows, his life came to a tragic but unmourned end at the battle of Bosworth Field in August of that year. It is also known of course that the Lancastrian Duke of Richmond became Henry VII very soon afterwards, but what is not known is how far the Lynam ménage survived this major change. Lynam himself did succeed in keeping a good post under the new monarchy although it was apparently at a less senior level and the date of his appointment is not known. He could not easily forget the existence of Richard because as later records show, Peter Curteys, the former Keeper of the Wardrobe to the late king, took action against Lynam upon a bond for £204 8s 4d concerning the wardrobe. The Inner Temple also sued him for dues in 1496/7 and again in 1510.[7] However, he had been granted a pardon in 1509 when he was apparently far away from London and from Hinxworth. He had been appointed as JP for Shropshire from 1502 until some unknown date, and from 1505 he was clerk or baron of the Exchequer at Chester. Unfortunately his name is similar to that of other civil servants of the time and as a result there is possible confusion about Thomas Lynam's later life and his death.

But what happened to his family? Did Jane go with him to Shropshire or had the marriage disintegrated? There is no means of knowing. If they had parted it was perhaps Jane's fault: it may have been that she could not tolerate exile from London, because it is hard to think of her in a provincial setting. Lynam is known to have died during or before 1518,[8] the ninth year of Henry VIII's reign, but the actual date of his death cannot be confirmed.

Of Jane herself during her later years nothing is known, except from the moving piece written by Sir Thomas More in his *History of Richard III*. He describes how she had reached her seventies in a state of wretched poverty and was reduced to begging, often approaching those who in the past had begged favours from her. It has been suggested by Nicolas Barker that she did not walk about with a begging bowl, a melodramatic touch that was to appeal to some later writers, but wrote begging letters to various people in the hope of finding some support. It is difficult to imagine how she survived. How could Thomas Lynam leave her without provision? Either he was in financial trouble after Richard III died or he was personally careless, as many professional people can be; or else the marriage had broken down angrily and there was nobody to help either of the partners.

Ever since More wrote his *History*, first in Latin and later in English with many editorial changes, it has been attacked by historians. However nobody can destroy what he wrote about Jane, if only because there is no other contemporary evidence about her life generally and particularly about her last years. Desmond Seward has mentioned[9] that in 1509 when Henry VII died, Jane strewed flowers along the path of the funeral procession, as was often done to celebrate the death of a former victor, but there seems to be no proof of this legend. According to More, Jane died well into Henry VIII's reign, possibly in 1527, implying that she was indeed in her seventies; presumably she had outlived her second husband and probably lost her young daughter, unless she had been forced to arrange some kind of adoption for her.

What happened to her three brothers? After all, William had entered the priesthood and might have been expected to show at least some Christian charity, in the best sense of the word, towards his solitary sister. None of these Lambert men has been traced; perhaps they did not share their sister's longevity. Jane may have chosen to be solitary, perhaps her second husband had disappointed her, but only the romantic novelists could make a choice among all these eventualities and explain the sad end to her long life. The historical novelist Jean Plaidy, who wrote *The Goldsmith's Wife* in 1950, apparently believed that Jane did not love Lynam, and for that reason had decided not to marry him. It is known now of course from the Lambert will that they did marry, but perhaps there was not enough love between them to keep them together for long. Perhaps Jane had been so anxious to find a new 'protector' and leave prison that she had accepted Lynam's offer of marriage for no other reason, and if any contemporary writers knew more about this marriage they chose not to mention it.

However, not long after her death, there was one eventuality which might have brought some consolation for Jane: she was soon taken out of the shadows, where she had lived for a long time, for as her mortal life ended, a second life, a kind of literary, half-legendary life, began. Her real life had not followed the classical pattern of rags to riches, she had known a comfortable start in a middle-class home, but she had been unable to tolerate an arranged marriage with no sexual content. In her bid for independence she took a great risk and when her lover the king died early she suddenly saw that she had lost. A second bid for independence, which involved remarriage, seems to have meant only short-term protection, followed by solitude and poverty. If only she could have been trained in order to earn a livelihood – but most women were not to have that security for many years to come. Instead, death released her from poverty and led her at once towards the writers who were to celebrate her existence in various ways, forgive her so-called 'sins' and reflect on the lessons that her successors might learn from her.

Jane was the first royal mistress in English history to be remembered by something more than a few anecdotes, but even modern research has not produced sufficient facts to explain all of her life. During most of the sixteenth and part of the seventeenth centuries the post of royal mistress did not exist, or was irrelevant. Henry VIII had preferred to marry his mistresses, for he was desperately in need of a legitimate son, while later James I did not desert his Danish-born wife despite acquiring several male favourites. From the time of Charles II the mistress returned to favour and then, after the happy marriage of George III, the occasional mistresses of George IV, the devotion between William IV and Dorothy Jordan, and the long reign of Victoria, the institution of mistress was restored again, first by her son Edward VII, later by Edward VIII and latest of all by Prince Charles, current heir to the British throne (who may of course prefer to see his eldest son as king of England in his place). In France the royal mistress had been an institution from early days and the long 'reign' of Diane de Poitiers; even François Mitterrand, the recent president, had enjoyed the company of a semi-official mistress.

Sadly, the date of Jane's death is vague, the place unknown, although it would be probably somewhere in London. No will is extant, no grave has been discovered, although as will be seen later, she was included in a family memorial in a Hertfordshire church.

A leader, whether king or not, can be forgiven for needing relaxation and entertainment and this was the reason that kept Jane Shore so close to

Edward IV for so long, especially because she was not seeking power in any way. When he died suddenly at forty she might perhaps have retired to a convent, as solitary women so often did. But no, she recovered, she wanted life, and her longing for independence outstripped any guilt she might have felt. After her own long life ended, memories of her story were not forgotten and subsequent generations of writers chose to see her as a potent symbol, the solitary woman who needed support and love. Her lover had deserted her by dying, his successor had punished her, but she had survived, apparently without any help from God. Despite her conventional upbringing, which would inevitably have had a religious background, there is no sign that she later asked for or expected any help from the Church. It is known that she had had a confessor, Pierre Bost, when Edward IV was alive but no more is heard about him or any successors afterwards. How did she pass the time after the disappearance of Lynam? If she had been with him in the provinces she would then, presumably, have come back to London, where she had been brought up and lived all her life. Now she waited for death. If Lynam had died in about 1518 her wait, although solitary, was not too long. Nor was her death the end: she who had been a minor historical figure now became an unexpected heroine of legend.

PART TWO

The Legend

EIGHT

'for yet she liveth . . .'

Jane is known to have died in 1527 or 1528 and therefore Sir Thomas More, who lived until 1535, might well have met her or heard about her directly from people who knew her well. He had begun to write his *History of King Richard III* in about 1513, producing two versions, one in English and one in Latin, although neither of them was completed. However, by one means or another the text became fairly well known. Unreliable versions were adapted and included in some of the *Chronicles* before More's nephew William Rastell, using a holograph version, finally published a sound text in 1557. Even today there is discussion among scholars about possible variations and differing interpretations between the English and Latin versions, but readers seeking to study all aspects of this much-quoted unfinished work will find detailed analysis in the introduction by Richard S. Sylvester, executive editor, to the third volume of the Yale Edition of More's Complete Works. In 1976 *The History of King Richard III and Selections from the English and Latin Poems* was published as a separate volume with useful annotations. For instance, footnote 18 on page xvii states that 'Most of what we know about Jane Shore is contained in More's narrative and her story was to prove immensely popular in Elizabethan verse, prose and drama.'

Jane's surviving legend therefore owes much to More, and he made a point of including those few words 'and yet she liveth' as he completed the last of the three separate sections in his essay which together provide his perceptive description of Shore's wife along with some mention of her later years. Her Christian name 'Jane' had not been invented in More's time but was used inevitably by Sylvester in his notes and index to the *History of King Richard III*.

The unfortunate More, who had introduced Jane to later writers and readers, was executed for alleged treason in 1535 by the tyrannical Henry

VIII and so never learnt how the legend continued. He did not live long enough to know that a little-remembered minor poet Thomas Churchyard, often dismissed as a hack, was probably the next person in the sixteenth century to write about Mistress Shore and see his work published.

Churchyard was a farmer's son, born probably in about 1520 in Shrewsbury, and spent most of his life as a soldier, sometimes fighting for England, sometimes working as a mercenary on behalf of other countries. His military life was eventful, moving between Scotland, Europe and Ireland but he could not give it up, especially since he had quickly spent all the money his father had given him and failed in his attempt to earn a private income by marrying a rich widow. He had constant bad luck in many ways; he had been fighting in the complex so-called Italian Wars in Europe which ended with the defeat of France and he had apparently helped to negotiate the terms of surrender. He then found himself in prison; the important treaty of Cateau-Cambrésis in 1559 might have included arrangements for his release, but only after he had paid a ransom. As usual in his case he had no money, could not find any means of paying and in the end had to return to England by promising payment and then breaking his word – he had to take the risk somehow. More adventures, too many to recount here, and an unhappy marriage followed. One of his patrons disowned him, and he managed to upset Queen Elizabeth for a time, although much later she granted him a small pension. On the whole Churchyard did not have a happy or successful life although he did not do much to help himself. But he found Jane.

Many of his contemporaries wrote better poetry though their lives may have been duller; few of them were helpful or partial to this unlucky man who could not resist trying to write and publish poetry; none of it was much good, everyone thought. However, they relented when he began to grow old and at least one of his poems is remembered: 'How Shore's wife, Edward IV's concubine, was by King Richard despoiled of all her goods and forced to do open penance'. It appeared in what would now be described as an anthology, a compilation with high moral content entitled *A Mirror for Magistrates*,[1] aimed at instructing readers through the examples given that they must behave well according to the rules of the religious and moral code and not be too ambitious, for pride comes before a fall; when that happened they would either die in misery, lose their honour or at least find themselves in court before a magistrate. The magistrates themselves, it was thought, could also profit from these examples and from the fate of the people concerned. There had been plans to publish the work in 1559 but this possible first edition was apparently suppressed for politico-religious reasons and after that it seems to have disappeared. There were eventually several later editions, all of value and gaining many readers, in 1563, 1564, 1578 and later still, into the next century.

The existence of this unusual collection of verse had been influenced by the free translation made in the previous century by the English poet John Lydgate, a monk at Bury St Edmunds in Suffolk, of an earlier Latin work by Boccaccio, *De casibus virorum illustrium*, known in England as *The Fall of Princes*, which had been very popular in the fifteenth century. In the reign of Henry VIII, when religious controversy was always in the air, serious or at least curious readers presumably wanted to learn just how and why the mighty had fallen, and such a book was regarded as a possible good influence on the moral climate of the country generally, even if some readers may have enjoyed moments of what is now called *Schadenfreude*, pleasure in the misfortunes of others. The original translation was no longer available in the mid-sixteenth century but George Ferrers, Master of the King's Pastimes, had an idea: there should now be a relevant follow-up, based on English history only and not on classical times or foreign notables. It would be appropriate for it to start with the deposition and death of Richard II in 1399–1400 and continue with real-life 'sad stories of the deaths of kings' and others, all highly placed, which had been enacted closer to the present day.

Eventually a careful plan was evolved: individual poets would compose monologues, supposedly addressed to the chosen editor, William Baldwin, by the spirits of the dead people concerned, 'wherein may be seen what vices bring men to destruction, with notable warnings how the like may be avoided', to quote from the title page of an edition of the Lydgate work. After the publishers had dealt with various administrative problems, the *Mirror* eventually appeared and when the revised first edition came out in 1559, it presented nineteen 'tragedies', as these monologue-poems were called, of which eight that belonged to the fifteenth century are relevant to the existence of Mistress Shore. They start with Jack Cade, whose rebellion had occurred in the year when she was presumably born, while later items include the story of Lord Hastings and the regrets of the dead Edward IV.

The latter piece, thought to have been written by the well-known John Skelton who lived from *c.* 1460 to 1529, is the only one of noticeable literary merit in this group. Nearly all the monologues in the *Mirror* are composed in the seven-line stanza style invented by Chaucer and known as rhyme-royal, with a set rhyming scheme patterned *ababbcc*, but Skelton himself chose a different form, writing longer stanzas and ending each one with a refrain in Latin, *Et ecce nunc in pulvere dormio*. The message is simple: King Edward asks himself, 'Where is now my conquest and my victory?' His vanity and self-indulgence have caused all to wither away: 'I have played my pageant: now am I past.' He sleeps now in dust, as the Latin says. He mentions his wife, 'Lady Bess', he mentions Windsor and Eton, all now lost to him, but he does not refer to his many concubines or to Mistress Shore personally, although he admits his own excesses in all directions.

'Why should a man be proud or presume high?' In the end every hero would become 'worms' meat'. So there was no point in overambition, it always led to a bad end. Skelton, a poet remembered now with admiration, at least did not write a plodding interminable piece, as most of the contributors to this collection did, but limited himself to seven stanzas of twelve lines each, achieving eighty-four lines in all. He made no attempt (fortunately) to write out the whole of Edward's life and the result is clearly more effective than a would-be verse autobiography, depressed and depressing from beginning to end. For the modern reader the poem is long enough, symbolic rather than comprehensive. The same readers may regret that there is no mention of the mistress rated so helpful to Edward by More and others, but that absence was to be remedied later, when she herself joined the cast of monologue-reciters.

In the first issue of the *Mirror* there were no contributions by women, possibly because Lydgate had earlier decided to 'forget' that Boccaccio had included some of them and had no objection to writing about them or their downfall. The contributions to this 1559 edition, nineteen in all, were restricted to the story-confessions of kings and nobles, plus, as mentioned earlier, the outsider and troublemaker Jack Cade. Most of the writers remain only slightly known today and their work is well meaning but pedestrian, despite the tragic stories they tell. In the 1563 edition two women were added to the list: Mistress Shore and Eleanor, Duchess of Gloucester; the duchess had lived a little earlier than Jane, was found guilty of witchcraft in the hope of achieving her ambitions and was to make a regretful appearance later in Shakespeare's *Henry VI* Part II, draped in the white sheet of a penitent.

The *Mirror* was assembled by the work of an ad hoc editorial committee: various of the writers would meet, listen to readings of new contributions as they became available and then discuss them. If Churchyard himself was not exactly popular as a poet he at least received a good response to his piece, the monologue delivered by Mistress Shore. 'This work was so well liked,' wrote the (assumed) editor, 'that all together exhorted me instantly, to procure Master Churchyard to undertake and to pen as many more of the remainder as might by any means be attempted at his hands.' It is not impossible that Churchyard wrote this himself, being a great self-publicist. However, in the end he was chosen to produce only one more monologue, the supposed utterance of a near-contemporary, the late Cardinal Wolsey who had died in 1530, not long in fact after Mistress Shore herself. For unknown reasons Churchyard did not like Baldwin: perhaps he thought that the editor, like most other people, underestimated him, although it became clear later that the poet considered the editor to be a hypocrite and a snob.

Setting aside all that was said or written during his lifetime and afterwards about the much-criticised Churchyard, it has to be admitted that in the monologue supposedly uttered by Mistress Shore he achieved an unexpected, near-convincing dramatic effect, which is more than can be said for most of the *Mirror* contributions, with the exception of Skelton's piece and the undoubtedly literate long piece about Buckingham by the sixth Earl of Dorset, the future Lord Sackville. After all, Churchyard knew all about living a tough life, as Mistress Shore had done, all the more difficult to accept when part of the suffering is known to have been self-inflicted. The Shore monologue is not interminably long – fifty-six rhyme-royal stanzas – and expresses the speaker's regret at the way she decided to leave her husband, how and why she gave in to temptation so easily. She attempts to explain why this happened: her beauty was in part to blame, 'For nature's gift was cause of all my grief,/A pleasant prey enticeth many a thief.' She laments her arranged marriage but for this she blames not her parents but her friends, perhaps remembering the 'Mrs Blague' who in later ballads advised Jane to accept the king's invitation:

> But clear from blame my friends can not be found,
> Before my time my youth they did abuse:
> In marriage an apprentice was I bound,
> When that mere love I knew not how to use.

She goes on to blame the 'strife' a forced marriage can bring – and here the writer touched on a theme that preoccupied the Elizabethans deeply, for they disliked such alliances – but it was her own weakness, she confesses, that

> made my youth a prince's prey.
> Though wisdom should the course of nature stay,
> Yet try my case who will, and they shall prove,
> The ripest wits are soonest thralls to love.

She admits too that she was deeply impressed by Edward, 'His royal state, his princely grace', and there was the promise of 'ease and wealth, the gifts that were not small'. She claims also that she had gained a certain power over the king:

> . . . to his death I was his chiefest hand
> I governed him that rulèd all this land.
> I bare the sword though he did wear the crown,
> I struck the stroke that threw the mighty down.

Exaggeration, surely, but later she admits that her power exposed her to danger, and realises that she should not have climbed so high:

> The wind is great upon the highest hills,
> The quiet life is in the dale below . . .

Then comes the cataclysm:

Portrait of a young woman, believed to be Jane Shore. *(Eton College)*

King Edward IV by an unknown artist. *(Royal Collection, by gracious permission of Her Majesty the Queen)*

Queen Elizabeth Woodville. *(Panel portrait, with the date 1464, probably added later)*

Cecily Neville, Duchess of York, wife of Richard, Duke of York. *(Getty Images)*

King Richard III. *(Getty Images)*

Sir Thomas More. *(Getty Images)*

Michael Drayton in middle age; after the engraved portrait by William Holle used in *Poems*, 1619

Chapbook illustration, from *The History of Mistress Jane Shore*, late seventeenth century. *(Pepys Library, Magdalene College, Cambridge)*

King Edward IV in middle age, from a sixteenth-century woodcut in *The Pastime of the People* by John Rastell.

Below, left: Jane Shore Doing Penance, engraved by Edward Scriven, after a drawing by W.S. Lethbridge.

Below: Engraving of Nicholas Rowe, from *The Works of Nicholas Rowe Esq*, in two vols, London, 1792.

Above: Mary Ann Yates playing Jane Shore, engraving in *The Works of Nicholas Rowe Esq.*

Above, right: Engraving of Horace Walpole. *(Getty Images)*

Right: The cover of the souvenir programme for the 1915 silent film, *Jane Shore. (Shelfmark M. adds. 110.66, Bodleian Library, University of Oxford)*

The King changed countenance, then endeavoured to rally her from her resolve, but she was inflexible. He paced the long and splendid apartment with unequal steps, then, approaching a table, wrote a few words on a slip of vellum, and handing it to Jane, exclaimed—"Shall your husband live—or die ?"

Jane and her daughter portrayed on a memorial brass, Hinxworth church. On the left stands her brother John Lambert.

Enlarged figure of Jane, memorial brass, Hinxworth.

Tomb of William Shore, Church of St Nicholas, Scropton, Derbyshire. *(Derbyshire Archaeological Journal, Vol. XV, 1986, by courtesy of Dudley Fowkes, editor)*

The Church of St Nicholas, Hinxworth.

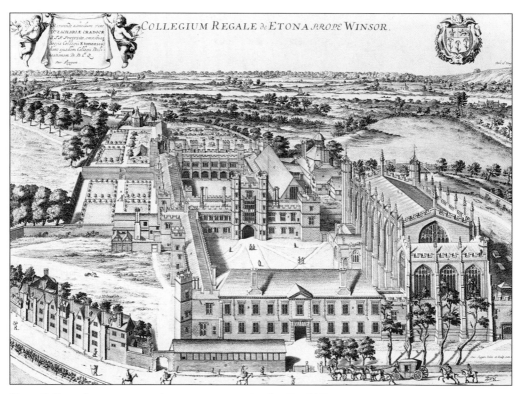

Eton College, late seventeenth century, engraving by David Loggan.

> King Edward died in whom was all my joy.

She cannot refrain from attacking her lover's successor, although his actual name is never mentioned:

> His brother was mine enemy most of all
> Protector then, whose vice did still abound,
> from ill to worse till death did him confound.

This brother accused her of trying to poison him, she infers; she then mentions that Lord Hastings's blood cried out for vengeance, but does not refer to the brief time she spent with the latter, her new lover. She describes the penance to which she had been condemned, calls on heaven to seek vengeance on the usurper and in the last few stanzas describes her terrible poverty and the desertion by her friends. The monologue ends on a note expressing the precise purpose of the *Mirror*, something which surely pleased the editor and the other contributors:

> Example take by me both maid and wife,
> Beware, take heed, fall not to folly so,
> A mirror make of my great overthrow:
>
> Defy this world, and all its wanton ways,
> Beware through me, who spent so ill her days.

Churchyard claimed that he had written his poem much earlier than 1563, when it was published in the *Mirror*, but thirty years later he was angered by possible plagiarism in the publication of a poem entitled 'Beauty Dishonoured or Shore's Wife',[2] signed by Anthony Chute, a poet even more obscure than himself, although perhaps a better one, and much less prolific. Chute is said to have been an attorney's clerk, was given to drink and destined to die in 1593 or 1594. He described this poem as 'the first invention of my beginning muse', a lengthy start indeed, for it consists of 197 stanzas of six lines each, telling the story of the adulterous wife's downfall and her harsh treatment by Richard III; it omits her penance but mentions the king's command that no one must help her. Chute seems to

109

have been deeply preoccupied with problems connected with beauty, how it might lead to 'wanton' behaviour, for instance. The poet also writes of Jane's husband as though he had been a really old man and his young wife had had to deal with his demanding behaviour.

The poem is full of misery and can only be described as tedious, until the very last page when Jane wants to die but can't and is afraid that she will never succeed in doing so. She is compared to 'a wither'd lily, dried and sapless quite', and the poet becomes unexpectedly a prophet: 'Her body went to death, her fame to life',[3] a line echoed by the British *Dictionary of National Biography* in its edition of 2004, which includes a reference to Jane's 'considerable literary afterlife'.

Chute would probably have known something about More's telling of Mistress Shore's life but he had also read Churchyard's poem and had copied him occasionally without giving any acknowledgement. Churchyard was an angry man at the best of times but now he flew into a rage, republished his own poem in what he called *Churchyard's Challenge* and added several new stanzas to his original 'monologue' for publication in the next edition of the *Mirror*. However Chute died in 1593, the year in which his poem was apparently published and therefore escaped Churchyard's anger. His poem, not easy to find outside *The Witchery of Jane Shore*, has always divided opinion, some readers finding it dull and overrated, others believing that it has been unfairly neglected, but it remains an early contribution to Jane's survival in legend and literature.

By the time of the 1587 edition of the *Mirror* Churchyard had begun to identify himself with the regretful Mistress Shore, and was so keen to speak in her own voice that with much irony he composed the lengthy prose link which preceded her own monologue, using the first person: 'I appeared first to one Baldwin, a Minister and a Preacher: whose function and calling disdain to look so low, as to search the secrets of wanton women, (though commonly a Preacher with sufferance may rebuke vice).' Jane has now decided to 'appeal and appear to some martial man', for such men were more experienced in 'defending women's honour, and know somewhat more of their conditions and qualities'. So she has chosen 'a writer of good continuance . . . whose name is *Churchyard*: he shall have . . . all the glory I can give him, if he lend me the hearing of my woeful tale, a matter scarce fit for woman's shamefastness to describe. But since without blushing I have so long been a talkative wench (whose words a world hath delighted in), I will now go on boldly with my audacious manner: and so step I on the stage in my shrouding sheet as I was buried.'

Churchyard was obviously his own public relations officer, ready to use any opportunity to earn public attention and praise, for he was convinced he deserved them. He had been falsely accused of claiming authorship for various works which had been written by others, but he was too prolific and apparently fair game: everyone seemed ready to attack him. If Chute, the recent cause of irritation to the older writer, died early, the robust ex-military man Churchyard lived another ten years or so and has survived mainly through references to his heroine Mistress Shore. In the end he was partly accepted and even received 'epitaphs' while still alive, including a prophetic one in 1592 from the writer Thomas Nashe, so often satiric, who told him, in his *Foure Letters Confuted*, 'I love you unfeignedly and admire your aged Muse, that may well be grandmother to our most grandiloquent Poets at this present . . . Shore's wife is young though you be steeped in years: in her shall you live when you are dead.'[4] The same idea was taken up cheerfully some nine years later when the students of St John's College Cambridge enacted the second part of *The Return from Parnassus*: 'Hath not Shore's wife, although a light-skirts she,/Given him a chaste long lasting memory?'

That was almost the end, but the elderly poet with the unfortunate name did not escape without raising a laugh:

> No, all light pamphlets one day discover shall,
> A Churchyard and a grave to bury all.[5]

Edmund Spenser, truly a great poet, in the long poem written after his return from Ireland in 1591, *Colin Clout's Come Home Again*, refers to many poets under invented fanciful names and Churchyard became

> . . . old Palemon free from slight
> Whose tuneful pipe may make the hearer rue,
> That sung so long until quite hoarse he grew.

The frustrated elderly Churchyard died in about 1604, thought to be at least eighty years old, and was buried in St Margaret's, Westminster, close to Spenser, whom he had greatly admired. Churchyard must have been a solitary man: perhaps he really had come too close emotionally to Mistress Shore, almost falling in love with her and adopting her unconsciously as his muse, for he had obviously failed to find anyone else. This situation recalls Francis Bacon's mention in his essay *On Love* of the way military men became so fixated on women; after all they needed women, real or imaginary, if only so that they could think about them when away from home – if Churchyard, about whom relatively few personal facts are known, ever experienced such a comfort as a home. He was obviously a different type of person from the long list of others who contributed to *A Mirror for Magistrates* but whose names are now forgotten. He was a minor writer, yes, but it is through his attention, even if he tried hard to share her publicity, that Mistress Shore became one of the very few women of the fifteenth century and the early Tudor years whose reputation survived to the end of Elizabeth's reign and far beyond.

She was useful to the Elizabethans – they needed a heroine whose life reflected two related problems which they had begun to take seriously, the question of the over-arranged marriage and the marital infidelity which could so easily result from it. There was no easy answer: romantic love was all very well, provided it remained in the romances, the ballads or even on the stage: it was not too welcome in real life, at least not yet, and the perfect marriage did not exist. However, the new preoccupation with women characters in all forms of literature was inevitably leading to what was virtually a new and developing genre – domestic tragedy. Another problem which worried the Elizabethans was the desertion of friends, again something which led them to see Jane as an icon; Thomas Deloney, of whom more later, was to write about this problem in at least one of his early fiction pieces, *The Green King of St Martin's* and in more than one of his famous ballads. The 'Green King' finds that when all at once he has no money his former friends don't want to know him any more, so, he asks, was he not still the same man? After King Edward died Jane Shore's 'friends', like the 'Mrs Blague' of the ballads, deserted her.

The 1590s, the last complete decade of Queen Elizabeth's reign, brought the publication or even performance of several important literary and theatrical works. For instance 1594 saw the appearance of *The True Tragedie of Richard III* which included the death of Edward IV, the assumption that the two young princes were smothered in the Tower and – on the title page of a surviving copy – a reference to 'a Lamentable End of Shore's Wife, an Example For All Wicked Women'. Unfortunately, this interesting but anonymous drama has not survived entire although it is known to have been printed in 1594; the only version available now is a fragmented series of detached scenes. Some of them are striking and show Mistress Shore receiving the news of Edward's death and later suffering King Richard's harsh treatment. It has been suggested that Shakespeare himself might have known this play and seen it acted; it might even have helped him decide not to include Mistress Shore in his own *King Richard III*, written about 1593. One of the memorable scenes from the early play is that where Mistress Shore's former friends and servants carefully obey Richard's instructions that she is not to receive help from anybody, even if she has previously helped them, a fact mentioned by More in his essay about Richard III. In *The True Tragedie* a man who had helped her is executed: later playwrights were to follow this example.

The late sixteenth century, with its crowd of poets, obviously found Mistress Shore a good subject and her story fitted in well with the legends of some previous royal mistresses. Samuel Daniel, who lived from 1563 to 1619 and was to be admired later by poets as different as Wordsworth and T.S. Eliot, wrote a well-remembered poem about one of the most popular of these early stories, the legend of Fair Rosamond, mistress of King Henry II and wickedly done to death, apparently, by the jealous Queen Eleanor of Aquitaine, as already mentioned. However, Eleanor was not the only jealous woman in history or legend, for in Daniel's poem Rosamond thinks she herself is forgotten or misunderstood, becomes convinced that she deserves better and seems to be jealous of Jane. She speaks in her own voice in 'The Complaint of Rosamond' (1592),[6] in an attempt to win sympathy, and it seems clear that Daniel is making an oblique reference to Churchyard's poem in *A Mirror for Magistrates*. The old legend had been described by well-known chroniclers such as Fabyan and Stow but they had simply recounted the story. With Daniel however, Rosamond tells the story herself and complains that 'she hath little left her but her name'; she is convinced that she had never received any sympathy:

No Muse suggests the pity of my case,
Each pen doth overpass my just complaint,
While others are preferred, though far more base:
Shore's wife is grac'd, and passes for a saint . . .

She seems to be referring to some of the ballads and/or to Churchyard's monologue, but forgets that she herself had been a mere legendary figure of no historical significance for many centuries. After all, Shore had been a real person not many years earlier and through Churchyard in fact had started to move from history into legend, the reverse of Rosamond's situation. As for passing 'for a saint', that was not true: Shore was regarded as a wanton woman who had had the bad luck to lose her lover early, then suffered for her sins and repented. But she was a realist and soon found a second husband, or at least a protector. Either this fact was not known to the Elizabethans or they chose to ignore it – did they think it would have ruined a good sad story? After all Rosamond had (allegedly) died at the hands of the jealous queen because the young girl and her lover the king had obviously not been realistic and vigilant enough, allowing Eleanor to become a murderer. Significantly, in later literary history the stories of the two women, Rosamond and Jane, as she had become by then, were often retold together. The obvious difference between them was forgotten: Rosamond belonged to legend, but Jane had once belonged to history. It had not taken long for her to move into legend, perhaps because the Middle Ages, after the transitional reign of Henry VII, intrigued the Elizabethans as part of a near-forgotten distant world, and Jane conveniently supplied a link between past and present.

NINE

A Female Icon?

The often despised Churchyard had started something, a kind of minor biographical trend, for after the success of Mistress Shore's monologue in *A Mirror for Magistrates* writers and readers began to realise even more clearly that they had found a useful female icon. This was someone who not only belonged to vaguely medieval 'legend', as they saw it, and had not been a member of the aristocracy, but who had been real, middle class too. She had broken the rules of marriage and had become aware of her 'sin', after deserting her middle-class husband for a married lover – who happened to be a king with a long reputation for acquisitive sexual curiosity. After his sudden early death she had suffered at the hands of her former lover's brother, made a mysterious marriage which nobody had learnt much about, and spent the last decades of a long life in neglect and poverty.

There were themes here to catch the attention of everyone, for the interests of Elizabethan readers were changing. All educated people were still deeply interested in legend and poetry but they were beginning to think more about social problems, especially, as mentioned earlier, the arranged marriage system with its attendant difficulties. Forward-looking people were beginning to see it as old-fashioned, partly because there were other reasons now for an increased interest in women. During the sixteenth century, after the early death of Edward VI in 1553, England was ruled by a queen, Mary I, who insisted on marrying a Catholic like herself, and a foreigner at that; when she died childless in 1558 she was followed by the pathetic nine-day reign of Lady Jane Grey, forcibly married for political reasons to a man she did not care for. Elizabeth I came to the throne in 1558, was never married and with much regret had to sign the death warrant of Mary Queen of Scots, who was related to her through a daughter of Edward IV and had herself been married three times. If Mary's first husband, François II of France, had lived, she might, with him, have even claimed the throne of England – and in any case now was regarded as a danger. Women with power, or potential power, could obviously not be ignored any longer. Women were important now, they were no longer mere wives and mothers, while some of Elizabeth's subjects had searched for and failed to find any heroine they could admire beyond those of classical times and foreign countries. It was not too easy to find a woman they could admire or even criticise, a woman who mattered. They could not openly admire Joan of Arc – obviously unsuitable for the English – and actresses had not yet invaded the fashionable and increasingly popular theatre, although women took part in court entertainments, assuming at least semi-dramatic roles.

However, even middle-class women were now well educated and read widely, while a few outstanding among them even translated or wrote themselves. They included, for instance, the Countess of Pembroke who wrote well and was said to give advice to her brother, Sir Philip Sidney. Among these women too were those scarcely known feminists *avant la lettre* who believed that women had been treated for too long as an inferior race. If, in the recent past, you had been a queen, a princess or an aristocrat you could of course have lived a comfortable life. However, you might have been born Queen Margaret of Anjou, who had been on the losing side; then if you had been Lady Margaret Beaufort, Duchess of Richmond, you would have been able to work hard for political change, leading to your son's transformation into Henry VII, but you would have worked in the secret shadows. Cecily of York, Edward IV's mother, had acted in the same way earlier. Her contemporaries near the court circle listened to her but did not take her too seriously. Shakespeare was probably the only writer who presented her as a real person, and that was long after her death. Many women of the merchant class surely achieved a happy and well-fulfilled life, and even if they didn't they tended not to complain; but if you had been born in the mid-fifteenth century the daughter of a successful mercer, married off young as part of a business arrangement to another successful mercer, you had to show initiative and courage before you could escape from the system. For where could you go, except into the arms of some rich and preferably unmarried lover? – and they were not easy to find. Otherwise there was only the convent.

So it was not long before the real-life legend of Mistress Shore, trailed, as would be said today, by Thomas Churchyard, attracted the attention of two much more valuable writers and she finally received her adopted Christian name, which made her seem much more 'real'. The earlier of these two writers was Michael Drayton, born in Warwickshire, reaching London in 1593 and publishing his early work three years later. Impressed by Spenser's *Shepherd's Garland* of 1579 he brought out his own *Shepherd's Calendar* in 1593. He is thought to have been influenced by the inevitable monologues published by Churchyard and others, whose work for *A Mirror for Magistrates* at least led younger writers to consider historical figures rather than idealised or legendary men and women as subjects for poems likely to please the public. Drayton chose historical figures and made some unlikely but noteworthy choices, including Piers Gaveston, Earl of Cornwall, the close, possibly homosexual, friend of the late twelfth- and early thirteenth-century King Edward I and he also wrote (at great length) the *Tragical Legend of Robert, Duke of Normandy*, who had been the father of William the Conqueror and was killed during the Crusades.

Drayton was a prolific writer of sonnets, at least one of which has never been forgotten by editors of anthologies; perhaps over the years the lovesick have quoted it to a partner: 'Since there's no help, come let us kiss and part'. However, history – his poem on Agincourt is a classic – and historical figures obviously fascinated him, and he took inspiration from the youthful Ovid, borrowing an idea from the *Heroides* which were popular with the Elizabethans. Ovid had chosen pairs of legendary lovers and imagined the letters written by the women to their absent partners: Helen and Paris, Hero and Leander, Dido and Aeneas among others. Some of the men even replied to their correspondents. Drayton himself chose not classical but mainly English historical figures for his paired correspondents, although some of the 'partners' belonged to legend, and their exchanges of letters became *England's Heroical Epistles* of 1597, easily the best-remembered series of poems he wrote. Among the couples he chose as correspondents were Fair Rosamond and King Henry II, inevitable favourites with the public, King John and the chaste Matilda, next Eleanor, Duchess of Gloucester, and her husband Humphrey; they were followed, surprisingly perhaps, by Lady Jane Grey and her nineteen-year-old unwilling husband Lord Guildford Dudley, and, unsurprisingly, Mistress Shore, as she was still named, with her royal lover King Edward IV.

For each pair of correspondents, readers are told the whole story as imagined by Drayton in passages of rhyming couplets, and the stories are sometimes more imaginary than true. In Mistress Shore's case the poet did not question the legend that had been believed for a long time. The king describes how he had seen the woman he wanted in the goldsmith's shop and how her husband Matthew had 'one jewel more . . . That I might not for love or money buy . . .'.[1] The king writes to Mistress Shore, tempting her with life in a palace, for a shop was no place for such a beautiful creature, she ought to be living 'in a prince's sumptuous gallery':

> . . . hung all with tissue, floored with tapestry;
> Where thou shalt sit and from thy state shall see
> The tilts and triumphs that are done for thee.

The king also hoped in an autocratic way that she would appreciate the grandeur of his kind of love:

> Then know the difference (if thou list to prove)
> Betwixt a vulgar and a kingly love.

Mistress Shore in her reply seems to regret that she was tempted with such attractive possibilities:

> Would I had led a humble shepherd's life.
> Nor known the name of Shore's admired wife,
> And lived with them, in country fields that range,
> Nor seen the golden Cheap, nor glittering Change.

It is difficult to imagine this correspondent living anywhere outside the city of London, the countryside was not her scene, to use a more modern expression. In the poem she reminds the king that she had been married very young and describes her changed attitude towards her unfortunate husband; and in any case it was all the king's fault:

> Thou art the cause Shore pleaseth not my sight,
> That his embraces give me no delight.

Perhaps Drayton never knew, or had decided to forget that these 'embraces' were limited, for the Shores had been divorced through the Court of Arches in 1476 which had accepted the allegation of the husband's impotence. On the other hand anyone who cared about the situation could have assumed that these alleged grounds for divorce had been a mere invention and decided to ignore the whole of the divorce proceedings, believing that Mistress Shore had not been free to leave husband and home. She had behaved like an irresponsible wanton woman.

It would have come as a shock to the real-life King Edward IV to learn that he, along with all the men of his time, was to blame for his high-handed treatment of his latest conquest. Jane spoke out:

> Blame you our husbands then, if they deny
> Our public walking, our loose liberty,
> If with exception still they us debar,
> The circuit of the public theatre;
> To hear the smooth-tongued poets' siren vain,
> Sporting in his lascivious comic scene . . .

At this point Mistress Shore began to be angry, she referred to the

> . . . passionate tragedian in his rage,
> Acting a lovesick passion on the stage;
> When though abroad restraining us to roam,
> They very firmly keep us safe at home . . .

(Drayton had forgotten that there was no 'public theatre' in Jane's time, but it suited him to mention this detail.)

At the same time there was nothing for women to do in this prison-like home, for there were plenty of servants, and the overprotected wife remained idle, without any worthwhile entertainments:

What sports have we, whereon our minds to set?
Our dog, our parrot or our marmoset;
Or once a week to walk into the field;
Small is the pleasure that these toys do yield . . .

Mistress Shore seemed to be trying hard to make the king feel guilty, as any other man might feel, reminding him that he is offering tempting promises simply because he is the king; but at the same time she knows that she is being tempted and she knows too that she cannot resist him:

Thou art the cause I to myself am strange . . .
Long winter nights be minutes, if thou here,
Short minutes, if thou absent, be a year . . .

It was all his fault, she wrote at the end of her 'heroical epistle', but she admitted that she had lost her battle with duty and could do nothing about it:

And thus by strength thou art become my fate
And makes me love, even in the midst of hate.

Who inspired this hate and who was hating whom? Was she trying to say that she hated giving in to the king? That was a strong word but perhaps she meant it – and of course it supplied a useful rhyme. She surely hated the system rather than the unfortunate Shore, for after all he had been caught up in the arranged marriage system too and might otherwise have remained a bachelor. Drayton was thought to be possibly homoerotic, attracted to men but not necessarily a practising homosexual, but as with many of the men in both groups his attack on the way men had usually treated women showed insights into women's problems, especially those of his own century. At the same time the poet's dramatisation of the well-known story is less interesting to later generations than the prose 'Annotations' that he thought necessary to add after each exchange of letters. In this instance he added a great deal, starting with a long quotation from Sir Thomas More's earlier references to Mistress Shore in his *History of King Richard III*, for over the previous century and beyond few writers felt they could or should forget or question this text. Drayton then repeated another detail mentioned by More, to the effect that the lady was not very tall, but added some additional details: her hair was 'of a dark yellow, her face round and full, her eye grey, delicate harmony being betwixt each part's proportion, and each proportion's colour, her body fat, white and smooth, her countenance cheerful and like to her condition'. No wonder King Edward fancied her.

Then came an interesting, tantalising description: 'The picture which I have seen of her was such as she rose out of her bed in the morning, having nothing on but a rich mantle cast under one arm over her shoulder, and sitting on a chair, on which her naked arm did lie.' Had the poet actually seen such a picture, now presumably lost, and not referred to by any previous or contemporary writer, or had he merely imagined it? He then went on to give a brief, undetailed biographical sketch of his subject: 'What her father's name was, or where she was born, is not certainly known: but Shore, a young man of right goodly person, wealth and behaviour, abandoned her bed after the king made her his concubine.' Drayton then referred to Richard III's treatment of her, 'not so much for his hatred of sin, but that by making his brother's life odious, he might cover his horrible treasons the more cunningly'.

In the second volume of Percy's *Reliques of Ancient English Poetry*, edited by Henry B. Wheatley and first published in 1765, the reader was brought up to date on Mistress Shore's life by the inclusion of Richard III's much quoted letter to the Bishop of Lincoln, his chancellor, about his 'Servant and Solicitor' Thomas Lynam and 'the late Wife of William Shore'.[2] Wheatley quoted these facts because he was about to include in his edition of Percy's collection one of the famous ballads about 'Jane Shore', to be described later, and mentioned these details presumably because he thought the author should have known them. The same is perhaps true of Drayton, but the Elizabethan poet was not so much concerned with biographical accuracy, as with writing a 'Heroical Epistle' and he clung to his vision, trying to evoke the characters of his two correspondents, the relationship between them and especially their self-defence; although the king did not defend himself credibly, he was in love and he was king, and he thought that was enough. A king must not be disobeyed: Jane must go to him when he commanded her. At the same time Drayton was obviously concentrating on the woman the king wanted and the reasons for her decision to obey him. Jane made the point that had not been mentioned by many writers about her life: a husband not only forces you to stay at home but forgets that you don't know how to get through the day, for there is nothing for a wife to do. So the moral and social lessons were there for the readers to absorb, wrapped up in several pages of readable poetry.

To return to Wheatley and his quotes from Drayton, Percy's editor himself added one more picturesque detail about 'Jane', admittedly based on a source probably far from reliable: '. . . the Duchess of Montagu had a lock of her hair which looked as if it had been powdered with gold dust'. The description may not be accurate, but who knows or in fact cares? Those few words bring a hint of glamour left over from the life that 'Jane' may have lived in the vanished world of medieval London.

These *Heroical Epistles* have remained the best remembered of Drayton's work not because they were the equivalent of later centuries' romantic fiction, but because they showed a memorable degree of psychological insight set within a series of mini-dramas already known to the readers. A great number of these readers would be women, pleased to read about women and the ways in which they had been treated in a high-handed manner by men, or had won minor battles with some of them, or unfortunately had made mistakes, as Mistress Shore had obviously done.

Among Drayton's vast output the heroines – there were some heroes too – and the poems themselves find no serious competition today from his other work; possibly he wrote too much, including at least twenty plays, some on classical or historical themes. The latter were apparently performed, some printed and many lost, but Drayton was not a born dramatist and at this period he would have found too many rivals. His other major work, *Poly-Olbion*, designed as a public relations exercise glorifying England, its history, geography and royalty, is not forgotten but it can never be a rival to the *Heroical Epistles*. The latter may be a minor work, but it embodies the preoccupations of the period, inheriting and extending in some ways the success of *A Mirror for Magistrates*, while any feelings of guilt the characters express can involve the readers without overwhelming them.

The first edition of the *Epistles* dates from 1597 and for later editions the author revised his work only slightly. If Drayton was a genuine poet but a half-failed dramatist, this set of poems was followed two years later by two linked plays written by someone who was definitely a dramatist, although not a genius. He was even more prolific than Drayton, wrote in virtually every existing genre and did many other things too. In fact, he wrote far too much. The plays relevant to Jane, and assumed to be his – for his prodigious output meant that his work was never carefully classified – were *The First and Second Parts of King Edward the Fourth* of 1599 or 1600, as set out on the title page, which then continued 'with His merry pastime with the Tanner of Tamworth, as also his love to fair Mistress Shore, her great promotion, fall and misery and lastly the lamentable death of both her and her husband'.

This sounds a little closer to the familiar story, but who was this enterprising playwright? He was Thomas Heywood,[3] a many-sided writer, who wrote or contributed to some two hundred plays, most of which are now lost. His best-remembered drama remains *A Woman Killed with Kindness* of 1603, and perhaps his best-known other work is that unexpected essay which now appeals to the feminists: *Gunaikeion*, or *Nine Books of Various History Concerning Women*. This production occupies more than 400 pages and after tracing the history of women from the Greek goddesses to Queen Elizabeth and her successor as queen, James I's Danish-born wife Anne, Heywood concluded that women had never been fully appreciated; but he stopped short of saying that they deserved full equality with men: it was too early for the public to accept that. However, the social climate was indeed changing. Heywood noted too that he had written this work in seventeen weeks because he was short of money. That aspect of the writing life has never experienced fundamental change, it merely varied from time to time.

Heywood had been born in Lincolnshire in 1573 and when later a student at Cambridge he saw every possible kind of play acted in public. From 1594 he never stopped writing and often appeared on the stage himself as an actor. This led him in 1612 to write a readable and useful book, his *Apology for Actors*, in which he emphasised that the performances of actors could supply more than mere entertainment, they could supply lessons in morality, and that was considered worthwhile. His two plays about Edward IV were probably first produced in 1599 and the story they tell is different from that told by every other writer so far about one of the king's mistresses, Mistress Shore. Surprisingly perhaps in these plays, Mistress Shore is happily married to the goldsmith Matthew Shore and they have a small child. At last Mistress Shore has a Christian name: both her husband and later King Edward IV address her as 'Jane'. Some parts of the two linked dramas seem almost farcical today but Heywood was intent on making any points he could about the behaviour of royal persons in contrast to that of their underlings and he had some ideas of his own about the relationships between the principal characters. In Part II the second scene in Act II is particularly hard to accept: surely even brilliant acting could hardly make it credible.

Queen Elizabeth Woodville enters with her son the Marquess of Dorset, 'leading Jane Shore who falls on her knees before the Queen, fearful and weeping'. The Queen's response is sarcastic:

> Queen Shore! Nay, rather Empress Shore!
> God save your grace, your majesty, your highness!
> . . . what! You kneel there? King Edward's bedfellow,
> And I, your subject, sit! . . .
> I may take your place; you have taken mine.
> I am sure you are our sister Queen at least:
> Nay, that you are. Then let us sit together.

Jane pleads for forgiveness, but the angry Dorset tries to intervene, telling his mother to scratch her eyes out, even threatening to do it himself. His mother tells him to keep out of the way. She then lectures Jane, asking how *she* would have felt if she, the queen, had taken *her* husband away. Heywood was nothing if not a realist, allowing the queen, temporarily at least, to speak like any suffering wife in any domestic scene:

> . . . Yes, I warrant thee
> There's not the meanest woman that lives,
> But if she like and love her husband well,
> She had rather feel his warm limbs in her bed
> Than see him in the arms of any Queen.

The queen probably did not know much about the Shore ménage. She then quotes the unhappy fate of Fair Rosamond, the woman so often linked with Jane, and warns her current rival that her life too could be in danger: might not she, the queen, like Eleanor of Aquitaine, now take her revenge? Jane, humble and prostrate, replies that she is ready for 'torture, poison, any punishment'. Dorset again tries to intervene and his mother sends him away. (It is known now that Dorset was later to become Jane's lover – if he had not already been so earlier.) The queen then threatens violence against her rival: she 'draws a knife, and making as though she meant to destroy Jane's beauty, runs to her', but she has a change of heart, 'and falling on her knees, embraces and kisses her, throwing away the knife'. But the drama is not over yet:

Enter King Edward, angrily:

> Why, how now, Bess? What, will ye wrong my Jane?
> Come hither, love! What has she done to thee?

Pure melodrama, unbelievably touching: at least that was what the dramatist had intended. Jane tells the king to love his 'beauteous queen',

> The only perfect mirror of her kind.

The two women kneel on either side of the king, they all forgive each other and Edward admits to 'Bess' later that he had been alarmed at what she might do to her rival.

Two women and one man: a triangle that has often been regarded as a situation more suitable for comedy than tragedy. No wonder Heywood needed two plays, for he was to include much more material, such as the appearance of the rebel Falconbridge (correctly Fauconberg), who incidentally hoped that he too might seduce Jane. Later in this two-part drama, Jane herself achieves great power through her closeness to the king, and rescues her husband and his associates from serious trouble; but the modern reader surely cannot accept the denouement: it includes too much suffering, with Jane and Matthew Shore finally dying in each other's arms. It is difficult today to take it all seriously, but this love-in-death ending was to appeal to many later dramatists and their audiences.

However, the drama was a great success for over a century. There were other memorable plays at this period; in the anonymous *Arden of Faversham* and *The Yorkshire Tragedy*, the heroines were more important than the other characters, and the latter play was apparently based on a true crime of the period; these two dramas, plus *King Edward IV*, marked a new genre, the domestic tragedy. Shakespeare's tragic lovers were all royal and seriously heroic, while the other lovers he created were usually aristocrats, or professional upper-middle-class people, rarely artisans or peasants and they were nearly always both of the same class. Many of the characters were still involved in the ever-present problem of arranged marriage. In *The Merry Wives of Windsor* Fenton, described as a 'gentleman', has to work hard to win Mistress Page as his wife, and when he is successful he reminds her father in the last scene of the play that *he* would not have treated his daughter well, he 'would have married her most shamefully', whereas he, Fenton, was marrying her for love, and sparing her 'a thousand cursed hours': she would not have been subjected to the virtual imprisonment in a boring home that Jane Shore, according to Drayton, had had to endure.

Social change was obviously imminent and in the early twenty-first century Richard Helgerson, in his absorbing study *Adulterous Alliances*, saw the importance of women's roles in what was developing into 'female complaint', followed in the eighteenth century by the 'she-tragedy'. Helgerson pointed out that Heywood's play was important to a changing public who were shocked to hear about 'a royal man in illicit relation to a bourgeois woman': that was new. The Jane Shore situation had not been forgotten, because it caused violent reaction: 'Invading the exclusively ruling class and masculine domains of social history,' Helgerson continued, '*de casibus* lament, national history play, and classical tragedy, that story has provoked repeated hostility. But,' he went on, 'it has also remade those generic domains in its own image and, in so doing, has helped remake the culture from which they arose. Tears that were shed over Jane Shore prepared the way for a world in which urban merchants, like the Londoners Jane came from, would take the place of kings, a world in which the middle class would have other luxuries than the luxury of grief.'[4]

So Jane, who had taken some risky independent action on her own, was seen as responsible, over-responsible perhaps, for the social change that was

126

now clearly on its way. Did the changing situation and the treatment of women in imaginative works provide an unexpected hint of democracy to come? Perhaps it was the first stage, a step towards the modern world. Heywood's play had certainly transformed Edward IV and his queen into ordinary domestic mortals, but Edward had not yet lost all the autocratic attitudes of monarchy: 'Jane, in the evening I will send for thee,' he announced as he left her, giving her a 'true-love kiss': he did not intend to come to the Shore house to claim her, and he was not yet relinquishing his kingly rights.

TEN

The Early Ballads of Mistress Shore

Jane's life in legend and literature had begun with her virtual promotion as a heroine through poetry and drama, but in fact her story had already reached a much wider public along a different route, through the ballads. These continued an age-old oral tradition in many European countries and a long history too of story-telling in verse. For people who did not read – and even in Elizabethan times there were many who had not had the chance to learn and in any case could never have bought books – these stories in verse supplied entertainment and education at the same time. Ballads were recited or more usually sung, often with harp accompaniment, and in their early existence there would probably have been dancing too, for the word 'ballad' is close to the Italian *ballare*, to dance. Jane would surely have heard many of these ballads when she was very young and may even have been taught to sing some of them herself. Their range was wide: they could be stories, simple, sad or even sinister, expressing a triumphant celebration of some hard-won battle or a lamentation for one that was lost; there was no limit to their scope and they included brief life-stories of many heroes and some heroines.

Shakespeare liked to introduce memories of old ballads into his plays: the sad 'Willow, willow' for instance is mentioned (ironically) by Princess Bona in *Henry VI* Part III, Act III, Scene 3, sung (pathetically) by Desdemona in *Othello* Act IV, Scene 3, and echoed by Emilia just before she dies in Act V, Scene 2. Thomas Heywood referred to a well-known lively ballad even on the title page of his two-part play about Edward IV: 'his merry pastime with the Tanner of Tamworth'. This presents a cheerful story of how the king asked the tanner to tell him the way to Compton Bassett (in Wiltshire); the tanner did not realise he was talking with his king and tried to do a business deal. Then he feared he might be hanged for disrespect, but instead the would-be democratic king generously gave him some land. The earlier ballads used the older themes, such as the inevitable story of Fair Rosamond, and there was even the *Confession of Queen Eleanor*, while new heroines appeared, including the brave Mary Ambree, and older heroes too, such as Sir Patrick Spens, the sea-captain, while the moving story of King Cophetua and the Beggar-Maid was not forgotten. The variety of subjects was immensely wide, for the ballad writers and performers, often composing ad lib, had to appeal to both men and women of all types while at the same time taking account of local taste as they moved round the country. All these ballads were anonymous or unreliably credited to various forgotten authors, many were told in different versions and most of them changed as the years went by, different themes becoming more or less popular if rumours about national news began to vary. They distributed new gossip, facts or even opinions, and any performer or listener could add or subtract from the verses as they wished.

Jane Shore had never faded from public attention since More's references to her had been included in several sixteenth-century chronicles, and the success of Heywood's play had prolonged her remembered life, for apparently she encountered no serious competitors, at least none seem to have been remembered. She and her miseries had impressed women in particular: mothers wanted their daughters to know what would happen to them if they strayed from dutiful behaviour and/or deserted their husbands. From the sixteenth to the early nineteenth century ballads were the tabloid news-sheets of their day, soon followed by the chapbooks, as will be shown later.

It is not known exactly when Thomas Deloney,[1] the silk-weaver turned pamphleteer and early prose fiction writer, who lived from about 1543 to about 1599 or 1600, composed his poem about Jane described as a 'sonnet', using the word in its meaning as a 'little song'. Since he did not refer to his heroine as 'Jane' he was obviously unaware of this as her 'adopted' Christian name through Heywood's play, and since he himself is thought to have died in 1600 or even earlier, he would probably not have heard it at all. His poem, a monologue spoken by the heroine, regretful but not desperate, reads easily and has a charm of its own:

Shore's wife I am,
so known by name:
And at the Flower-de-Luce in Cheapside
   Was my dwelling:
The only daughter of a wealthy merchant man,
Against whose counsel evermore,
   I was rebelling.

Young was I loved:
No affection moved
My heart and mind to give or yield
   To their consenting.
My parents thinking richly for to wed me,
Forcing me to that which caused
   My repenting.

Then being wedded
I was quickly tempted,
My beauty caused many Gallants
   To salute me.
The King commanding, I straight obeyed:
for his chiefest jewel then,
   He did repute me . . .

When the King died,
My grief I tried:
From the Court I was expelled
   with despite.
The Duke of Gloucester being Lord protector,
Took away my goods, against
   All law and right.

In a Procession
For my transgression,
Barefoot he made me go,
   For to shame me.

A Cross before me there was carried plainly,
As a penance for my former life,
   So to tame me . . .

Wherefore, Fair Ladies,
With your sweet babies,
My grievous fall bear in your mind,
   And behold me:
How strange a thing, that the love of a King
Should come to die under a stall,
   As I told ye.

The 'stall' may be another reference to the rumour that Jane died in a ditch, hence the name Shoreditch, but this place-name had been used since much earlier times and any link with Jane is invalid.

In the late seventeenth century too came the anonymous ballad that was to find even more long-lasting popularity: it fascinated the public and was to appear in at least twenty separate editions. This was *The Wofull Lamentation of Mistris Jane Shore*, the title followed by an immensely long sub-title: '*a Goldsmith's Wife in London, Sometime King Edward the Fourth's Concubine, Who for Her Wanton Life came to a Miserable End. Set Forth for the Example of All Lewd Women*'. It was followed by *The Second Part of Jane Shore, Wherein Her Sorrowful Husband Bewaileth His Own Estate, and his Wife's Wantonness, the Wrong of Marriage, the Fall of Pride, Being a Warning for all Women to Take Heed by.*

This full title of the second part does not appear in Volume II of Percy's *Reliques* in its various nineteenth-century reprints, the most easily accessible publication where the first part of the ballad can be read today.

As printed by Percy, the ballad begins with the near-inevitable reference to Fair Rosamond, as made earlier by both Samuel Daniel and Drayton:

If Rosamond that was so fair
Had cause her sorrows to declare,
Then let Jane Shore with sorrow sing,
That was beloved of a king.

In thirty-seven four-line stanzas, each one consisting of two rhymed couplets (*aa bb*) with a further two lines repeated after each stanza, Jane tells her own sad story, referring to her supposed earlier life in Lombard Street:

> Where many gallants did behold
> My beauty in a shop of gold.
>
> I spread my plumes, as wantons do,
> Some sweet and secret friends to woo,
> Because chaste love I did not find
> Agreeing to my wanton mind.

This seems to indicate a new twist to the story: did Jane perhaps, dissatisfied with her impotent husband, decide to sleep around? But there came an exciting possibility:

> At last my name in court did ring
> Into the ears of England's king.
> Who came and liked, and love required,
> But I made coy what he desired.

At first she did not give in to him, she said. Then another new twist, not forgotten by later writers, for Jane claimed that she received advice:

> Yet Mistress Blague, a neighbour near
> Whose friendship I esteemèd dear,
> Did say, It was a gallant thing
> To be beloved of a king.

So she gave in, and deserted her wedded husband.

Many of these ballads were long-lived, remaining in folk-memory. When Wordsworth visited Scotland in 1803 he heard a 'solitary girl reaper' singing as she worked in the fields and wondered what the song was about: 'Will no one tell me what she sings?' he asked:

> Perhaps the plaintive numbers flow
> For old unhappy, far-off things,
> And battles long ago:
> Or is it some more humble lay,
> Familiar matter of today?
> Some natural sorrow, loss, or pain,
> That has been, and may be again?

The girl singer could have been remembering 'The Battle of Otterbourne' or perhaps 'Mary Ambree'. It is unlikely to have been 'The Wofull Lamentation of Mistris Jane Shore', although the ballad singers had probably brought it to Scotland in the seventeenth or eighteenth century; at least one of the chapbooks, which told the tale later, had been printed in Edinburgh in 1750. At the end of the sixteenth century, and throughout the seventeenth, the popularity of Heywood's two-part *King Edward IV* had made more people than ever aware of Jane's story; later editions of *A Mirror for Magistrates* were still read, so were Drayton's *Heroical Epistles*. According to Professor James L. Harner there was even popular accompanying music, for another ballad about three deserters from the army was sung to the 'Tune of Shore's Wife's Lamentation' and several other ballads were also supported by this melody.

Jane's story went on:

> From city then to court I went,
> To reap the pleasures of content;
> There had the joys that love could bring,
> And knew the secrets of a king.

She was able to help Mrs Blague, for the king gave her a 'living', presumably money, but William Shore, whom Jane charitably described as 'a prince of peerless might' left the country. She, or rather the composer of the ballad, added that he died overseas, which was not true, but this imaginary sad end suited the story. It also tells how Jane devoted herself to good works possibly out of guilt:

But yet a gentle mind I bore
To helpless people, who were poor;
I still redressed the orphans' cry,
And saved their lives condemned to die.

It has to be remembered that in the fifteenth century at least, charity had been virtually the only help available to the disadvantaged, and if records of the time prove the generosity of the upper and middle classes, expressed in a variety of ways, it nearly always depended on personal gifts or the carefully managed charitable companies – very little of it, if any, was state organised. Jane described how she cared for widows and small children:

And never looked for other gain
But love and thanks for all my pain . . .

This was the attitude that had earned the notice and praise of Sir Thomas More much earlier.

Unfortunately, after the king's death, Jane's so-called friends let her down. Mrs Blague, to whom she had entrusted her jewels, denied that she had ever seen them and would not even allow her into the house. This behaviour, the desertion of friends was, as mentioned earlier, apparently another favourite theme that often occurred in Elizabethan writing, and people became afraid that it might happen to them. Jane had suffered of course from 'crook-back Richard', lost all her former friends and according to at least one ballad, when one of them was hanged for helping her she wished that she had died instead.

If Jane had not merely emerged from the merchant class and failed to join the aristocracy – only the truly high-born could describe themselves as aristocrats – she might have grown into a tragic heroine, but for the time being she was merely a downtrodden young woman out of luck, and she had only herself to blame, for she should not have left her husband. However, the 'Wofull Lamentation', often without the second part, which is concerned mainly with the imagined travels and death of the unfortunate 'Matthew' Shore, never lost its popularity.

Jane described how she was totally penniless and reduced to begging; she also slept in the streets, or at least she claimed so. The details are horrifying if, of course, they are even partly true, but most of the ballad-makers probably exaggerated them for dramatic effect:

> My gowns beset with pearl and gold,
> Were turn'd to simple garments old;
> My chains and gems and golden rings,
> To filthy rags and loathsome things.

It sounded as though the end of her world had come:

> Thus was I scorn'd of maid and wife,
> For leading such a wicked life;
> Both sucking babes and children small,
> Did make their pastime at my fall.

Of course there had to be strong emphasis on the moral:

> You wanton wives, that fall to lust,
> Be you assur'd that God is just;
> Whoredom shall not escape his hand,
> Nor pride unpunished in this land.

Then comes the lesson which repeats the one already included in Drayton's *Heroical Epistles* and also in Shakespeare, through the words of Fenton at the end of *The Merry Wives of Windsor*. Jane warns everyone:

> You husbands, match not but for love,
> Lest some disliking after prove;
> Women, be warn'd when you are wives,
> What plagues are you to sinful lives.

It should be remembered that after every quatrain of the ballad two extra lines were to be sung as a kind of refrain in order to reinforce the simple lesson, too often forgotten, that time passes:

> Then, maids and wives, in time amend,
> For love and beauty will have end.

Wordsworth had been right to wonder if the Highland girl had been singing 'some more humble lay,/Familiar matter of today'; for centuries the sufferings of women had been largely ignored and their misdeeds rarely forgiven, while Jane's situation was only too familiar by now, the ballad-writers intent on emphasising her misfortunes.

Jane had to defend herself through the ballads, and Shakespeare for one did virtually nothing to help her. In his *King Richard III*, written probably as early as 1593, he could have omitted all mention of her but he chose to refer to her in a way that was quite different from that of the unknown earlier author of *The True Tragedie of Richard III* who seemed to sympathise with her. The new king was uninterested in Jane's emotional plight or her earlier good works; he saw her only as a collaborator in witchcraft with Edward IV's widowed queen, responsible, he said, for his withered arm, and later alleging that she had acted as a messenger between the queen and Lord Hastings.

Richard had learnt that Hastings had moved into her house after Edward's death, but that did not deter him from ordering the latter's immediate execution. In Act III of the play, soon after Lovell and Catesby had entered (scene 5) 'with Hastings' head', the Lord Mayor of London admitted that Richard's former friend deserved his fate, and explained why:

> I never look'd for better at his hands
> After he once fell in with Mistress Shore.

According to John Stow, in his *Survey of London*, the Lord Mayor in 1483 was Robert Bilisden, a haberdasher. In this scene Shakespeare, through various characters, seems to have been anxious to blacken Jane's character: he referred again to Richard's description of her in the previous scene, which evoked the dramatic meeting in the Tower, as that 'harlot strumpet Shore'. This was the harshest description ever made of her in this play, but it expressed Shakespeare's purpose – he was presenting a melodrama with the wicked Richard III as the central character. He succeeded so well in convincing generations of playgoers that his hero was a villain that efforts are still being made today, six centuries later, by biographers and The Richard III Society, to prove that this king was not unduly wicked, but simply a man of his times.

Shakespeare missed no opportunity in this play for some character to attack Jane, emphasising Richard's cruel revengeful treatment of her. Perhaps he believed that the ballad-writers had gone too far in allowing her to explain herself and utter her endless repentance as a warning to others. However, it is only fair to add that in the twentieth century various directors and producers of *Richard III* in Britain decided that Jane should appear in person on the film or television set, feeling that she belonged to the play. Obviously she was not given a speaking part, but controversially, her presence seemed essential to some and in her *Harlot or Heroine? Re-Presenting 'Jane Shore'*, Maria M. Scott examined these decisions from a feminist standpoint.[2] However, these 'appearances' by Jane, their significance unexplained to the audience, do not seem to have added anything to the central theme of the play. Perhaps the ballad-writers had been too preoccupied with Jane's sufferings and as a result had helped to create some opposition to her, so that readers and listeners had grown tired of her; but at the same time she was still seen as a mysterious and potentially interesting character. Surely though it is more fitting that her story should retain at least some mystery, rather than decline into mere romantic fiction. If she had not been mysterious in so many ways the legend would not have appealed to so many writers in so many genres, for it gave them the opportunity to explore her personality and her story in an imaginative way.

It was left to one of Shakespeare's editors in the eighteenth century to choose Jane as the subject of his own most popular tragedy: he was Nicholas Rowe, whose *Tragedy of Jane Shore* came to be admired for over a century in England, Europe, Mexico and later in the United States. In the meantime other people became intrigued by her, and if poets and playwrights in different ways had created and prolonged her legend, it was not going to fade away just yet.

ELEVEN

More Ballads, New Chapbooks

During the late sixteenth century the well-remembered Jane Shore had, through Drayton and Heywood, entered literature and finally acquired a Christian name, but her constantly recurring appearance in the ballads obviously brought her closer to the area of trade. The printers issued endless editions and reprints of those ballads that were most popular, including the much quoted 'Wofull Lamentation of Mistris Jane Shore', in broadsheet format, before the chapbook printers and the travelling salesmen began to achieve even more profit from her sales potential. But the ballads continued: and as late as 1671 there appeared 'A New Ballad of King Edward and Jane Shore', performed to a new tune, *St George for England and the Dragon*, a change from the usual accompaniment, which seems to have been very popular so far, *Come live with me and be my love*, presumably used originally with Marlowe's famous idyllic poem. The 'new ballad' is said to have been composed by Samuel Butler, a farmer's son who lived from 1612 to 1681 and was later known as 'Hudibras' Butler after his successful mock-heroic poem published between 1663 and 1678 which had earned the praise of the restored King Charles II.

There was a very different atmosphere to the 'New Ballad', sung to its new tune and printed in London in 1671. It seems a very masculine piece of work and would be enjoyed by men who didn't care a damn about Jane and her lost king. It was full of sexual innuendos with the king losing every round, a cheerful change from all the woeful lamentation in so many of the ballads and other surviving pieces. The anonymous writer, or possibly 'Hudibras' Butler himself, if he was responsible, went to great trouble with his versification and the references to mythology and history. The fourteen stanzas all follow the same pattern: the first five lines evoke legendary or classical heroines, then line six of each stanza always contains Jane's name repeated once and tells what she did. As the ballad went on the references became progressively more bawdy; for instance the writer refers to Arthurian legend:

> Queen Guinevere and Arthur fought singly hand to hand,
> In bed, though afterward she made horns on his head to stand,
> And to Sir Mordred pictish Prince a paramour became,
> But Jane Shore, Jane Shore, she made King Edward tame.

Each stanza ended with two chorus lines:

> Jane Shore she was for England, Queen Fredrick was for France,[1]
> Honi soit qui mal y pense

Towards the end of its many stanzas references to King Edward become more physically crude, including presumably a reference to the highly sexed medieval Queen Joan of Naples:

> And Naples Joan, would make them groan yet ardently did lov'r,
> But Jane Shore, Jane Shore, King Edward he did shov'r

while the corresponding fifth and sixth lines in the last stanza are a final, total put-down for Edward:

> But brave King Edward who before had gained nine victories
> Was like a bond slave fetter'd with Jane Shore's all-conquering thighs.

Men had presumably composed all those earlier first-person lamentations by Jane and now at last another group of men had remembered how the story had started and what it had all been about: sex. Jane had enjoyed what had obviously been a good sex-life for nearly thirteen years, and she had had an exciting time, so why not remember the fun she and Edward had known together, and why not imagine that she could get the better of him sexually? Perhaps the writer was remembering Edward's reputation as a womaniser and how, later in life, he got his deserts through early death. It was a refreshingly new angle, more than welcome after all those woeful lamentations and tearful warnings.

The sixteenth century had inevitably brought great changes to the social scene, especially after the death of Edward VI, Henry VIII's son, who had reigned for only six years. His unpopular half-sister and successor, the committed Catholic Mary, reigned only for five. Elizabeth, who became queen in 1558, had kept the throne for forty-five years, a record contested by Edward III, who had been king for fifty years in the fourteenth century, later by George III who reigned for sixty (with minor gaps due to mental illness) in the eighteenth and nineteenth. Elizabeth kept an important Privy Council, consulted closely when she chose but remained authoritarian whenever she encountered strong opposition. However, there was time in her long reign for crucial improvements such as the various reforms of the Poor Law, which finally led to its enactment in 1601. This would have helped Jane, who seems to have been beyond charity at the end of her life, especially after King Richard had vetoed any help to her.

There were of course hard-to-solve problems of a different sort, such as the choice of a successor to Elizabeth, all candidates for the queen's marriage having been refused in varied circumstances; in addition there had been a potential power bid from Mary Stuart, who had abdicated as queen of the Scots and then had come to England. There was censorship of the press, there were plots of various kinds, but the threat from the Spanish Armada was removed, there was overseas exploration and in the cultural context this, especially in the last two decades of the reign, was a golden age of literary and theatrical art.

The public and the officials of the government were now forced to accept the importance of women, starting with the intelligent queen, even if William Cecil, Lord Burghley, once complained in 1560 that a diplomatic despatch from Paris was 'too much for a woman's knowledge'. However, Elizabeth was not Henry VIII's daughter for nothing: she knew how to get her own way. The most potentially dangerous problem of the reign was of course the antagonism between Catholics and Protestants, but fortunately it did not develop beyond local rebellions and frequent changes of personnel in the queen's administration, except for one tragic case: it led in the end to the execution of Mary Stuart. She was regarded as a threat, and thought to be involved in a plot against Elizabeth. The queen, after keeping her in prison eventually signed her death warrant only after much hesitation. She was not told by her civil servants that the document had been sent on its way and very soon it was too late for any last-minute change to her orders. If her officials had accepted a queen to rule the country they still found ways to ignore her, especially in a case like this when another woman, regarded as a danger, was concerned.

These ever-present, inescapable images of women automatically led to continued concern about the problem of arranged marriages and unhappiness among both married and single women. The term 'female complaint' had come into use to describe what these women felt but rarely expressed directly, and that dramatic-sounding term unfortunately fitted the case of Jane Shore only too well. Memories of her sorrows were not affected by the religious arguments of the period because the desertion of a husband was liable to earn disapproval from all Christian people, not merely Catholics, but Protestants and Puritans as well. Her closeness to the king was less important because Edward IV, like many of his predecessors, had had many mistresses but never showed the slightest intention of deserting his queen. His sudden death was Jane's misfortune, but both she and the king had unwisely failed to be vigilant, for in those days, especially with the inescapable haunting presence of the Black Death, life could be devastatingly short and medical science had not progressed as far as might have been expected.

Jane's punishment by Edward's illegal successor Richard III was part of that unpopular man's behaviour in general. It followed his insistence in trying to prove that his brother Edward had been born illegitimate, pursuing Cecily of York's admission of infidelity when her eldest son insisted on marrying Elizabeth Woodville. Later research in Rouen by Michael K. Jones during the twenty-first century may even prove in the end that she was not inventing this story about herself, although the situation was complicated. In his book *Bosworth 1485: Psychology of a Battle*[2] Jones discusses at length the possible evidence that Edward IV was conceived by his mother Cecily at a time when her husband was known to be away at the war front. Jones mentions the many uncertainties that can affect the date of conception but does not allow for the fact that, even if away from home, York may still have been in reach of Rouen and could have rejoined Cecily if he had so wished. However, in 1483, the possibility of Edward's illegitimate birth was helpful to Richard. It was also alleged that Edward married illegally on another count, because he had set aside the pre-contract made with Lady Eleanor Butler. Finally he had taken up with a wanton woman, and Richard, who hoped to show a good example of high morality in himself, was determined to destroy her or at least silence her before she caused him more trouble.

He had tried to prove she was a witch, closely allied with the former queen Elizabeth Woodville but failed in that attempt and then sent her to prison twice, since after her penance had won her more friends than enemies there was little else he could do. He was apparently defeated when she met Thomas Lynam in Ludgate jail. It is a strange fact that Jane's second marriage was either unknown to the general public later or else it was ignored, perhaps owing to the lack of records or because it might have spoilt a good story. The popular ballad-makers knew a good dramatic tale when they heard one and did not want it destroyed by any incursion of reality. The story, without Lynam, continued to appeal to the audience for ballads and, after the long Elizabethan era and the ensuing reign of James I were over, a new set of entertainers and profiteers took up Jane's story, for they could see it had all the elements they wanted; these were the men who had studied the audience and customers for ballads and now devised the chapbooks, arranging their distribution round the country.

Apparently these chapbooks, small-format unbound books of twelve pages or so, illustrated with often irrelevant woodcuts or crude drawings, had been originally developed in France. They were printed cheaply and then hawked from door to door by travelling pedlars, known as chapmen. The term 'chapbook' does not seem to have been used before the early nineteenth century and most of them do not include any publication date. All that can be said of them is that they were published at various times from the mid-to-late seventeenth century and on into the early eighteenth. At first the 'books' were designed for the semi-literate, and later for children, telling them stories like that of Tom Thumb or Jack the Giant-killer. However, they soon made a different appeal to the more sophisticated of the period including the well-known Samuel Pepys, the London civil servant who became and has remained world famous through his valuable, immensely readable diaries. He had already been fascinated by ballads and collected five folio volumes of them, now carefully preserved in the Pepys Collection at Magdalene College, Cambridge. As one would expect of an experienced civil servant he classified them carefully – there were ten different types altogether, varying from tragedy, which included 'murders, executions, judgements of God' to 'Love pleasant, love unfortunate' and also 'Marriage, cuckoldry'. In addition to this collection, and also preserved in Cambridge, there were four little duodecimo volumes, each including different sections: 'Penny Merriments, Penny Witticisms, Penny Compliments and Penny Godlinesses'. Pepys seems to have bought these chapbooks when he happened to see them and later they would be bound tightly in small volumes which means that reading them today is not very easy.

At least one of the four 'merriments' includes that still popular heroine, Jane Shore. The titles vary, some fairly simple: 'The History of Mistress Jane Shore with her Life and Death', another one even more simple: 'The Description of Mrs Jane Shore', yet another is 'The History of Mistress Jane Shore Concubine to King Edward Fourth, who was wife to one Matthew Shore, a Goldsmith in London. Wherein is declared her wanton life with her miserable End, and Death of her Husband'. This is accompanied by crude drawings showing Jane in the goldsmith's shop, she and her husband wearing what the artist regarded as medieval dress. It was the habit of these cheap printers, whenever they needed illustrations, to use whatever woodcuts or any other images came their way and so Jane is usually portrayed as a well-dressed lady who looks like Queen Elizabeth, although sometimes her face is concealed. In the depiction of Jane's penance, she is accompanied by a man in seventeenth-century dress, obviously anxious that she should not escape; whereas Jane, draped in her penitent's sheet, looks like a nun and carries an enormous candle. The text ends with poor 'Matthew Shore's' unhappy exodus from the country. In the end he hanged himself, he was so miserable. It is known now of course that the real William Shore led a successful and adventurous existence after his divorce, made money and finally died in England where he was buried in a marble tomb. However, the chapbook telling the 'Matthew Shore' story closes with a drawing that shows a forlorn figure hanging from a tree.

For some reason an additional incident in the supposedly wretched life of 'Matthew' Shore, taken from the ballad quoted, was used in the chapbook concerned: he had been reduced to criminality and was condemned to death in England for 'clipping gold in secrecy' – though he complained that it was all Jane's fault:

> And so by gold my life decayed.
> Thus have you heard the woeful strife
> That came by my unconstant wife.
> Her fall, my death wherein is shew'd
> The story of a strumpet lewd.
> In hope thereby some women may
> Take heed how they at wanton play.

Readers of the chapbooks were not interested in biographical truth, they wanted drama, preferably melodrama, and they certainly found it. Centuries later, some writers of stage plays and film scripts were to work in the same way and achieved the same degree of success without any hint of truth: truth was unimportant and it got in the way; so Jane, the 'wanton', took all the blame.

The writers of the chapbook texts were not embarrassed by any copyright questions and borrowed the wordage they needed wherever they found something suitable, including paragraphs from Drayton's annotations to his *Heroical Epistles* and, in fact, any anonymous poem or ballad they came across. Apparently these cheap little books had an educational function, because they were read and enjoyed by people who probably never owned a book in their lives. Children enjoyed the nursery rhymes and probably also, as they grew up, the sad little adult stories which had only a slender link with truth. These rough and ready booklets were often the only help available to children learning to read, and at the same time they began to know about the heroines of the past, including the inevitable Fair Rosamond and Jane Shore.

The chapbooks brought Jane's story into the area of useful trade and they seem to have reached the United States by the nineteenth century at the latest when five editions, some excluding the imagined fate of her ex-husband, were published in New York between 1821 and 1834. So ballads and chapbooks had carried on the story from the middle of the sixteenth century when the chronicles used More's text and *A Mirror for Magistrates* had included Churchyard's original monologue for Jane. Infinitely more elegant versions had been published in the meantime, written and read by educated people, but they had probably not earned their authors much money. The interesting thing is the amount of attention that was paid to Jane's story over such a long period of time.

That situation was to change in the early eighteenth century. In the meantime the seventeenth century brought the 22-year reign of Elizabeth's successor, James I of England and VI of Scotland, who was the son of Mary Stuart. The policies of James's son, Charles I, unfortunately led to the civil war and finally to his own execution in 1649. During Cromwell's Protectorate which followed, Jane Shore was not forgotten, even if women counted for less during these painful years. However, with the exuberance of the Restoration in 1660 women returned to the forefront, partly because Charles II found them essential to his life and also because theatres could reopen, even if the attempted ban imposed during Cromwell's time had not been strictly enforced.

Samuel Pepys in fact made several references to Jane Shore in his diaries. She seems to have been remembered partly for her own sake and partly because there was now a whole bevy of royal mistresses; their profession had lapsed during the sixteenth century after the time of the many-wived Henry VIII but now it was fashionable again. These women found it useful to quote Jane as a bad example, for they enjoyed any chance to be thoroughly nasty about their predecessors and/or current rivals. They were quite unmoved by Jane's bad luck. In his diary entry of 9 April 1661 Pepys referred to Jane in a casual way: with a friend he had gone up what he called 'Jane Shore's Tower' and enjoyed a singing session. Sir Robert Birley, writing in *Etoniana*, identified this building as the Wardrobe Tower at Baynard's Castle in the city, the former home of Cecily of York, Edward IV's mother. Why it should be named after Jane is not clear, but it may have been some private joke. Jane was obviously not forgotten because on 21 April 1662 Pepys went after dinner to see his friend Sir Thomas Crew, who apparently was 'still ill'. But not too ill to pass on a story about two of the current royal mistresses: 'He tells me,' wrote Pepys, 'how my Lady Duchess of Richmond and Castlemaine had a falling out the other day, and she calls the latter Jane Shore, and did hope to see her come to the same end that she did.' How convenient that Jane had existed and been unlucky – she could now be quoted as an example by the new breed of courtesans if they wanted to be thoroughly insulting to or about any other woman who had taken up the profession of royal mistress and was threatening to cause rivalry and general trouble.

The succession of Charles II's concubines provided good entertainment for a specialised public, and writers of all kinds did not neglect these opportunities, especially the anonymous rhymester who recounted a supposed dialogue between a pair of the ladies, the Duchess of Cleveland (Barbara Villiers) and the Duchess of Portsmouth, the English title awarded by the king to the French Louise de Kérouaille: the 'Dialogue between the D of C and the D of P at their meeting in Paris with the ghost of Jane Shore'. It consists of three pages of rhymed couplets in which these two women attack each other bitterly, the first telling the second that she has lost her beauty while she herself is of course still young, beautiful and powerful. It is a splendid display of cattiness and the older of the two feline creatures hopes that the London apprentices will scratch the other's eyes out.

Then the two women get a shock:

> What spectre's that?
> Oh Heav'ns what have we here?
> My joints do tremble and my soul doth fear.

The ghost of Jane Shore [comes] to them:

> *Ghost:* Perhaps you know me not, yet take a view,
> See what I am, I was once such as you.
> I was a whore, a Royal Mistress too
> I was a woman of egregious fame
> And like you two I gloried in my name . . .

Jane, or rather her ghost, tells her own sad story and warns the two women that they will go to hell.

> Rivals, look on me and contend no more,
> What you are now I once was long before.
> Yet I am damned although a Royal Whore.

146

Who wrote the poem, and why, remains unknown. Did he – or even she – write it as a joke, or did the writer disapprove of Royal Whores, or of whoredom as a way of life? It probably was a joke, but a serious kind of joke, for these women were far from popular, while Jane was the right person to read them a lesson and utter those solemn warnings, like the ones she had received herself, if too late, from the ballad-writers. The only one of Charles II's mistresses who was or had been accepted was Nell Gwynn, who called herself the 'English whore', for she was a good-hearted, unpretentious young woman who had worked hard to escape from a poor background.

Whatever the background to that amusing poem, preserved in the Huntington Library, the writer had it printed in London by one J. Smith and some unknown contemporary dated it in handwriting typical of the time: 28 March 1682. It might have seemed by now that apart from the relevant ballads and chapbooks, all constantly reprinted, that Jane and her sad story had been too much written about; wasn't it time to forget this unlucky woman who after all had brought all the trouble upon herself? The new generation of dramatists, Congreve, Farquhar, Wycherley and their followers would not have found any hint of their favourite themes here: King Edward IV and his brother Richard did not interest them in any way and an actress such as Mrs Anne Bracegirdle, much admired by Congreve, might not have been attracted to the role of Jane. However, that situation did not last very long.

TWELVE

The 'She-Tragedy'

Jane Austen was fifteen when she wrote her short *History of England* in 1791, illustrated by her sister Cassandra with thirteen unrecognisable portraits. Jane said that 'One of Edward IV's Mistresses was Jane Shore who has had a play written about her, but it is a tragedy & therefore not worth reading'. It *was* a tragedy and it *is* worth reading, if only because Nicholas Rowe's drama of 1714, *The Tragedy of Jane Shore*, was and remained for a long time amazingly popular in England, in the United States and in continental Europe. It also attracted a series of leading actresses, keen to take the roles of the heroine and her 'friend' Alicia, who closely resembled the 'Mrs Blague' of the ballads. Rowe's play obviously made a major contribution to the popularity of the 'she-tragedy', as the author himself called this and others of his plays, mentioning the term in the prologue to *The Tragedy of Jane Shore*. It has remained a useful phrase ever since to academic and other critics writing about dramas or domestic disasters which were in themselves tragic enough for a few characters but could not strictly speaking be entitled 'tragedies' as Shakespeare's had been classed.

As mentioned earlier there had already been two plays in England in which women were the undisputed heroines: the anonymous *Tragedy of Mr Arden of Faversham* of 1592, telling how the heroine and her lover succeeded, after various attempts, in killing her husband, and also *The Yorkshire Tragedy* of 1608 which is said to have been based on a series of contemporary murders. It should be added that when the former play was revived in the twentieth century, presented in the actual Faversham house where it was said to have originally happened, the modern audience felt no pity or terror, and were not all convinced that they were watching an early example of the 'she-tragedy'. However, it seems the play has not been forgotten.

On the other hand, among the many writers of the late seventeenth and early eighteenth centuries who concentrated on drama, Nicholas Rowe seems to have been neglected by many critics and others who enjoyed the theatre, perhaps because his themes were tragic, as Jane Austen indicated, unlike those popular successes by his contemporaries such as Wycherley or Farquhar whose entertainingly frivolous comedies, which followed the restoration of Charles II in 1660, are cheerfully enjoyable today. At the same time the remarkable Rowe was qualified to do many other things, both in and out of the theatre. He was born in 1674 in Little Barford in Bedfordshire, attended Westminster School and when he was fifteen his lawyer father entered him at the Middle Temple. The young man was called to the Bar in 1696 but did not enjoy legal work and soon took up creative writing, especially plays. He never had to live in Grub Street and did not need to spend his time anonymously rewriting work by others, although like so many of his contemporary dramatists he was happy to borrow from his predecessors if it suited him. When his father died he inherited a useful private income which allowed him to write without worrying about money or even performance. In this his destiny was totally different from that of the earlier Thomas Otway, whose celebrated *Venice Preserv'd* of 1682 was admired by Rowe and most other dramatists of the time. Sadly, Otway died in poverty at the age of thirty-three.

The year 1700 saw the production of Rowe's first play, *The Ambitious Stepmother*, and in the words of Dr Johnson, it 'was received with so much favour, that he devoted himself from that time wholly to elegant literature.'[1] Two years later came *Tamerlane*, a political satire, also successful, followed by *The Fair Penitent* in 1703, about which Dr Johnson was almost lyrical in his praise: it was 'one of the most pleasing tragedies on the stage, where it still keeps its turns of appearing, and probably will long keep them, for there is scarcely any work of any poet at once so interesting by the fable, and so delightful by the language.'[2] The 'fable', which relied heavily on *The Fatal Dowry* by Massinger (*c.* 1618) is also described as a 'she-tragedy', the type of drama that, as mentioned above, was not in itself tragic, but usually emphasised the problematic role of a woman, inevitably ending with her unhappiness, suffering or death. This was the case of the 'fair penitent' Calista, whose lover, Lothario, was a heartless young seducer with a name that has remained familiar: Richardson's Lovelace in *Clarissa Harlowe* of

1747/8 inherited his behaviour, and who could deny that the seducer attitude remains a persistent element in male psychology? Lothario possibly anticipated Casanova, who was born in 1725. Rowe's tragedy was set in late medieval Genoa and again the problem of the arranged marriage was central to the theme, for Calista's father, Sciolto, had arranged for her to marry Altomont and assumed she was ready to do so.

Far from it: she was desperately in love with Lothario, who was not interested in marriage and believed in having a good time with any willing partner, but it was understood by both that the fun would have no future. He maintained that he had once asked Calista's father for permission to marry her but had been turned down; however, this was not the whole story, for he had succeeded in seducing Calista during one exciting, unforgettable night – the modern word would be 'torrid' – and now of course, having lost her virginity, she was no longer a suitable bride for a respectable husband. In the early eighteenth century this situation fascinated women in particular; they were attracted by the idea but frightened of it at the same time. If it happened to them, whatever would they do? Naturally all parents were frightened too, especially those of the upper and middle classes, who continued to arrange marriages for their daughters; even if the girls were not always ready to accept the system, it was still hard to escape, for money and property were inevitably involved.

To return to Rowe's play: it is, in one sense, a conflict for Calista between love and duty, a common theme in the earlier classical French plays by Corneille and Racine that would have been well known to the dramatist. Calista decides that she will be a dutiful daughter and marry Altomont but her father realises she has probably not given up Lothario. The play becomes a complex drama between the two families, one of them expecting to be united through Altomont and the other aware that the young seducer Lothario might cause trouble.

In the end Lothario is killed and the last act of the play[3] opens with a stage-setting reminiscent of Gothic horror:

SCENE, is a room hung with black: on one side, Lothario's body on a bier; on the other, a table with a skull and other bones, a book, and a lamp on it. Calista is discovered on a couch in black, her hair hanging loose and disordered.

After the performance of a sad song, Calista throws away a book from which she had hoped to learn about true penitence. Her father comes in, argues with her and even suggests that she kills herself, but then changes his mind. She does, of course, manage suicide in the end despite efforts to restrain her. The intended husband, the respectable but unloved Altomont, faints and is taken away. The trouble is obvious: Calista was never a true penitent and even gave up the idea of retiring to a convent. This drama or, in fact, melodrama, was a great success and Mrs Bracegirdle, the actress who played Altomont's sister, Lavinia, spoke an epilogue after the premiere which many women in the audience must have enjoyed, for there are no kind words for husbands:

> Had we the pow'r, we'd make the tyrants know
> What 'tis to fail the duties which they owe;
> We teach the sauntering squire who loves to roam,
> Forgetful of his own dear spouse at home,
> Who snores at night supinely by her side,
> 'Twas not for this the nuptial knot was tied.

The epilogue ends with a hopeful plea:

> No foreign charms shall cause domestic strife,
> But that ev'ry married man shall toast his wife.
> Phillis shall not be to the country sent,
> For carnivals in town to keep a tedious Lent:
> Lampoons shall cease, and envious scandal die,
> And all live in peace, like my good man and I.[4]

Such a civilised attitude had been far from current in Jane Shore's day and the problem of how to help the situation of a wife, considered indirectly by Michael Drayton earlier, was to preoccupy Rowe later. A radical change was needed, and still is, for society could not, and still cannot, achieve a transformation quickly.

The success of *The Fair Penitent*, premiered at Lincoln's Inn Fields in March 1703, encouraged Rowe to write four more tragedies during the next fifteen years before his early death in 1718. His one prose comedy, *The*

Biter of 1704, was a total failure, to Rowe's great surprise. When he was writing it he would laugh out aloud at his own jokes, but the theatre audience did not laugh nearly enough. In 1707 came *The Royal Convert*, which reflected the union of Scotland and England that year.

Rowe was so adaptable that in the next few years he applied himself to other work, first as secretary to the Duke of Queensbury and also to his valuable, but easily forgotten, editorial work on Shakespeare's plays. He added a cast list to each one, for none had ever been printed with the text, and divided the plays into acts and scenes, which nobody had undertaken earlier. He even made some small editorial changes but at least Dr Johnson approved of the enterprise when the six volumes were published in 1709. Five years later Rowe was appointed Land Surveyor of the Customs by the new King George I.

On 2 February 1714 *The Tragedy of Jane Shore*, dedicated to the Duke of Queensbury, opened at Drury Lane Theatre with Elizabeth Barry in the title role. Later, at the same theatre, the part was taken by Sarah Siddons, Mary Ann Yates and other leading actresses, while the play was so successful that it was performed regularly until the nineteenth century. Rowe described it as 'written in imitation of Shakespeare's style', the predecessor whom he had studied and edited so carefully. Dr Johnson's comment here was honest and straightforward: 'In what he thought himself an imitator of Shakespeare, it is not easy to conceive; the numbers, the diction, the sentiments, and the conduct, everything in which imitation can consist are remote in the utmost degree from the manner of Shakespeare; whose dramas it resembles only as it is an English story and as some of the persons have their names in history'.[5] One wonders, therefore, why the play was destined to have such an extended popularity, but the great critic made that clear: 'This play, consisting chiefly of domestic scenes and private distress, lays hold upon the heart. The wife is forgiven because she repents, and the husband is honoured because he forgives. This, therefore, is one of those pieces which we still welcome on the stage.'[6]

Rowe's five acts are not lengthy and move fast. King Edward is dead, and as Act I ends Jane entrusts her jewellery to Alicia, her close friend, who happens to be the mistress of Lord Hastings. Then she makes what can only be described as a feminist statement:

Why should I think that man will do for me
What yet he never did for wretches like me?
Mark by what partial justice we are judged;
Such is the fate unhappy women find,
And such the curse intail'd upon our kind,
That man, the lawless libertine, may rove,
Free and unquestion'd through the wilds of love;
While woman, sense and nature's easy fool,
If poor weak woman swerve from virtue's rule,
If strongly charm'd she leave the thorny way,
And in the softer paths of pleasure stray;
Ruin ensues, reproach and endless shame,
And one false step entirely damns her fame,
In vain with tears the loss she may deplore,
In vain look back on what she was before,
She sets, like stars that fall, to rise no more.[7]

If the word 'feminism', in its modern sense, was not used until 1895, Rowe, through Jane, was surely stating a feminist attitude here. He had not been led to support the cause of women as the result of any turmoil in his private life, he was merely forward-looking and presumably knew some contemporary women, the bluestockings as they were called, whose views must have interested him, including the poet Anne Finch, Countess of Winchilsea, an unconscious feminist of the time.

Rowe was inventive in various ways, introducing new themes into the plot. Hastings has spoken to Gloucester on Jane's behalf but he, still the 'protector', soon becomes hostile and ready to punish her. Rowe also gave his version of Shakespeare's great scenes in the Tower (Act III, Scenes 4 and 5) where Jane is condemned to death, and Hastings of course is destined for the same fate. The audience knows, but Jane does not, that Hastings' mistress Alicia, jealous of Jane, with whom Hastings has fallen in love, has betrayed her. Alicia pursues Hastings, still declaring her passion for him, but to no avail, it is too late. He will soon be dead.

The abandoned Jane comes to beg food from Alicia, who refuses to see her. Alicia's servant Bellmour introduces Dumont, who is in fact Shore in disguise, still in love with Jane. Like Heywood before him Rowe changed the story to suit himself and presumably his audience: Shore does not die away from home, he has returned to London secretly and has been watching Jane closely, presumably hoping for a reunion. He has even rescued her from Hastings, who had tried to seduce her. But once more it is too late, for Jane is dying of hunger. The play ends with a melodramatic reconciliation scene in which Jane repents her desertion of Shore, who forgives her. He tries to feed her, but she is too weak to eat. Shore breaks away from the guards who have come for him (for he had disobeyed Richard by helping the destitute woman), and kisses Jane but she dies and he is led away. The dramatist had pleased the audience by inventing a kind of happy ending, even if Jane dies and her husband is destined to the same fate. No wonder Dr Johnson reported that this was 'one of those pieces which we still welcome on the stage'. Towards the end of his essay on Rowe, in which he criticises him on various points, including the lack of high tragedy, he asks, 'Whence then, has Rowe his reputation?' His reply to himself and the reader is typical of Johnson and his age: 'From the reasonableness and propriety of some of his scenes, on the elegance of his diction, and the suavity of his verse'.[8] Johnson then makes it clear what aspects of his work he regards as valuable: 'He seldom moves either to pity or terror, but he often elevates the sentiments; he seldom pierces the breast, but he always delights the ear, and often improves the understanding.' He also adds a special mention of *Jane Shore*, for it portrayed the woman 'who is always seen and heard with pity'. This play was, he thought, the one that truly had a marked effect on the audiences.

There was a Shakespearean element in *The Tragedy of Jane Shore*, as Rowe had made clear in his sub-title but he introduces a new theme by making Jane's so-called 'friend', Alicia, the mistress of Hastings. Hastings' attempt to seduce Jane, and her rescue by Shore in disguise was new, if improbable. Rowe's play also provided roles for two actresses who both had to be first-class performers; that delighted the theatre audiences.

When Sarah Siddons played Jane the intensity of her acting must have been amazing: it brought about sobbing and shrieking from the women spectators, and men, after struggling to suppress their tears, 'at length grew proud of indulging them', as described by the memoir writer James Boaden, remembering the great actress in 1827.[9] Ever since Elizabethan times the middle and upper classes had been shocked by the true story of how a middle-class woman had allowed herself to be seduced by a king and left her husband as a result. Then another king, her late seducer's brother, had victimised and punished her as though she were a common harlot. Not even Shakespeare's exclusion of her from his *King Richard III* lessened the concern about her fate expressed by so many ordinary readers and spectators, as her developing legend proves so clearly. Rowe, with the help of his actresses, had presented her story with inescapable realism, or so he hoped. The choice of Jane as a heroine never seemed to fail. Although he had many useful friends, including the young Alexander Pope and Richard Addison, Rowe suffered a few hostile critics, especially the journalist Charles Gildon, who at least noted the audience reaction to the Jane Shore play and its successor, the sad story of Lady Jane Grey, which ended with her execution. Gildon wrote that 'The Whore found more favour with the Town than the *Saint*'. Hardly surprising, surely in fact inevitable.

The story of that unfortunate nine-day queen was perhaps too close in time for the audiences to relish it, especially the melodramatic realistic ending, when Lady Jane walked towards the scaffold, which could be seen on the stage. Her young husband had already been executed.

It may seem strange that a fifteenth-century young woman should mean so much to an eighteenth-century lawyer, classicist and Shakespearean editor, and that his work should later find so much success abroad, from Mexico City to Boston and Philadelphia, but Rowe was obviously a far-sighted man who knew both political and literary history and also foresaw certain social changes. His career continued, and he was created Poet Laureate in 1715 in place of the poverty-stricken Nahum Tate, who had been reduced to living in the Royal Mint, presumably at public expense. Rowe had one more triumph although, unfortunately for him, the work concerned was not published until after his early death. This was the verse translation of the best, if unfinished, work by the Latin poet Lucan (Marcus Annaeus Lucanus, AD 39–65) known as the *Pharsalia*, which recounts the civil war between Caesar and Pompey.

To return to *The Tragedy of Jane Shore*: after the play was a success in London it brought about an amazing amount of related writing, from more ballads, additional reviews and comments of various kinds to the Epilogue written by Anne Finch which had been spoken by Mrs Oldfield the day before the public premiere. Various rewritten versions of More's early account of Jane were published and in 1719 there was a new send-up of the story, which was bound to happen at some time. 'Jane Shore. A Celebrated Droll' was followed by an immensely long title, ending 'With the Comical and Diverting Humours of Sir Anthony Noodle, a Foolish Courtier, and His Man Weezel.' Unfortunately no text for this intriguing piece has survived, but it was performed at least during the years 1719, 1723, 1727, 1733 and 1745. So Jane was not only a tragic figure, she could be good for a laugh too, as 'Hudibras' Butler had possibly discovered earlier. As for Jane, described earlier as the 'merriest' of Edward's mistresses, she might possibly have been amused by her appearance as a 'droll'.

It is hardly surprising perhaps that several of Rowe's plays remained popular in England for a long time, but not as easy to understand the lasting success of *Jane Shore* abroad. However, news of its many performances in London crossed the Channel and in 1771 a German translation appeared, *Jane Shore, ein Trauerspiel von Nicholas Rowe, Esqr.* The translator's name appears only as 'S', and there is no indication that the play was performed, although it was published in *Lindforschen Schriften*. In 1784 came the first translation into French, the work of the Baronne de Vasse, published in Paris, while performances in France had to wait until the next century, after three more translations had been published. That of 1797 acknowledged 'Mr Row' but was entitled 'Jeanne Shore, or the triumph of fidelity to the country, and to royalty, tragedy in five acts'. The translator is acknowledged only by a set of initials.

The play continued to attract translators and in 1824 a French dramatist well known at the time was impressed by the story: this was a man with a grand name, Louis-Jean-Népomucène Lemercier (1771–1840), famous for the utterly boring quality of his many works. This did not prevent his success, including later election to the Academy, and in fact it might have helped him. Lemercier seems to have been left over from the eighteenth century. As a young man he had received the patronage of Marie-Antoinette's friend Madame de Lamballe, who was torn to pieces by the mob for supporting the unpopular queen, but Lemercier had a first triumph in the theatre when he was only seventeen: he had written a tragedy about Meleager, the Greek poet. He then entitled his new play *Richard III and Jane Shore, historical drama in five acts and in verse, in imitation of Shakespeare and Rowe*. The manuscript of what is presumably the second edition, also in 1824, has been preserved in the French National Archives, but the name of Richard III was dropped from the title.

In one sense, Lemercier's life and character were much more interesting than his plays, for he at least thought for himself and would not accept obedience to any monarch who revealed dangerous signs of tyranny: he refused to take the oath to Napoleon. He based his whole existence on the ideas of the eighteenth-century *philosophes* and had perhaps been impressed by Jane's independent decision to desert her husband and also by the tyranny of Richard III, which it was his duty to condemn. When Lemercier died his place in the Academy was taken by Victor Hugo.

Another translation of Rowe's drama appeared in 1824, prepared by a captain in the royal artillery, and also preserved in the French National Archives. It was apparently produced at the second of the two national theatres in the same year: in fact this was Jane Shore's year in Paris, for 19 April saw what must have been an extraordinary event at the Théâtre de la Porte Saint-Martin: this was a 'melodrama in three acts, *à grand spectacle*', complete with music, a ballet and special scenery. Such an adaptation of Jane's story may have pleased the Parisian public, for this was the Romantic period and all was grist to the theatrical impresarios of the time: any highly coloured dramatic theme could be made popular. England too was popular in some ways, for three years later Rowe's drama was included in a series of 'English plays produced in Paris'. Further translations into French are listed at the British Library, and there was further travel for Jane, Shakespeare and Rowe, when Lemercier's play took the fancy of opera composers and librettists in Italy. One Ferdinando Livini wrote an opera libretto which was published in 1829, and the same year saw *Giovanna Shore, melodramma serio in tre atti* produced at La Scala with a libretto by Antonio Fontana and music by Carlo Conti.

After the Italians, the Spanish were impressed by the dramatic story of Jane, and Felice Romani composed another *melodramma serio*, again with a libretto by Antonio Fontana. This was produced in Mexico City at the Teatro Principal in 1827, and one edition of the work was printed with Spanish and Italian text on facing pages. For this production the music was composed by Lauro Rossi, an immensely prolific composer. Professor Harner, who has bravely explored all these post-Rowe developments, has also noted three other operas entitled *Giovanna Shore*, two of them in

Italian and one in French. (Details can be found in *The Dictionary Catalogue of Opera and Operettas* edited by John Towers and published in 1910 with a New York reprint in 1967.) These seem to be the last-known adaptations of Jane Shore's story as dramatised by Rowe but it should not be forgotten that on 30 October 1819 the play had been performed at the Chestnut Street Theatre in Philadelphia and it was also published there. It is amusing to note that the performance was followed by 'the comic opera of Love laughs at locksmiths'. Perhaps the audience needed some light-hearted entertainment after the sadness of Jane's repentance and death.

The next century, however, was to add further new dimensions to Jane's past existence which persistently returned to the present. As late as 1901 in France a play was written about her by Eugène Morand, a popular dramatist, Vance Thompson and Marcel Schwob. The latter was a well-known intellectual of the time who became a friend of the writer Colette. Described by Maria M. Scott as 'a melodramatic tour de force of hysterical proportions', it was never published or performed but has survived through a manuscript deposited in the Library of Congress in 1901.

But this was still not the end of the Jane Shore story.

THIRTEEN

Facts, Fiction and Fantasy

Jane's story did not concern the great male novelists of the eighteenth century, who preferred to devise their own plots, and if moral issues preoccupied Samuel Richardson, who found a wide public with *Pamela* and *Clarissa* both in England and in France, he would not have chosen for his heroine a controversial figure from the Middle Ages who had appeared so often in poems, ballads, chapbooks and plays. However, Jane was still a favourite heroine for minor poets, who usually preferred to remain anonymous, like the one who in 1749 composed *Jane Shore to the Duke of Gloucester*, in which Jane asks him why he treated her so badly and destroyed his own brother's reputation at the same time, condemning him for consorting with a harlot. Much of the poem – in twenty-five stanzas mainly of ten or fourteen lines each – is taken up with Jane's memories of her dead lover and her shame at having indirectly 'murdered' Edward's reputation. She asks forgiveness and prays for Richard too – an unusual theme, not heard before in any supposed utterance from Jane or indeed from anyone else, with the exception of Horace Walpole's defence of 1768. The anonymous poem of 1749 is a late curiosity, possibly written by a woman, for no man surely would have made Jane feel guilty on Edward's behalf and it is unlikely that he would have mentioned forgiveness in the case of Richard, especially in a poem.

It was later in the century that Horace Walpole, a very different writer, very much the *littérateur*, involved Jane in a totally different and polemical piece of work. He was the fourth son of Sir Robert Walpole, Prime Minister of England from 1721 to 1742, and for twenty-six years a member of parliament himself, but is known to literature as Horace Walpole. Thanks to his family's social status he encountered few setbacks in life, attended Eton College, then King's College, Cambridge and completed the first part of his life with the Grand Tour of France and Italy. In 1747 he bought a

159

former coachman's cottage, sometimes described as a 'villa', in Twickenham near London and over twenty years converted it into the still-existing pseudo-Gothic mansion of Strawberry Hill. There he set up a printing press and published some of his own works, including in 1768 his only drama, *The Mysterious Mother*, never performed, although fashionably Gothic, probably because its theme of incest was considered to be 'gruesome'.

In the same year, 1768, Walpole also published his controversial work *Historic Doubts on the Life and Reign of Richard III, the Great Debate*. This is best studied in the Folio Society edition of 1965 edited and introduced by Paul Kendall, who included also More's *History of King Richard III*, for Walpole constantly refers to it. Ever since the death of Edward IV and the short reign by his younger brother, which had ended at Bosworth in 1485, there had been controversy, a 'great debate' in fact, which still continues today, about Richard's personal character and much of what he did or did not do – thanks mainly to the energetic Richard III Society, with its worldwide and well-informed membership.

Controversy had begun in 1616 when Sir William Cornwallis the Younger had discreetly published an attempt to discredit the anti-Richard attitude of Shakespeare in his famous early play. Thirty years later Sir George Buc, Master of the Revels to James I, published a seriously hostile anti-Tudor attack entitled *A History of the Life and Reign of Richard III*, in which he hoped to prove that the last Plantagenet Yorkist king had been an honest and much misunderstood man. This view gradually became fashionable, and impressed Walpole, although in 1941 George Sampson described the 1768 book as 'valueless' because Walpole was 'too languid to undertake research'.[1] Although the public thought they were buying scholarly academic research, which they were not, the book was very popular, apart from some dissent by the historian David Hume, which upset the author, who had always respected him.

Walpole was one of the first to attempt proof that Richard was no killer of young princes and even described him as 'patient and gentle', surely as different from the Shakespearean 'hero' as anyone could be. Walpole carefully established fifty 'points' calculated to invite discussion, starting with the supposed falsehoods of the pro-Tudor Sir Thomas More which had been repeated in many of the chronicles. Some of Walpole's interpretations seem strange and hard to justify today, including the execution of Hastings as an act of self-defence, and especially his own belief that Perkin Warbeck, the second of the two claimants for Henry VII's throne, really *was* the younger of the princes in the Tower, the Duke of York, who had somehow escaped from imprisonment with help from outside.

The very last of the contentious fifty points asserts that Richard's early proclamation against 'Jane Shore, for plotting with the Marquess [of] Dorset, not with Lord Hastings, destroys all the credit of Sir Thomas More, as to what relates to the later peer'. Walpole's editor, Paul Kendall, who remains fair-minded throughout his introduction to the book, felt that Walpole had made 'heavy weather of Jane Shore', mainly because he believed that the puritanical Richard worried too much about Jane's marital status, suspected she was not legally divorced from her husband and assumed that she did not marry Lynam. He was not alone in that. Walpole, who described her as 'that unhappy fair one', also believed that Richard was too kind-hearted to have ordered her penance, instead merely asking the churchmen to consider some form of suitable punishment for her. Admittedly this might not have been impossible. The *Historic Doubts* raises other problems today, some for which evidence is not available, but it is still required reading in any context involving Jane Shore and her relationship with Richard III. It also reveals how and when the pro-Richard movement had begun and was set to gather strength – earlier than is generally believed.

For the time being however Walpole was alone, for the eighteenth century was dominated by other more popular writers, especially some of the best and most lasting of English novelists. They were with few exceptions men, concerned with creating both men and women characters with whom their readers could easily identify, and the delightful, perceptive Fanny Burney is most unlikely to have chosen Jane as a subject for her fiction. In the next century, as education continued to spread, fiction took the place of the ballads and chapbooks, although they still circulated. Jane Austen and the Brontë sisters had become successful partly because they included so many varied women characters, and women were their principal readers.

It was partly due to a different kind of woman writer, Mrs Mary Elizabeth Bennett, that historical novels by women and about women became so popular. Originally Mary Saunders, born in 1813, she married

John Bennett who was a journalist and novelist himself, and also a publisher. She had followed the success of the writer Harrison Ainsworth with interest and soon embarked on a series of novels herself. They often carried titles including the word 'girl': there was *The Cottage Girl*, *The Canadian Girl* and others, but this prolific writer was never short of themes: she also wrote *Orphan Sisters*, *Broken Heart*, *The Gipsey Bride, or The Miser's Daughter*, and *The Jew's Daughter*. Some of these titles were advertised as 'By the author of *Jane Shore*' (1839) for which she presumably did some research and added much invention.

It is worth noting that the novel about Jane Shore went through at least twenty editions and there seems to have been a possible further one as late as 1873. Mrs Bennett acquired some professional skills by working closely with her husband, for together they edited and published the *Boys' and Girls' Companion* after 1857. Unfortunately this promising novelist ran out of luck: after the deaths of her husband and her brother she seemed incapable of managing her own life and despite help from the Royal Literary Fund, died in poverty. Harrison Ainsworth, whose historical novels such as *The Tower of London* remain readable today, was not lucky either when he wrote a story about Jane Shore, entitled, unsurprisingly, 'The Goldsmith's Wife' and included in a group entitled *Bow Bells*. Despite his early successes no publisher wanted these stories and they appeared in print in 1874 only in cheap popular collections. Unsurprisingly too Ainsworth remained more interested in colourful descriptions than in any attempt to understand Jane.

By the end of the century stories by romantic novelists were soon all-important at one social level, and their numbers increased during the next century for soon many more people, including women of all classes, could read and it was essential to keep the circulating libraries supplied with books. In fairness, it must be said that the qualities of these stories was variable, some being earnestly educational and some unashamedly tearful.

The nineteenth century in Britain belonged, in literature, to novelists and poets; the list of major novelists included the names of Scott, Dickens, Thackeray, Trollope and Hardy, to select just a few from the many well-known authors. One of those was the popular Mark Twain who in 1884 mentioned Jane Shore in *The Adventures of Huckleberry Finn* as though she were a household name, as in fact she had been to many, including

Lord Byron, earlier in the century. As he gave his friend Jim some off-the-cuff, near-surrealist education Huck informed him that 'all kings is rapscallions' and ready to be rough and tough, especially where women were concerned. As for Henry VIII, he 'was a blossom,' he used to 'marry a new wife every day and chop off her head next morning. And he would do it just as indifferent as if he was ordering up eggs. "Fetch up Nell Gwynn," he says. They fetch her up. Next morning, "Chop off her head!" And they chop it off. "Fetch up Jane Shore," he says; and up she comes. Next morning, "Chop off her head" – and they chop it off.' 'Fair Rosamun' also received the same treatment. 'And he made every one of them tell him a tale every night; and kept that up till he had hogged a thousand and one tales that way, and then he put them all in a book, and called it Domesday Book – which was a good name and stated the case.' In his cheerful, garbled history lesson (Chapter 23 in the novel) Mark Twain seems to have remembered both the Queen of Hearts in *Alice's Adventures in Wonderland* and the story-telling talent of Scheherazade: the mention of Jane is unexpected, disconcerting but good fun in this comical if alarming context: it proves also that her name was not forgotten.

There was so much reading to be done, and all the novels were long, so it seems possible that many people were left with little time to go to the theatre. But various plays from the previous century were still popular, including Rowe's *Tragedy of Jane Shore* – which had travelled far by now – and audiences were delighted when they could see revivals of cheerful and witty comedies by Sheridan and his contemporaries, but these were not nineteenth-century names. Most talent for writing, apart from poetry, had been absorbed into fiction and as a result it is not easy to find enduring names among the playwrights of the century. Dion Boucicault (*c.* 1820–90) had a splendid name which belied his Irish origins. After attending London University he became an actor for a time in London and then took to writing plays. He was nothing if not inventive in the theatre, developing a form of melodrama which depended on amazing stage effects such as a house burning down or a Mississippi steamboat exploding. He also wrote plays with Irish titles and themes, which lasted fairly well and were even revived in Dublin and London in the 1960s.

He was not an isolated case, having succeeded in developing the late Victorian taste for melodrama, and some audiences could never have enough. It seemed essential in fact to watch a melodrama rather than read it, for melodrama was intended for direct response in the theatre itself. It was a contemporary of Boucicault, William Gorman Wills (1828–91), another Irishman, who soon achieved immense success with melodrama and became something of a theatrical character himself.

When Wills first moved to London he exercised a different talent, also in the visual field: he painted portraits, and although he tended to be absentminded and often forgot his appointments he was surprisingly successful. He also worked in journalism but then, noticing the public taste for melodrama began to write it, and for subject matter he preferred history, mainstream history with characters well known to the general public. If Shakespeare had been ready to adjust history to suit his plans for drama, Wills merely disregarded it. The twentieth-century critic George Sampson said of him that having chosen to write about a well-known villain – and no melodrama could exist without one – Wills became 'almost farcical in the intensity of this villainy'. His Cromwell in *Charles I* (1872) and John Knox in *Mary Stewart* (1874) belonged to this category, but it should not be forgotten that brilliant actors such as Sir Henry Irving often excelled in bad plays, minimising the importance of the text and enabling audiences to forget the dramatist: only the actor mattered.

It was not difficult for Wills to choose Richard III as the villainous hero of his play *Jane Shore, An entirely New and Original Drama*: he was an obvious choice. In 1876 the work was produced at the Amphitheatre in Leeds, then in other provincial theatres and finally at the Princess Theatre, London, in 1876. Wills was lucky, as there had been a gap in the theatre's programme and his play was chosen to fill it, surprising everyone by its success, which earned it a long run. Sir Robert Birley, writing in *Etoniana* of 4 June 1972, gave extracts from this supposed Jane Shore story, which he had courageously read. The resulting melodrama was grotesque, although it attempted to tell the story of Jane and the good works she carried out to help the poor, earning of course the anger of King Richard. It falls to Jane to break the bad news to the widowed queen that her sons are dead, and the two women weep together, although the queen had earlier told Jane to leave the palace at once following the king's death.

Jane returns to what had been her home with Shore, but finds he is far from welcoming. He tells her, 'I loathe thy sin.' She wants to see her son but is told the 'child' is dead. The author's sense of time was non-existent, for since Jane had left home some thirteen years earlier this son would no longer be a little boy, but evidently that problem did not concern Wills. Shore relents and produces the 'child' for his repentant wife to see.

Richard of course, the arch-villain, orders Jane's penance and tries to seduce her. By the start of the last act snow has fallen in London, and as Jane begs for food the king and his attendants abandon her in the wintry street. Since this was a melodrama there had to be several crowd scenes, which Wills readily supplied, and when Grist the baker (a well-chosen name) tries to give Jane some bread a rough mob attacks him. Then Shore arrives, rescues Grist and Jane too, for he has obviously had a change of heart.

The play ends with a touching reconciliation between the deserted husband and the erring wife who is now dying in the snow. In reality of course nothing could have been further from the truth, for Shore went abroad after his divorce and there was no reconciliation, but the audience had to have their happy ending and this barely historical melodrama was a great success. Freeman Wills Croft, the author's brother, denied later that the eighteenth-century tragedy by Nicholas Rowe had influenced the composition in any way because he believed this earlier work had no value as a play. The author of *The Witchery of Jane Shore*, C.J.S. Thompson, thought the same about Wills' work and in support of his own findings quoted an anonymous critic of the time: 'it was rendered a success by means of a snow scene, but it was a tedious and inartistic play.'[2] That snow scene, invented to emphasise total and utter desolation, which presumably made the audience tearful, was to survive in at least one early film. Yet it has to be said that however much fashions changed, from poetry to tragedy, to fiction, melodrama and beyond, Jane's story was never forgotten; she may have deserted her husband but she tried to make amends by helping the poor; when her lover, the king, died nobody was ready to help her; but then, after her own death, she was to acquire a kind of immortality through the varied creative imagination of poets, dramatists and also, importantly in its way, through the writers of melodramatic entertainment for the masses.

During the nineteenth century women novelists did not follow Mrs Bennett with more stories about Jane. Nobody saw her at that stage as a feminist or even a feminine icon, although the forward-looking Mary

Wollstonecraft had brought out her *Vindication of the Rights of Women* as far back as 1795. Most of Jane's memorable reappearances have not been in fiction for the word implies something fabricated or made up. If there are insufficient recorded facts for telling the story of Jane's life in its entirety, facts themselves cannot be invented, and if invention is thought to be essential it must be imaginative, something best left to poets and dramatists who do not pretend to be telling hard truth; their role has always been that of interpretation, a kind of gloss, explanation, even a forecast. A good novelist can be imaginative and interpretative, obviously, but they are rare.

The next hundred years brought a great deal of social change, most of it forward-looking, and if by 1900 women did not all choose their own husband or make a romantic marriage, often for various reasons many could not marry the man of their choice. Against this changing background playwrights and novelists no longer found it essential to write about these emotional agonies in the same way as their predecessors, for clear-cut Christian morality no longer dominated the scene.

However, very late in the nineteenth century, but more importantly in the next, came a new and influential medium, cinema, bringing further change to the social scene and the moral climate.

FOURTEEN

The Image of Jane Shore

With the coming of cinema the visual sense began to dominate the entertainment world. It needed less effort than reading and it was soon cheaper to go to the cinema than to the theatre. Figures from the past came out of the history books and could now be presented against wider and moving décor, while royal personages, famous and infamous, heroes and villains were suddenly more popular than ever. Women of course had to be glamorous. The story of Jane Shore led to four early films about her, the first in 1908 and the last of them in 1922, with Sybil Thorndike in the part of the heroine. After a long gap Jane appeared again, played by Sandra Knight in a second version of *The Tower of London* in 1962.

The film of 1915, known in England as *Jane Shore* and in the United States as *The Strife Eternal* is memorable through the sheer complicated horror of the screenplay, which was credited to both Rowe and Wills. Rowe would certainly not have recognised it as having been partly inspired by his work but the garbled story would have suited Wills through its total disregard of history and biography. For good measure there are two Shore brothers, William and Matthew, there is treachery, jealousy and every melodramatic incident possible. The Duke of Gloucester tries to bribe Jane into sex by saying that if she refuses him her husband will be killed. When King Edward is dying he asks Hastings to look after Jane. They are to get married but the wedding ceremony is interrupted by Gloucester's order for Hastings' arrest. Then Jane is arrested too, for witchcraft, this event being overtaken by a snowstorm, the episode invented earlier by Wills in his melodrama and found by his audiences to be deeply impressive. Matthew finds Jane in the snow (of course) and they are to be reconciled, presumably, which seems to be the end; but in fact the film is not complete. A detailed and well-illustrated booklet presenting the whole drama was produced for publicity reasons and fortunately a copy has been preserved in the Bodleian Library; it expresses the atmosphere of the film with all its muddled history and inventions. It is unfair to say that it saves the trouble of watching the film but it is helpful to anyone who feels overwhelmed by the complications of the plot. Only film historians would recognise any names in the cast list, but the film, produced by Barker Motion Photography, obviously combined some vague hints of the true story with the added attraction of swashbuckling excitement and a heavy dash of romantic melodrama.

As the visual sense developed in all spheres and film-making became an essential part of the cultural scene, the inevitable question was asked about Jane as about any heroine from history: what did she really look like? Jane was always one of the most mysterious of royal mistresses and now designers hoped to find a reliable image of her somewhere. But where? Searching through history for clues to her appearance still remains a confusing and disappointing task. In the Middle Ages the art of portraiture was not highly developed in England and had still to catch up with the Italian and French painters, while Holbein did not come to London until 1526. However, it was usual for a royal personage to be painted, often in connection with diplomatic marriage arrangements, and the same was true of certain aristocrats. As mentioned earlier, the handsome King Edward IV is only remembered in painting through disappointingly boring work, although the anonymous painter of the portrait in the Royal Collection seems to have been tolerably interested in portraying the king's decorative clothes. Edward's wife, Queen Elizabeth Woodville, known to be beautiful, fared much better, fortunately for her. Nobody would have troubled to produce portraits of Edward's many mistresses, for none of these ladies lasted long enough. The so-called authentic portrayals of Jane, who lasted about thirteen years at the king's side until his death, never seeking publicity, seem to have been completed long after her youth or even after her death; most of them were imaginary or unfortunately lost. Even her colouring remains mysterious: the poet Michael Drayton referred to her hair as 'dark yellow', while her eyes were grey. Over the centuries her eyes were sometimes blue, her hair was occasionally black but most of the time it remained safely blonde. This was almost inevitable, and in the seventeenth century Robert Burton, in his analysis of beauty as one cause of 'Love-Melancholy', emphasised, with many examples from the classical world, the irresistible power of fair hair, among gods, heroes and women. More, in his description of Jane, does not mention details of this kind, being preoccupied with her character, not her physical appearance, but he did indicate that she could have been a little taller.

As the name of Jane Shore became famous or infamous during the late fifteenth century and later, many engravings were made, perhaps from sketches or lost portraits, but they may not have had much relation to truth. The Archive Collection in London's National Portrait Gallery includes many attractive images of Jane, some with attributions or references, most without. Some became well known through constant reproduction, especially the early portrayal of her penance by Edward Scriven, based on a painting by Walter Stevens Lethbridge, in which she casts her eyes up to heaven as though yearning pathetically for forgiveness.

In this context nothing can equal the drawing made by William Blake in 1778 when he was a young man of twenty-one. The figures of Jane and those accompanying her are all strategically placed, while the draping of the penitential sheet that she wears over her 'kirtle', a shift or petticoat, seems to follow the rhythm of her walk. Blake never made any direct or detailed reference to this work, not even in his notes to the catalogue of his 1809 exhibition, where it is given as Number XVI, the last in his list of drawings. He presumably regarded it as one of his 'Historical Inventions' and uses its inclusion to make a point that he regarded as important: 'This Drawing was done about Thirty Years ago, and proves to the Author, and he thinks will prove to any discerning eye, that the productions of our youth and of our maturer age are equal in all essential points.' Blake had obviously been attracted to this moment in Jane's life by her lonely, dignified independence: she had broken the rules of middle-class Christian morality, been deserted by friends and punished severely, all of which surely explains why he chose to perpetuate her memory: she was the kind of character who interested him. It is the most memorable of all the imaginary and imaginative portrayals of Jane, although it does not pretend to be a likeness; in his poem 'Jerusalem, Part II', Blake had written one line that could be relevant to the way he saw her: 'Every Harlot was once a virgin: every Criminal an Infant Love.' The work illustrating Jane's penance is now in the Tate Britain Gallery in London.

For at least two centuries after Jane's death the engravers were certainly busy, reproducing portraits of her by successful artists such as Lethbridge and Scriven. Blake disapproved (could he have been envious?) of his successful contemporary, the Italian-born Francesco Bartolozzi, who was responsible for many attractive images of Jane. The Archive Collection of the National Portrait Gallery includes work by him and by many unknown engravers reproducing equally unknown paintings or sketches, most of them reasonably attractive.

These portraits, all created after Jane's youth and even after her death, include one of Jane apparently defending herself against an accusation of witchcraft at a court held in the Tower of London, ordered or at least threatened by Richard III, of which there seems to be no record: possibly it never took place. The image shows Jane wearing a dashing hat with a brim, enhanced by jewellery and a white plume, clad in smart clothes which look much more Elizabethan than medieval. If any such trial took place – and the print concerned is wrongly dated 1482, before Edward's death, in fact – Jane would surely have escaped any trouble because she looks so confident and dignified. It has been assumed that Richard III ordered her penance because in the end there was no reliable proof that Jane and Edward's widowed queen had together used witchcraft to bring about his withered arm: everyone knew that it had always been in that condition.

There are many more of these unsourced reproductions which can only supply a partial answer to the question, What did Jane look like? A few paintings exist which are as controversial as almost everything else about this mysterious woman, and none more so than the anonymous works preserved at Eton College and Queens' College, Cambridge, assumed to have been acquired by both establishments because she is said to have dissuaded Edward IV from any action he might have taken against them. Few welcome remarks have ever been made about these portraits although one was cited in an early tourist account (1818) of 'England, Wales & Scotland'. The apparently learned author, Thomas Welford, Esq FSA, FLS, refers to Eton College as 'a beautiful building near Windsor. In the Provost's apartments is a portrait of Jane Shore upon a panel, supposed an original'. This terse sentence is all this long-forgotten writer has to say about Eton, leading Nicolas Barker, who quoted it in *Etoniana*, 2 December 1972, to add 'surely the strangest description of the College ever written'.[1]

The so-called 'learned author' was presumably referring to the best-known portrait of Jane accessible today which was included in the 2004 edition of the *Dictionary of National Biography* accompanying the relevant entry. Undoubtedly the artist could not have known much about her appearance or character, for her expression is sour: one cannot imagine that Jane ever looked like that. However, efforts had been made to give her the fashionable look favoured in her time, with her forehead made higher by shaving her hair at the front, a treatment that can be seen in other contemporary portraits of women. The unknown artist had given her a small pursed mouth and omitted any possible sign of charm from her expression. The jewellery, an important part of the portrait, appears also in the portrait at Queens' College, Cambridge, and in several engravings: two rows of pearls high up, close to the neck, while below them is a heavy necklace set with jewels and carrying a pendant which hangs slightly above the high-placed, youthfully firm bare breasts. Far preferable is the engraving by Bartolozzi, who may well have set aside some reality for the sake of charm: the jewellery is the same as in many other likenesses, but there are extra jewels in her hair and there is even a hint of a smile on a young and pretty face.

The view among art experts today is that the paintings at Eton and Cambridge have little to do with Jane as she was in reality; they are thought to be at the most copies, possibly of some earlier likenesses but made to look like the fashionable portraits from the sixteenth-century School of Fontainebleau showing Diane de Poitiers, mistress of Henri II of France. Perhaps this is correct, for the high forehead, the jewellery and the bare breasts are common to both the English and French portraits, even if Diane looks sexily attractive and Jane does not. Perhaps however it took the Italian Bartolozzi to remember that Jane had once been a beautiful and attractive young woman. In the seventeenth century Nell Gwynn was luckier, being painted by Sir Peter Lely, although it must be admitted that many of his women sitters look very much like each other.

During the early nineteenth-century Romantic period in France, English subjects were popular with dramatists and also apparently with some painters. Eugène Delacroix painted an imaginary portrait of Jane, said to be now in private ownership in Switzerland, according to information received from Geoffrey Wheeler.

So what was the reality of Jane's appearance? Was it that reality of remembered beauty described by Keats in a letter to his friend Benjamin Baily dated 22 November 1817: 'What the imagination seizes as beauty must be truth, whether it existed before or not'? It has to be imagined also from what is known of her life, her character and how others reacted to her. In 1933 C.J.S. Thompson divided his description of her existence into two parts – *Jane Shore in History and Romance* and *Jane Shore in Poetry and Drama*. He also included portraits and engravings of Jane, few of them reliable and none of them attractive. Forty years later, in 1972, Nicolas Barker published his groundbreaking discoveries in *Etoniana*, with detailed references to all his sources, while Sir Robert Birley, formerly Head Master of Eton, contributed *Jane Shore in Literature*, followed by *Some Further Appearances*, admitting the danger of using the word 'final'. In December 1981 Professor James Lowell Harner listed in *Notes and Queries* some seventy-seven items of literature relevant to Jane, including ballads and chapbooks, poems and dramas of many kinds, some perhaps close to history, some merely revisions of known texts and some clearly invented. He also added novels based on her story, details of the early films, together with articles in academic journals and several relevant PhD dissertations. He added for 1972 his own unpublished PhD dissertation: 'Jane Shore: A Biography of a Theme in Renaissance Literature'. All these details build up the elements for a life and understanding of the mysterious Jane, but there can never be a gallery of authentic portraits representing her fabled beauty.

Taking a further look back, the great actresses of the eighteenth century no doubt after some professional advice brought Jane a new lease of life, and transmitted their version of what she had possibly looked like and how she might have dressed, although actors and actresses preferred on the whole to appear in the clothes of their own era. Fortunately prints of Mrs Oldfield, Sarah Siddons, Mary Ann Yates and others as they took part in Rowe's successful play about Jane can all be seen in the National Portrait Gallery and some at the Victoria and Albert Museum in London. They cannot be regarded as portraits of Jane, but they represent something of her personality and the ambiance about her that remained mysterious and intrigued the theatre audiences. They seem to prove the validity of the proverb: 'Seeing's believing, but feeling's the truth'. Those who drew these representations of Jane, either from real life, based on their own theatre experience, from memory or from imagination and hearsay, transmitted something about her which has to be accepted even centuries after her death, for there is no other way of knowing at least something about her presence. In the end it is only possible to be aware of her essence from what the poets and dramatists wrote about her, whether they admired or criticised her.

Such has been the curiosity about Jane that she was even introduced into various twentieth-century films and television productions of *Richard III*. Shakespeare did not include her in his tragedy and merely allowed some of his characters to make cynical or disapproving remarks about her; he may have distrusted the rumours that she worked secretly, surprisingly no doubt, with Queen Elizabeth Woodville by taking messages to Hastings before Richard was declared king. Perhaps Shakespeare did not care for a woman who had been condemned as a harlot, but she was undeniably present in the background to the play, undeniably also as anathema to Richard. In any case the decisions by some recent producers that Jane should be visible, silent and smiling, were little more than an experiment that is not likely to be repeated.

In the early chapbooks the resourceful but forcibly economical editors and printers often needed illustrations of Jane, and, as mentioned earlier, they often used whatever images were available, notably those of Queen Elizabeth I. Occasionally they included crude drawings of Jane dressed in a penitent's robe. Presumably these images must have convinced the uneducated readers that the figure did somehow actually represent Jane. This seems to have been Jane's fate – one can never see her as she truly was, one has to accept some degree of approximation. Even in the twentieth century people in the city of London wanted to remember Jane and see an image of her if they possibly could. The directors of Barclays Bank, convinced, as were many other Londoners, that she had often walked down Lombard Street, where their head office was situated, commissioned from the sculptor Alan Gourley a series of curved metal panels representing early scenes of city life. They were erected in the entrance hall at 54 Lombard Street, their head office until May 2005, and included make-believe scenes from Jane's life. A few well-known lines from Shakespeare's *Richard III* were added: 'Shore's wife hath a pretty foot and cherry lip,

A bonny eye, a passing pleasing tongue'. The panels were moved to 33 Old Broad Street during redesign work and finally put into storage.

Occasionally tantalising references to portraits of Jane are found in unexpected places, but in the end the portraits themselves have always vanished. For instance in 1868 the National Gazetteer of Great Britain and Ireland mentioned 'Southam-with-Brockhampton, a hamlet in the parish of Bishop's Cleeve, hundred of Cleeve, count Gloucester, 2 miles N.E. of Cheltenham. It is situated near Cleeve Cliff, and its principal attraction is Southam House, built by Sir J. Huddlestone in Henry VII's time. The interior contains relics of great antiquity, with portraits of Jane Shore, Edward VI., &c'. (Did the editor mean Edward IV?)

The two villages are now linked together as Southam and the old house has become a luxury hotel. The newly refurbished bedrooms 'are named after the Kings and Queens of England and other historic families'. Those who make use of the 'good function rooms and leisure facilities' can enjoy views over Cheltenham racecourse but they will not see any portrait of Jane, which must have disappeared a long time ago. Perhaps there is a bedroom named after Edward IV.

As an icon, Jane nowadays represents not so much the wife who disobeyed the Church and the social rules of her time by deserting her husband and going to the arms of a lover, for this happens every day now and if it is sad, it is no longer shocking; Jane is still relevant because she represents a truly independent woman, a rare figure in the fifteenth century.

Her life was no average rags-to-riches story. Jane had not had a deprived childhood: there was no shortage of money in the Lambert household, but it was never wasted on useless things such as fashionable clothes for a teenage girl – they would come later, it was assumed, when she was a safely married woman. Shore was not a poor man, but his impotence may have meant that he did not know how to deal with an unsatisfied wife, and the result may have been a lack of generosity towards her. It is known that when she had escaped from the marriage she was particularly delighted with the 'gay apparel' she now possessed, and nearly all the engravings of her, plus the Eton portrait, show her wearing impressive jewellery. Her story is of great interest to all women, not only to feminists: she was an essentially feminine person who wanted a normal relationship with a normal man; through her flight from William Shore she was unconsciously trying to tell everyone that the arranged marriage could not necessarily work, it was a 'civil contract' indeed, a business arrangement, potentially unnatural and leading only to infidelity and unhappiness. It so happened that the man who became her long-term partner also happened to be king of England, hardly a 'normal' profession. Yet he himself had married for love, and despite lifelong political and social objections to his choice of queen, the marriage had been happy. Many royal mistresses who are remembered now were ambitious seekers after power and publicity, ready to grant favours to others provided they received due appreciation in return. They were nearly all insecure, the exceptions being Nell Gwynn and Dorothy Jordan, who were professional women; Jane herself was only partly secure, for the Lambert parents, people typical of their times, had brought her up with nothing more than marriage in view and therefore she could not have escaped unhappiness and poverty after the king's death. She accepted a second husband, for how else could she have supported herself?

Her formal education had been minimal, but then she presumably learnt fast, observed and listened as the years with Edward passed. By the time he died she would have developed into a person quite different from the unhappy teenage bride who had fled respectability: she had matured in all ways but now she was without support, a fact seized upon by Richard III, who realised how vulnerable she was. He took advantage of this, especially by removing Hastings from the scene as soon as he could, otherwise Hastings, although a married man, might even have become her regular lover. His wife could even have accepted the situation: most aristocratic wives did so. In the crisis time immediately after Edward's death Jane was alone, and that should not be forgotten. She did not spend much time lamenting her fate, even if the ballad-writers picked up that theme and developed it to the full. If Jane had learnt something about independence, she still had to accept a second marriage; there was no alternative for her, and she was not drawn to a repentant life in a convent. There seems to have been no other way of escape for a solitary woman in the late fifteenth century and there is no way of knowing the attitude of her parents, who may or may not have helped her.

The end of the twentieth century brought some reminders of what she had achieved when close to Edward IV. Earlier mentions had been scanty, none by Polydore Vergil or Dominic Mancini, while the editor of *The Great*

Chronicle of London ended his account of Edward IV's reign with a few disparaging lines about 'a woman named [blank] Shore' whose movable possessions were taken by the sheriff of London and she 'lastly as a common harlot was put to open pennance, for the life she led with the said Lord Hastings and other great estates'.[2] The editor, assumed to have been Robert Fabyan, had not troubled to add a Christian name, for 'Jane' had not been invented and he obviously knew no other. In the margin he added simply 'Uxor Shore'. These stern comments were ignored by the later poets and dramatists who saw Jane as their heroine, their icon, and the images they created, although obviously not visual, brought her to life.

In the twentieth century professional academic historians tended to mention Jane in a few terse sentences or footnotes. Understandably she did not interest them, for there is no evidence that she tried to intervene in affairs of state. However, a very different chronicler, Roy Strong, in his *Story of Britain*,[3] quoted again the words of More about Jane's skill in reconciling differences between the king and others, inevitable in any assessment of her persona. Queen Elizabeth Woodville had dutifully given her husband ten children while Jane, who had no royal bastards, was, accordingly to this author, 'hugely intelligent and attractive'; she had become the personal diplomat who somehow knew how to deal with the king's problems encountered while doing so much to bring administrative order to the country after the Wars of the Roses. Roy Strong implied that Edward deserved to escape the fate of being 'one of England's great forgotten kings', but he had hardly survived as a famous one. Just as Louis XV of France, four centuries later, is less remembered than his long-term mistress Madame de Pompadour, it has been Jane Shore's legendary 'life' in literature, and her reputation as 'the merriest' of Edward's mistresses, that have helped her king to survive among those who care about English royalty but are not themselves professional historians. In his survey Strong referred to no other royal mistresses, apart from a passing mention of Alice Perrers, and memorably described Jane as 'an influence for the good'.

It is only fair to remember this about Jane, and not to be overwhelmed by the more melancholy works of the earlier poets and dramatists who were moved by her situation but did not see all aspects of her personality. She was more than just one name in the long list of Edward's mistresses;

Drayton and Rowe in particular had realised this, for the former wrote about the potential boredom of middle-class married life and the latter promoted her into a heroine of the new 'domestic' tragedy, the 'she-tragedy', a term which he claimed to have invented. If Rowe's presentation of her had not been so impressive, with its barely mentioned overtones about the inequality of women, his play would not have travelled the world in the way it did. Although no clear image of Jane has survived showing us what she looked like or precisely what good works she performed, over many centuries the shadows have at least begun to fade, and if her real life may probably never move into the full glare of publicity – something she never wanted – Sir Thomas More's much-quoted phrase is still justified, 'for yet she liveth'.

ENVOI

Jane has not disappeared. During her lifetime she survived several contrasting periods of existence: a normal family background at first, despite the uncertainties of war, then a violent and risky breakaway to a completely changed life which brought several years of happiness; then a second violent break, a few surely happy years, then finally poverty and loneliness. She still remains mysterious. However, in the end she may have experienced something like peace. During her very last years she may have lived briefly close to her own family again in the countryside, for there is one place where unexpectedly an image, if not a portrait of her, can be seen, in the village of Hinxworth at the northern tip of Hertfordshire.

In the twenty-first century Hinxworth still possesses most features of the ideal English village: cottages and small houses with well-kept thatched roofs, a welcoming pub, also thatched, neat gardens, wild flowers in the hedges, surrounding lanes with well-maintained farms situated some way from the roads with their rows of trees, and notably the small, simple, beautifully maintained church of St Nicholas. It is approached through a short avenue of lime trees leading towards the large churchyard which includes just a few ancient lichened headstones and hardly any modern ones.

Some parts of the building date from the early fourteenth century and so when John Lambert decided to retire to this village in the late fifteenth century, he and his family would attend what was for them a fairly

modern church. It is known from his will that he had had a chapel in his
own house, which had been true of his city home in Silver Street and
presumably also of the house he bought in this village, possibly the grand
and well-preserved Hinxworth Place of today. It seems likely that if
members of his family came to stay, they might all have gone to St
Nicholas' church together, but in any case they are all together there now,
commemorated in a set of brasses affixed to their tomb, which is marked
by a large slab of marble in the floor of the chancel, a few feet from the
altar itself. This setting was described by the seventeenth-century
antiquary Henry Chauncy in *History of Antiquities in Hertfordshire*. The
brasses, ordered apparently by the eldest Lambert son John, show eight
figures in all, two large ones representing John Lambert and his wife Amy,
and beneath his figure a row of much smaller ones, led on the left by that
of a tall man, presumably the eldest son, John. Since John Lambert the
elder seems to have had only three sons, the fourth figure has been taken
to represent Jane's second husband, Thomas Lynam, John's son-in-law,
mentioned in his will. Opposite this row of men, beneath the figure of
Amy, is a tall female figure wearing the married woman's headdress,
assumed to be Jane. Behind her is one small figure thought to represent
her little daughter, Julian Lynam, also mentioned in her grandfather's will;
when he died, in 1487, she would have been about three years old. This is
the only record of her that has survived, for she may have died young. In
addition to the figures, the marble slab is embellished with various coats
of arms and the individual merchant's mark originally used by John
Lambert. The link between the Lambert-Lynam family and the Hinxworth
church was discovered, like so much else in this story, by Nicolas Barker
whose research is described in *Etoniana* in 1972,[4] enhanced by reproductions of the brasses on the tomb, including one set out in diagram-
matic form.

Inevitably, over the centuries, the brasses were damaged as members of
the congregation walked over them when they came to the altar rail to take
communion. In the end a carpet was laid down covering the tomb and on
its underside there is a plea for it to be replaced neatly 'over the lady',
presumably the large figure of Amy Lambert. Some time ago the church
representatives asked the Mercers' Company in the city if they could help
with the expense of transferring the brasses to the wall, where they would

escape damage; but it was decided in the end to leave them in the chancel beneath their protective carpet, for otherwise these valuable artefacts might have been stolen. However, when a new cloth was recently added to the altar the small carved diagram on the tomb which represented the Lambert merchant's mark was embroidered on to it, along with other motifs from the church decoration. Copies of the brasses have apparently been placed in the Barbican Centre in the city of London.

So if Jane herself had been no saint, and no early writer seems to have noticed that she showed any obvious signs of devotion, visitors to the church can examine the brasses and read a short account of her life prepared by the Church Recorder in a contribution to The North Hertfordshire Decorative and Fine Arts Society Newsletter of 2003. The date of her death may remain uncertain but her memory has been preserved in an essentially peaceful place where for once tranquility surrounds her. She will be remembered for ever in this quiet village. It may have been the scene of family reunion, and the tomb in St Nicholas' church is a moving memorial that shows how even a once-broken family can be reunited in death and then remembered. As George Eliot wrote in *Adam Bede*: 'our dead are never dead to us until we have forgotten them'.

By a coincidence the dramatist, Nicholas Rowe, remembered for his drama *The Tragedy of Jane Shore*, produced in 1714, was born at his maternal grandfather's house in the village of Little Barford, Bedfordshire in 1674, about 20 miles away. It seems unlikely that he ever knew of Jane's memorial in Hinxworth. Neither would he ever have known that after the later success of his play, his heroine would be remembered, after more centuries had passed, in such contrasting works as early films and academic theses in Germany and the United States.

Soon after her death Jane had been remembered differently, especially in popular ballads and that tradition has never been lost, for in 1954 the Irish poet, Donald MacDonagh wrote what may be the last ballad ever composed about her, 'The Ballad of Jane Shore'.[5] It takes the reader back to her early days in the city of London, along with remembrances of Sir Thomas More's description of her. Some details are out of date but the fact that they belong in the end to legend rather than to history is an essential part of Jane's story – after all, some seven centuries have passed since she was close to an English king:

As she went down through Lombard Street
To make her open penitence
Her cheeks that never blushed before
Were warm in her defence.

A linen skirt her only dress
All London stopped and wondering
A taper in the little hand
That once had held a king.

Bare to the waist, as though she rose
From the reluctant, amorous sea,
Raindrops were pearls that garlanded
Her hair's pale filigree.

Her body, white as waxen taper
Crowned at the head with golden light,
Had ripened in a shop of gold
To be a queen by night;

And she was young and womanly,
None saw her without love or pity,
Now stripped, who lived for gay apparel,
Now shamefaced, who was witty.

Proper she was and fair of body.
A grey eye merry, a slender figure,
An ankle that a man might span
Between a thumb and finger;

And she had been the king's gay love
Who now must beg forsakenly
From those that would be beggars still
But for her charity;

> But love that's light – once lovers die
> Is as a blade that courts the rust:
> The evil deed men write in marble,
> The comely one in dust.

So poets, dramatists and film-makers have all remembered Jane. The story of her independent behaviour, her sufferings and struggles after Edward IV's death impressed them, for women, and men too, could learn from her. Women of later centuries, and not only feminists, continue to discover unexpected heroines in history and legend from all times and locations. Among these half-mysterious figures Jane has not been forgotten. In the end that prophetic line by Anthony Chute in the last stanza of his poem 'Beauty Dishonoured or Shore's Wife' has proved especially far-sighted:

> Her body went to death; her fame to life.

APPENDIX I

Claims to the English Throne by Lancastrians and Yorkists

The origins of these rival claims to the English throne date back to Edward III, who reigned for fifty years from 1327 to 1377 and had five sons. The most outstanding of these were his eldest son, the Black Prince, father of Richard II, and the third son, John of Gaunt (named after Ghent, where he was born). The latter's first and second wives, Blanche of Lancaster and Constance of Castile, brought him land and riches, and by 1390 he was Duke of Aquitaine. After he had become a widower for the second time he married in 1396 his long-term mistress Katherine Swynford, and his three sons by her were legitimised, although they were later barred from inheriting the throne. By his first wife, Blanche, he had a son, Henry IV, who was followed by his own son Henry V. The latter's son, Henry VI, became king in 1422, before he was two years old, continuing the Lancastrian line, but he had no heir until 1453.

Shortly before this event Henry VI suffered his first attack of mental illness and Richard, Duke of York was appointed Protector, which gave him the confidence to put forward his own claim to the throne. He had not yet made this public but he was known to be highly ambitious and was soon suspected of planning hostility towards Henry VI. York was in a strong position: his own father, son of Edward III's fourth son, Edmund, Duke of York, had married Anne Mortimer, herself a direct descendant of Edward III's second son, the Duke of Clarence. This meant that *both* the Duke of York's parents could claim direct descent from Edward III, while the current king, Henry VI, could not. Henry V's widow, Katherine de Valois had married a second time, although this cannot be proved, and in any case this widow had been a French princess. (However, Katherine's second 'marriage' produced a son, Edmund Tudor, whose own son, known as the Duke of Richmond, eventually became Henry VII.)

Appendix I

In 1450 the rebel Jack Cade added the name 'Mortimer' to his own for he supported the Duke of York's claim and hoped to win support for himself in return.

The Duke of York's double descent from Edward III meant that his claim was sound, but the birth of Henry VI's son in 1453 changed the picture. Henry VI had a second attack of mental illness but recovered quickly, and now that York was no longer Protector, there was an attempt at reconciliation and a compromise decision: York was eventually to inherit the throne but not until after the death of Henry VI. However it was obvious, especially to his Queen Margaret, that the rights of Henry's son Edward, Prince of Wales, could not be set aside and the reconciliation plan came to nothing. Fighting between the supporters of Lancaster and York then broke out in September 1459 with the inconclusive battle of Blore Heath, and soon York became more aggressive, marched on London and defeated the Lancastrians at the battle of Northampton in July 1460. Five months after that, in December, when York himself was killed at the battle of Wakefield, his eldest son Edward assumed that he had inherited the claim to the throne and took charge of the Yorkist troops. He was crowned Edward IV in 1461.

However, there were still supporters for the Lancastrian claim, including the Earl of Warwick, who gradually became convinced over the next few years that his achievements had not been fully rewarded. By 1470 he had gathered sufficient supporters round him to drive Edward into exile, and the Lancastrians were so convinced of their success that Henry VI was once more crowned king. But Edward's exile lasted only a few months. Warwick was defeated and killed and Henry VI imprisoned and killed too, as described in Chapter Five.

Even these events did not end Lancastrian claims. The marriage in 1485 of the Duke of Richmond to Princess Elizabeth, the eldest daughter of Edward IV, was a convenient reconciliation arrangement and the duke became Henry VII. His reign however was uneasy, and the king had to deal with two claimants to the throne: early in 1486 a baker's son, the young Lambert Simnel, masquerading as the young Earl of Warwick who had escaped from the Tower, invaded England through Cornwall, after first achieving support in Ireland and hoping to seize the throne as Edward VI. He was soon defeated and then pardoned.

In 1491 Perkin Warbeck attempted a claim but was less successful in the end, after a promising start. This Belgian boy had claimed to be Edward IV's younger son, Richard Duke of York, who had escaped from the Tower. He too was well received in Europe and in Ireland, and also in Scotland. However, when he attempted invasion through Scotland he was eventually defeated, tried and imprisoned. He then tried to escape and Henry VII ordered that he should be hanged. This was 1499: fourteen years had passed since Richard III, the last Yorkist king, had been defeated by the future Henry VII at Bosworth Field.

APPENDIX II

Public Penance

In early centuries public penance was ordered by the Church in cases where no form of secular punishment was considered appropriate. It had been first instituted by the Church of Rome, and according to the *Shorter Oxford Dictionary* is defined as 'The sacred ordinance in which remission of sins is received by a penitent through the absolution of a priest, the necessary parts being contrition, confession, satisfaction and absolution.' Richard III decided on this punishment for Jane Shore after he had failed to subdue her through allegations of witchcraft and for concealing the whereabouts of the Marquess of Dorset, a Woodville and therefore an enemy. Immorality in women was a charge seen to be deserving of penance in public, mere confession in a church not being regarded as punishment enough. As for Jane Shore, Richard had a strong case, for her life with Edward IV, Lord Hastings and possibly the Marquess of Dorset would surely be public knowledge, and she was charged with harlotry. Her short walk through the city streets ended in St Paul's church, where according to old engravings the priests who had accompanied her were still by her side, so that the conditions of the 'sacred ordinance' were presumably met.

Richard knew that he could not order this punishment himself, but had to ask the Bishop of London to arrange it. In the past there had been one outstanding case of public penance when no other form of suitable punishment could be instituted. This occurred in the twelfth century after Henry II had angrily arranged the murder of the man he called 'this turbulent priest', Thomas à Becket, Archbishop of Canterbury. The Church insisted that the king must be punished, and since no secular punishment could be ordered it was decided that the king himself must carry out this penance, which he did close to Becket's tomb in Canterbury Cathedral in 1174.

One other memorable case occurred much later, not long in fact before Jane Shore had been born. This was the punishment of Eleanor, Duchess of

Gloucester, who had been accused of witchcraft in her attempt to help her husband Duke Humphrey move closer to the throne, perhaps ultimately to occupy it. She denied the charge and maintained that any witchcraft she had carried out was due to her efforts to conceive a child. Nobody believed her, and she was sentenced to public penance which involved being forced to walk to a church, clad only in a white sheet, an incident which Shakespeare included in *Henry VI*, Part II. She also had to carry a burning taper in her hand. Women of the middle and upper classes could not easily be punished otherwise, but those of the working class, including the infamous Margery Jourdemayne, who were seen as guilty of witchcraft, were burnt at the stake.

The end of the Middle Ages did not mean the end of public penance, but if it became less dramatic it seems to have been imposed frequently; so much so that the churchwardens' accounts for Wakefield Cathedral recorded the loans of sheets for both women and men 'to do penance in', at a usual cost of six pence. Penance of this kind was demanded mainly for 'immorality, cheating, defamation of character, disregard of the Sabbath and other transgressions'. In 1534 the vicar of a Hull church was punished for preaching a 'heretical' sermon. He had to walk round the church on a Sunday, 'clad only in his shirt, barefooted and carrying a large faggot in his hand'.

Perhaps the dramatic aspect of the punishment helped to maintain the custom, just as it had helped Jane Shore, who had been punished as a so-called 'harlot' but earned the sympathy of the spectators. In Scotland, in the nineteenth century, any wrongdoers were made to sit on a stool throughout a church service, wearing a black shawl over their head, while sometimes a man would suffer a public rebuke from the minister.

In twenty-first-century Britain public penance has been replaced by public apology, as for instance at the blessing for the marriage in 2005 of Prince Charles, heir to the throne, and the former Mrs Camilla Parker Bowles. The more dramatic aspect of public penance as known in the past has not been forgotten in the English language, as witness the still extant phrase 'to stand in a white sheet', implying guilt, regret and apology.

APPENDIX III

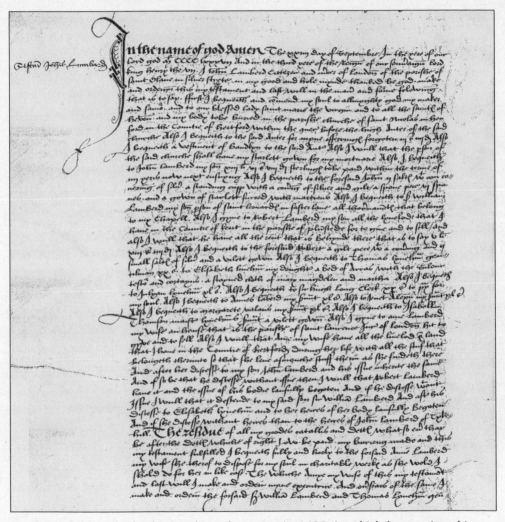

Part of the will of John Lambert, drawn up in 1485, in which he mentions his daughter Elizabeth Lynam, in line 23. *(The National Archives, Kew)*

Notes and Sources

PART ONE

Essential material for the life of Jane Shore is contained in *Etoniana* No. 125 of 4 June 1972, pp. 383–91 and 408–14, the valuable research work of Nicolas Barker. The *Great Chronicle of London*, the 1938 edition of the *Chronicles of London*, in addition to many other chronicles published during the Elizabethan period, supplies detailed historical background but most of the latter group include passages taken directly from Sir Thomas More's *History of Richard III*. The best version of the latter, as mentioned in Chapter Eight, is that edited in 1976 by Richard S. Sylvester which formed part of the Yale edition of More's works but was published separately in 1976 along with some of the author's English and Latin poems.

The writings of two visitors to England, Polydore Vergil and Dominic Mancini, are important for their contemporary reactions to the people and events of the time, although neither include any reference to Jane Shore. Quotations from Hall's *Chronicle* are from the 1805 edition, based on that of 1548, edited by Richard Grafton and known in the original spelling as *The Union of the Two Noble and Illustre Famelies of Lancastre and Yorke*.

Two works by J.R. Lander, *The Wars of the Roses* (History in the Making series, 1965) and *Crown and Nobility* (1976), are useful, the former for its inclusion of many hard-to-access documents and the latter for its analysis of social conditions at the time. The biographies by Charles Ross of Edward IV (1974) and Richard III (1981) are valuable and so too is *The Wars of the Roses* (1995) by Desmond Seward, especially since the *Lives of Five Men and Women* that it describes includes that of Jane Shore, one of the five 'survivors' of the wars.

One: Early Days, Early Years

1. N. Barker, 'Jane Shore, Part I: The Real Jane Shore', *Etoniana*, No. 125, 4 June 1972, pp. 383–91.
2. Quoted by J.R. Lander, *The Wars of the Roses*, Secker & Warburg, 1965, p. 46.
3. G.L. Kittredge, *Witchcraft in Old and New England*, Harvard University Press, 1929, p. 177.
4. Lander, *Wars of the Roses*, p. 58.
5. *Ibid.*, p. 59.

189

6. The name refers to the order of canons regular founded by St Norbert in 1119 at Prémontré near Laon in the Aisne.

7. Hall's *Chronicle*, ed. R. Grafton, in *The Union of the Two Noble and Illustrious Families of Lancaster and York*, London, 1809, p. 223.

8. A.H. Burne, *Battlefields of England*, Penguin Classic Military History, 2002, p. 214.

9. Lander, *Wars of the Roses*, p. 42.

10. *Ibid.*, pp. 144–6, quoting *The Great Chronicle of London*.

11. *Ibid.*, p. 125.

12. Burne, *Battlefields*, p. 241.

Two: *Growing Up*

1. King Edward's collection of books was presented to the (then) British Museum by King George II and is now included among the Royal Manuscripts Collection of the British Library.

2. C. Barron and M. Davies, 'Ellen Langwith, silkwoman of London', *The Ricardian*, The Richard III Society, Vol. XIII, 2003, pp. 39–47.

3. From *Historical Poems of the XIVth and XVth Centuries*, ed. R.H. Robbins, New York, 1995.

4. P. Ackroyd, *London, the Biography*, Chatto & Windus, 2000, pp. 627–8.

5. R. Burton, *The Anatomy of Melancholy*, Everyman's Library, 1948, Vol. II, p. 2.

6. Professor J.L. Harner, in his 'The Wofull Lamentation of Mistris Jane Shore', *Papers of the Bibliographical Society of America*, Vol. 71, Second quarter, 1971, refers to a note by Allen B. Friedman in *The Ballad Revolution*, 1961, p. 108, quoting an editor who knew children 'who would never have learnt to read, had they not took a Delight in poring over *Jane Shore* or *Fair Rosamon*'.

7. Ackroyd, *London*, pp. 627–38.

Three: *Marriage is Destiny*

1. M.K. Jones, *Bosworth 1485: The Psychology of a Battle*, Tempus, 2003, pp. 65–8.

2. Hall's *Chronicle*, ed. R. Grafton, p. 264.

3. Jones, *Bosworth*, pp. 24, 65–71.

4. Hall's *Chronicle*, ed. R. Grafton, p. 264.

5. Sir Thomas More, *The History of King Richard III*, ed. R.S. Sylvester, Yale University Press, 1976, p. 65.

6. *Ibid.*, p. 66.

7. J. Ashdown-Hill, 'The Endowments of Lady Eleanor Talbot and of Elizabeth Talbot, Duchess of Norfolk, at Corpus Christi College Cambridge', *The Ricardian*, The Richard III Society, Vol. XIV, 2004, pp. 82–94.

8. J.R. Lander, 'Marriage and Politics', *Crown and Nobility 1450–1509*, Edward Arnold, 1976.

9. Kittredge, *Witchcraft*, pp. 84–5, 106–7.

10. D. Mancini, *The Usurpation of Richard III*, tr. C.A.J. Armstrong, Alan Sutton, 1984, p. 67.

Four: A Civil Contract

1. Sir John Selden's *Table Talk* was a collection of his *obiter dicta* published in 1689 after his death.
2. C.D. Ross, *Edward IV*, Eyre Methuen, 1975, pp. 248–9.
3. Sir Thomas More, *Utopia*, tr. and ed. P. Turner, Penguin Classics, 1965, pp. 83–5.
4. *Ibid.*, Notes, pp. xxiii–xxiv.
5. A. Hanham, 'The Stonors and Thomas Betson; Some Neglected Evidence', *The Ricardian*, Vol. XV, 2005, pp. 33–52.
6. Information from the Group Archives Unit, Barclays Bank plc.
7. A. Sutton, 'William Shore, Merchant of London and Derby', *Derbyshire Archaeological Journal*, 1986, Vol. 106, pp. 127–39.
8. J. Stow, *Survey of London*, intr. H.B. Wheatley, Everyman's Library, J.M. Dent & Sons, 1960, p. 339.
9. More, *History of Richard III*, p. 56.

Five: Marriage, Divorce and Love

1. Barron and Davies, 'Ellen Langwith', pp. 39–47.
2. D. Seward, *The Wars of the Roses and the Lives of Five Men and Women in the 15th Century*, Constable & Co., 1995, p. 240.
3. *Ibid.*, p. 251.
4. Sutton, 'William Shore', pp. 127–39.
5. More, *History of Richard III*, p. 49.
6. Barker, 'The Real Jane Shore', pp. 389–91.
7. P. de Commynes, *The Memoirs for the Reign of Louis XI, 1461–1483*, tr. M. Jones, Penguin, 1972, p. 184.
8. *Ibid.*, p. 188.
9. P.M. Kendall, *Richard the Third*, Allen & Unwin, 1956, p. 104.
10. Sir Robert Birley, 'Jane Shore, Part II: Jane Shore in Literature', *Etoniana*, No. 126, 2 December 1972, p. 406.
11. J.L. Harner, 'Jane Shore: A Biography of a Theme in Renaissance Literature' (unpublished dissertation), University of Illinois, 1972, pp. 15–16.
12. More, *History of Richard III*, p. 57.
13. *Ibid.*, p. 57.
14. Harner, 'Jane Shore: Biography', p. 30, referring to 'Love Melancholy' in the Third Partition of R. Burton, *The Anatomy of Melancholy*, Everyman's Library No. 888, 1948, Vol. 3, p. 108.
15. More, *History of Richard III*, p. 58.
16. C.D. Ross, *Richard III*, Eyre Methuen, 1981, p. xxix.

Six: Loss, Punishment and Penance

1. Mancini, *Usurpation*, p. 59.
2. *Ibid.*, p. 59.
3. Seward, *Wars of the Roses*, p. 258.
4. Kendall, *Richard the Third*, p. 125.
5. N. Barker, 'Jane Shore, Part III: Jane Shore and Eton', *Etoniana*, No. 126, 2 December 1972, pp. 408–10.
6. More, *History of Richard III*, p. 59.
7. C.J.S. Thompson, *The Witchery of Jane Shore*, Grayson & Grayson, 1933, pp. 148–9.
8. More, *op. cit.*, p. 50.
9. Kendall, *Richard the Third*, pp. 212–13.
10. Mancini, *Usurpation*, p. 61.
11. C. Lethbridge Kingsford, ed., *The Stonor Letters and Papers*, Camden Society, 1919, Vol. II, p. 161.
12. Stow, *Survey*, p. 37.
13. Ashdown-Hill, 'Endowments', pp. 82–94.
14. More, *History of Richard III*, pp. 55–6.

Seven: Last Years

1. Barker, 'The Real Jane Shore', pp. 390–1.
2. Ross, *Richard III*, pp. 137–8.
3. Barker, 'The Real Jane Shore', pp. 389–90.
4. Seward, *Wars of the Roses*, p. 369.
5. *Ibid.*, p. 379, quoting from the Goldsmiths' Company Minutes Book A, pp. 170–2.
6. *Ibid.*, p. 169.
7. Letter to the author from Professor Sir John Baker, 5 August 2004.
8. *Ibid.*
9. Seward, *Wars of the Roses*, p. 361.

PART TWO

Two crucial texts are to be consulted throughout Part Two: in *Etoniana*, 4 June 1972, No. 125, Sir Robert Birley wrote 'Jane Shore, Part II: Jane Shore in Literature', pp. 391–407, followed by 'Jane Shore: Some Further Appearances', in No. 128, 1973, pp. 448–57.

All material relevant to *A Mirror for Magistrates* is based on or quoted from the 1938 edition, edited by Lily B. Campbell, pub. Cambridge University Press.

The quotations from Michael Drayton's *Works* are from Volume II of the J. William Hebel edition of 1932.

Dr Samuel Johnson's essay on Nicholas Rowe is available in his *Lives of the English Poets*, Everyman's Library, Volume One.

The Witchery of Jane Shore, by C.J.S. Thompson (1933), and subtitled *The Romance of a Royal Mistress*, includes several hard-to-find texts, among them *Beauty Dishonoured* by Anthony Chute.

Dr J.L. Harner's unpublished dissertation of 1972, *Jane Shore: A Biography of a Theme in Renaissance Literature*, deals with the sixteenth century.

Eight: 'for yet she liveth'

1. *A Mirror for Magistrates*, ed. L.B. Campbell, Cambridge University Press, 1938.
2. Thompson, *Witchery*, pp. 190–215.
3. *Ibid.*, p. 215.
4. R.B. McKerrow, ed., *The Works of Thomas Nashe*, Oxford, 1904–1910, revd F.P. Wilson, 1958. Quoted by Samuel J. Pratt in 'Jane Shore and the Elizabethans, Some Facts and Speculations', *Texas Studies in Literature and Language*, Boston: Twayne, xi (1970), pp. 1293–1306.
5. Pratt, 'Jane Shore and the Elizabethans', p. 1300.
6. A.C. Sprague, ed., *Poems and A Defence of Rhyme*, Harvard University Press, 1930.

Nine: A Female Icon?

1. M. Drayton, *Works*, ed. J.W. Hebel, Basil Blackwell, 1932, Vol. II, pp. 247–51, 254–8.
2. Thomas Percy, *Reliques of Ancient English Poetry*, ed. H.B. Wheatley, George Allen & Unwin, 1927, Vol. II, pp. 267–8.
3. T. Heywood, *Dramatic Works*, ed. R.J. Shepherd, 1874, rep. New York: Russell & Russell, 1964.
4. R. Helgerson, *Adulterous Alliances*, University of Chicago Press, 2000, p. 56.

Ten: The Early Ballads of Mistress Shore

1. An early publication of Deloney's ballad was in the *Garland of Goodwill*, 'written by T.D.', 1631, later reprinted in the *Roxburghe Ballads* and other collections.
2. M.M. Scott, *Harlot or Heroine: Re-presenting 'Jane Shore'*, Ashgate, 2004, pp. 123, 125.

Eleven: More Ballads, New Chapbooks

1. The repeated references to 'Queen Fredrick' are obscure.
2. Jones, *Bosworth*, pp. 65–70.

Twelve: The 'She-Tragedy'

1. Dr Samuel Johnson, *Lives of the English Poets*, London, 1779–1781, Vol. I, pp. 320–1.
2. *Ibid.*, p. 320.
3. N. Rowe, *The Fair Penitent*, Act V, in *The Works of Nicholas Rowe*, London, 1792, pp. 200ff.

4. *Ibid.*, p. 208.
5. Dr Johnson, *Lives*, pp. 321–2.
6. *Ibid.*, pp. 321–2.
7. N. Rowe, *The Tragedy of Jane Shore*, in *The Works of Nicholas Rowe*, London, 1792, pp. 146–7.
8. Dr Johnson, *Lives*, p. 326.
9. J. Boaden, *Memoirs of Mrs Siddons*, London: Henry Colburn, 1827 (2 vols).

Thirteen: Facts, Fiction and Fantasy

1. G. Sampson, *The Concise Cambridge History of English Literature*, Cambridge University Press, 1970, p. 540.
2. Thompson, *Witchery*, p. 277.

Fourteen: The Image of Jane Shore

1. N. Barker, 'The Story of Jane Shore: A Postscript to Part I', *Etoniana*, No. 126, 2 December 1972, pp. 408–9.
2. Hall's *Chronicle*, ed. R. Grafton, p. 60.
3. R. Strong, *The Story of Britain: A People's History*, Pimlico, 1998, p. 140.
4. Barker, 'The Real Jane Shore', pp. 383ff.
5. D. MacDonagh, in anthology pub. Dublin: Dolmen Press, 1954, repr. in *A Warning to Conquerors*, Chester Springs, Pa: Dufour Editions, 1968, pp. 20–1.

Bibliography

Ackroyd, P., *London, the Biography*, Chatto & Windus, 2000

Austen, J., *Volume the Second*, ed. B.C. Southam, Oxford at the Clarendon Press, 1963

Baldwin, D., *Elizabeth Woodville, Mother of the Princes in the Tower*, Sutton, 2002

Barker, N., 'Jane Shore, Part I: The Real Jane Shore', *Etoniana* No. 125, 4 June 1972, pp. 383–91

——, 'Jane Shore, Part III: Jane Shore and Eton', *Etoniana* No. 126, 2 December 1972, pp. 408–10

——, 'The Story of Jane Shore: A Postscript to Part I', *Etoniana*, No. 126, 2 December 1972, pp. 410–14

Beith-Halahmi, E.Y., *Angell fayre or strumpet lewd: Jane Shore as an example of Erring Beauty in 16th Century Literature*, 2 vols. Institute for English Speech and Literature, University of Salzburg, 1974 (unrevised), Boston University, 1970

Birley, Sir Robert, 'Jane Shore, Part II: Jane Shore in Literature', *Etoniana*, Nos 125, 126, pp. 391–407

——, 'Jane Shore: Some Further Appearances', *Etoniana*, No. 128, pp. 448–57

Brown, R.D., 'A Talkative Wench . . .', *Review of English Studies*, New Series, Vol. 49 No. 196 (1998)

Burne, A.H., *The Battlefields of England*, Penguin, Classic Military History, 2002

Canfield, J.D., *Nicholas Rowe and Christian Tragedy*, Gainsville: The University Presses of Florida, 1977

Carlton, C., *Royal Mistresses*, London and New York: Routledge, 1990

Castor, H., *Blood & Roses, The Paston Family in the Fifteenth Century*, Faber & Faber, 2004

Collis, L., *The Apprentice Saint* (Biography of Margery Kempe), Michael Joseph, 1964

Commynes, P. de, *The Memoirs for the Reign of Louis XI, 1461–1483*, tr. M. Jones, Penguin, 1972

Drayton, M., *Works*, ed. J.W. Hebel *et al.*, Vol. II, Basil Blackwell, 1932

Given-Wilson, C. and Curteis, A., *The Royal Bastards of Medieval England*, Routledge, 1984

Great Chronicle of London, The, ed. A.H. Thomas and I.D. Thornley, London, 1938

Hall, E., *The Union of the Two Noble and Illustre Famelies of Lancastre & Yorke etc.*, ed. R. Grafton, London, 1548, reprinted 1809

Bibliography

Hanham, A., *Richard III and his Early Historians 1483–1535*, Oxford, Clarendon Press, 1975

Harner, J.L., 'Jane Shore: A Biography of a Theme in Renaissance Literature', 1972, University of Illinois at Urbana-Champaign. Unpublished dissertation

——, ed., *Samuel Daniel and Michael Drayton, A Reference Guide*, Boston, Mass., G.K. Hall & Co., 1980

——, 'Jane Shore in Literature: A Checklist', *Notes and Queries* 28 (December 1981), pp. 496–507

Harriss, G., *Shaping the Nation, England 1360–1461*, Oxford, Clarendon Press, 2005

Helgerson, R., *Adulterous Alliances: Home, State and History in Early Modern European Drama and Painting*, University of Chicago Press, 2000

Heywood, T., *Dramatic Works*, ed. R.J. Shepherd, 6 vols, 1874

Hole, C., *Witchcraft in England*, illus. Mervyn Peake, Batsford, 1945

Johnson, M.L., 'Images of Women in the Works of Thomas Heywood', *Salzburg Studies in English Literature*, University of Salzburg, 1974

Jones, M.K., *Bosworth 1485: Psychology of a Battle*, Tempus, 2002

Kendall, P.M., *Richard III*, Allen & Unwin, 1956

——, *The Yorkist Age, Daily Life during the Wars of the Roses*, Penguin, Classic History, 2001

Kerrigan, J., ed., *Motives of Woe: Shakespeare and 'Female Complaint', A Critical Anthology*, Oxford: Clarendon Press, 1991

Kieckhefer, R., *European Witch Trials: their foundations in popular and learned culture, 1300–1500*, University of California Press, 1979

Kittredge, G.L., *Witchcraft in Old and New England*, Harvard University Press, 1929

Lander, J.R., *The Wars of the Roses*, Secker & Warburg, 1965

——, *Crown and Nobility 1450–1509*, Edward Arnold, 1976

Mancini, D., *The Usurpation of Richard III*, tr. and intr. C.A.J. Armstrong, Alan Sutton, 1984

Mirror for Magistrates, A, ed. L.B.Campbell, Cambridge University Press, 1938

More, St. Thomas, *The History of King Richard III*, ed. R.S. Sylvester, Yale University Press, 1976

More, Sir Thomas, *Richard III: The Great Debate*, including Walpole, Horace, *Historic Doubts on the Life and Reign of King Richard III*, ed. and intr. P.M. Kendall, The Folio Society, MCMLXV

Norwich, J.J., *Shakespeare's Kings*, Penguin, 2000

Percy, Thomas, *Percy's Reliques of Ancient English Poetry*, ed. H.B. Wheatley, 3 vols, George Allen & Unwin, repr. 1927

Pratt, S.M., 'Jane Shore and the Elizabethans: Some Facts and Speculations', *Texas Studies in Literature and Language*, 11 (1969), pp. 1293–1306

Ross, C.D., *Edward IV*, Eyre Methuen, 1975

——, *Richard III*, Eyre Methuen, 1981

Bibliography

Rowe, N., *The Works of Nicholas Rowe, Esq. In two volumes. A new edition*. London, 1792

——, *Dramatick Works*, Vol. II. republished Gregg International Publishers Limited, 1971

——, *The Fair Penitent*, ed. M. Goldstein, Regents Restoration Drama Series, University of Nebraska Press, 1969

Rubin, M., *The Hollow Crown, A History of Britain in the Late Middle Ages*, Allen Lane, Penguin, 2005

Scott, M.M., *Re-Presenting 'Jane Shore' Harlot and Heroine*, Ashgate, 2004

Seward, D., *The Wars of the Roses and the Lives of Five Men and Women in the Fifteenth Century*, Constable, 1995

Stow's Survey of London, intr. H.B. Wheatley, Everyman's Library, J.M. Dent & Sons, 1960

Strong, R., *The Story of Britain, A People's History*, Pimlico, 1998

Thompson, C.J.S., *The Witchery of Jane Shore*, Grayson & Grayson, 1933

The True Tragedy of Richard III, 1594, edited by W.W. Greg, Malone Society Reprint, 1929

Thrupp, S.L., *The Merchant Class of Mediaeval London (1300–1500)*, University of Chicago Press, 1948

Vergil, P., *Three Books of Polydore Vergil's English History comprising the Reigns of Henry VI, Edward IV, and Richard III*, ed. Sir Henry Ellis, K.H., Camden Society, 1884

Walpole, H., *Historic Doubts on the Life and Reign of King Richard III*, ed. P.M. Kendall, The Folio Society, 1965 (see also More, above)

Index

Index